Marian Shrines

of France

Rue du Bac, Paris La Sallete
Lourdes Pontmain

IMPRIMATUR:
✠ Most Rev. Sean P. O'Malley, OFM Cap.
Bishop of Fall River, Mass., USA
December 8, 1998, Immaculate Conception

The nihil obstat and imprimatur are official declarations that a book or pamphlet is free from doctrinal or moral error. No implication is contained therein that those who granted the nihil obstat or imprimatur agree with the contents or statements expressed.

OUR COVER:

This book, *Marian Shrines of France*, was formerly titled *You Will Make This Known to My People*. In this revised, up-dated edition of the same book, we changed the cover art and have added chapters on Pontmain to make it more complete and to complement the other book currently in our series on Marian Shrines, *The Marian Shrines of Italy*.

The four major shrines of France are illustrated on the cover as follows: top, La Salette; right, the Basilica of Pontmain; bottom, Lourdes; left the chapel of the Miraculous Medal, Rue du Bac, Paris. The illustration of Our Lady in the center is of a statue in the garden of the convent in Nevers where St. Bernadette spent her last years. She would often pray before this image, and remarked that it bore the closest resemblance to the Lady of the Grotto.

Rue du Bac, Paris   La Sallete
Lourdes   Pontmain

Marian Shrines

of France

Franciscan Friars of the Immaculate
Our Lady's Chapel, New Bedford, MA USA

Acknowledgments

How does one go about thanking two communities of Franciscan Friars for their contribution that made this book possible? First, the Marytown community in Libertyville, Illinois, who supplied me with so much resource material, both illustrations and written text from past issues of IMMACULATA magazine. Without the majority of black and white photos used in this book, which they generously lent me, the book would not have been nearly as attractive and easy to read. As a former editor of IMMACULATA, I had the double advantage of knowing where to look in their picture file for the illustrations I needed. Having a whole set of past IMMACULATA magazines, I had excellent resource material on which to base some of the chapters of this book. Bro. Charles Madden, a member of the Marytown Conventual Franciscans, helped me again with the proofreading and this time contributed a chapter, "The Ballad and the Message." Incidentally, this last September 1998, the friars of Marytown celebrated their fiftieth anniversary. They have an interesting, well illustrated special issue of their magazine, IMMACULATA, that gives the history of Marytown, their ideals, as well as describing their many apostolic activities, not least of which is their sanctuary of Perpetual Eucharistic Adoration and their promoting Eucharistic Adoration over the decades.

The other Franciscan community, my present community, the Franciscan Friars of the Immaculate, with their Guardian, Fr. Peter Damian Fehlner, have been very supportive in the work of producing the series of books on Marian Shrines and Saints. It is a big order for me and the community as it requires many man-hours. Our community also has Eucharistic Adoration and follows in the ideals of St. Maximilian Kolbe. Without their help and expertise on the computer, I would not have been able to begin to edit and write chapters for these books. Incidentally, the chapters that do not have an author under the title were authored by yours truly. And I might add without the spell check of this computer and another proofreader, Roy Schoeman, this book would no doubt have its share of typos. Roy, a convert from Judaism, also contributed two articles to the book. One of our dedicated Secular Franciscans, Madeline Nugent, SFO, who has authored several books herself, was asked at the last minute to write a couple of chapters. To one an all who have contributed to this latest in the series of Marian Shrines and Saints, my heartfelt thanks and prayers. May Mary bless you with her loving Child.

Bro. Francis Mary Kalvelage, F.F.I.

Introduction

This third book in the series, *Marian Saints and Shrines*, can readily be used to support Catholic apologetics. You may ask, how does a book on the four major Marian Shrines of France in the last century answer the challenge posed by what the Pope speaks of as modern man's "flight towards easy irrationalism" in his latest encyclical, *Fides et Ratio,* on apologetics. He makes it clear that there is no conflict between faith and reason. At a time when rampant rationalism, materialism and secularism are leading many to despair, when the spiritual side of man (intellect and will) is being ignored, at the expense of his dignity and supernatural destiny, Our Lady appears to children and the childlike to remind man that he has an eternal destiny, that through Grace, he has been raised to the dignity of sons of God.

In the nineteenth century, following upon the so-called "Enlightenment," when the supernatural was considered passé, when science promised to have all the answers, when human reason alone (as unreasonable as it then is) no longer needed faith, when technological progress in human affairs excluded God as unnecessary, when the "here and now" was all that counted, an uninvited guest appeared on the world stage—none other than the Mother of God herself.

Why is it that, "Mom always manages to turn up at the wrong time?" It is because she knows our propensity to get into trouble. Our Lady, too, knows better than any earthly mother could when things are not right as they should be. She loves us, and is ever keenly aware of our need of her guidance, intercession and reconciliation with the Father. There you have it! Man thought that he had come of age and was quite sure he was in control. Actually, the Nineteenth Century was the fertile ground from which in the first part of the Twentieth Century was spawned three totalitarianisms, and two world wars, accounting for more deaths than all pervious wars put together.

In the social, political, economic, even more so in the religious and moral spheres, man was making a mess of God's beautiful creation, so badly that one can envision the Triune God taking counsel. Knowing man and his great need for a mother, God the Father sends His predestined daughter, the perfection of all created love into the world. God the Son sends His mother, whom He ever obeyed on earth, saying to Himself, "They wouldn't pay attention to me while on earth, maybe they will to my mother?" God the Holy Spirit, the fire of Divine Love and Spouse of Mary places His divine seal of ratification on this counsel of the Father and the Son.

So she came to this sick world grown cold through lack of charity, blinded by the attachment to material things, so desperately in need of the truth—that elusive truth which the intellect seeks for happiness in this life and the next. But the fullness of eternal beatitude is found only by the humble of heart, recognizing and submitting to God's Will, acknowledging that reason must be enlightened by Faith and Grace.

When Mary appeared in the last century, she showed quite clearly there is no conflict between reason and faith. She gave that unbelieving self-confident age a lesson in apologetics. What do we mean by"apologetics"? It is that branch of theology which deals with the defense and justification of the Christian Faith, not only in the face of sincerely put objections, but especially in view of sophisticated and ambiguous interpretation of what truth is. Central in any defense and justification of the faith, is the firm conviction that man has been given an intellect which has as its object the truth. That truth is nothing less than God Himself who said, "I am the Way, the Truth and the Life." Truth, then, is not a projection of man's experience (subjectivism) but exists prior to and apart from and above man (objectively). And so man is responsible for conforming his life to that objective truth and must not adjust truth to fit what is most convenient for him at any particular time or place. Man will be held accountable for not using this talent to know the truth, as Christ made it clear in the parable of the unprofitable steward. And again, as Scripture says, "The truth will set man free." (Jn 8,32)

The latest Encyclical of our Holy Father, *Fides et Ratio* (Faith and Reason) published in the fall of 1998, deals with Apologetics, not so much as an *apology* for the Faith, but as a means of evangelization. By giving uncontestable truth rather than suppositions, to the most fundamental questions man is ever asking, the groundwork of conversions is being laid. The Holy Father did not plan this Encyclical to coincide with the twentieth anniversary of his ascent to the papacy, but it couldn't have been better timed. Cardinal Joseph Ratzinger sees it as representing a *Summa* or maximum expression, thus far, of this Holy Father's pontificate.

The Pope, a deep thinker and philosopher in his own right, providentially canonized another philosopher and intellectual, Edith Stein, who had been an atheist, who found the completeness of her Judaism in the Catholic Church, and who eventually joined the Carmelite Order where she found intimate union with Christ and heroic holiness. The publication of the encyclical and the canonization were within a week of each other, so underscoring the connection of faith and grace with reason.

The approved apparitions of Our Lady (in particular those in this book) are very much a part of the evangelization envisioned by Pope John Paul II. Those who would deny the worldwide import of these private revelations do not seem to be aware that the Mary of the Gospel is

Contents

---

the same prophetess who has made more spectacular appearances in the last two hundred years than in the previous twenty centuries of the Church. One would have to turn to the parting of the Red Sea to find a comparable miracle of the sun "dancing" at Fatima, witnessed by 70,000 people. The weeping Madonna at La Salette is the same *Woman* who stood at the foot of the cross. The miracle worker of Nazareth is the son of the miracle worker of Lourdes, and the Redeemer who died on a cross twenty centuries ago is none other than the Son of the Mother who cooperated so thoroughly and intimately in the plan of redemption as to be designated by the Church Co-redemptrix, along side of her Son, our Redeemer and hers. The truth therefore, is the same now as then. Miracles were a sign of Jesus' claim of being God and miracles and conversions today, through the wearing an inexpensive medal, are a clear sign that we must pay closer attention to what the Mother of God is saying to us, individually and universally. She is our only hope.

In conclusion, I quote a well used but appropriate passage from that great Catholic philosopher, G. K. Chesterton. He briefly and succinctly expressed the nub of the problem in today's confused world: "Truth is not so much difficult to find as it is living up to the truth once one has found it."

— Bro. Francis Mary Kalvelage, F.F.I.

Preface

Fr. John Hardon, S.J.

Saints and Marian Shrines are gaining in popularity. Thus, the series of Marian Saints and Shrines, of which this book is the third, is well-timed. The present Holy Father, Pope John Paul II, has been criticized for the numerous men and women, clerical and lay, whom he has beatified and canonized in the last two decades, much more than any previous pontiff. Recently, he announced that there will be many more beatifications and canonizations in celebrating the second millennium of Christianity. All of this points to the fact that we are living in extraordinary times. As the saying goes "where evil abounds, good abounds that much more." St. Louis de Montfort predicted in his great spiritual classic, *True Devotion to Mary,* "God will raise up great saints towards the end of time," and these saints will be noted for their true devotion (total consecration) to the Blessed Mother.

In recent decades there has been a diminution of the cult of the saints. One has to but look at the number of lives of the saints, books that have been written in the last thirty years, compared to the previous thirty years. But one can say today that the trend is gradually changing. The series of books on *Marian Saints and Shrines* published by the Franciscan Friars of the Immaculate, is one indication to that fact. Ignatius Press, possibly the largest Catholic book distributor in the country, has carried in their catalogues the first two books in this series, *The Guadalupe Handbook* and *St. Thérèse, Doctor of the Church.* They have found that there is a growing market for books of this type.

One might very well say, "about time!" The topic of lives of the saints should always be of great interest and importance to Catholic readers. For as the *Catholic Catechism* points out, "All Christians in any state or walk of life are called to the fullness of Christian life and to the perfection of charity (*Lumen Gentium*, 40, 2). All are called to holiness.

"Be perfect, as your heavenly Father is perfect" (Mt 5:48). And let no one say that the eclipse in lives of the saints was due to the Second Vatican Council. In the counciliar decree *Lumen Gentium* we read:

"In order to reach this perfection [of holiness] the faithful should use the strength dealt out to them by Christ's gift, so that... doing the will of the Father in everything, they may wholeheartedly devote themselves to the glory of God and to the service of their neighbor. Thus the holiness of the People of God will grow in fruitful abundance, as is clearly shown in the history of the Church through the lives of so many saints (LG 40, 2)."

The Church is ever interested in promoting the saints and their heroic lives, as this is the primary mission of the Church—to evangelize and sanctify all men. She supplies in her Sacraments, especially the Eucharist, which is both Presence and Sacrifice (the Mass) of Jesus, the primary means of attaining that holiness. Mary, the Mediatrix of All Graces and Spouse of the Holy Spirit, is ever by her Divine Son's side in the distribution of the Graces He won on Calvary. Thus the vital importance of realizing the place Mary has in the sanctification of individuals and society as a whole. There simply is no thought of holiness without Mary's intervention as the *Refuge of Sinners,* the *Gate of Heaven* through which all must pass.

Thus again, the vital importance of showing Mary's presence in our times, in particular through her apparitions and her admonitions at Lourdes, La Salette and other Church-approved apparitions. It is a well-known fact, besides the physical cures at these shrines, there are countless spiritual lepers, or sinners, who have been cleansed and reconciled to God. So I welcome this latest and third in the series of Marian Saints and Shrines. May it increase the number of those who are sincerely striving to become Saints. As Mother Theresa used to say to priests, even at this time of shortage of vocations, "We do not need more priests but holy priests." That can apply to all of us. For the Church, the Mystical Body of Christ is built up by "little people," the saints, and will triumph ultimately united to the Immaculate Heart of Mary.

PART I

19th Century Apparitions in Historic Context

The Eldest Daughter of the Church Is Marian

When France was chosen to be the host of the four most important apparitions of Our Lady in the Nineteenth Century — Lourdes, La Salette, the Miraculous Medal apparition in Paris, and Pontmain — one might pose the question, "Why France?" One has to study the history of France to understand, "Why France?" In modern times, it seems, France has been more a prodigal daughter of the Church than her "Eldest Daughter." The history of Catholicism in France has been a glorious and turbulent one: at times France has been a great defender of the Church and at other times, her greatest adversary.

Christianity arrived there in the middle of the Second Century in the area around what is now the city of Lyons, at that time a part of the Roman province of Gaul. Its first bishop, Hilary, was martyred but by the middle of the Third Century, there were over 30 bishoprics. Much of this expansion was due no doubt to the first Saint to be canonized other than a martyr, namely the popular St. Martin of Tours. When the Vandals and Franks overran the country, they brought with them the Arian heresy, which caused much confusion and falling away from the Faith. Following the conversion and baptism of King Clovis in 496, the Franks were converted. But it wasn't until two centuries later that the Christianization of France was completed. From that time on virtually every development and important event revolved around the Catholic Church—through the periods of the Carolingians, feudalism, the—

Middle Ages and monarchies right up to the Eighteenth Century and the French revolution.

It was that revolution and the bloody persecution of the Church that caused a devastating break between church and state and the introduction of the strictly secular state. This break with the past Christian roots of France was symbolized and made visible in her national flag. For centuries the French flag had the *fleurs-de-lis* on a blue field. They ever symbolized the Christian virtue of purity, and the Immaculate Virgin in particular, thus uniting Mary and the Church with French patriotism. The present tricolor was introduced at the time of the French revolution when religion was being exiled from public life. But love and loyalty to the Church could never be taken away from the hearts of Frenchmen. Our Lady saw to that.

The high point of the integration of Catholicism and French love of country was without a doubt during the Middle Ages. It was French Crusaders who supplied many of the knights and material support that liberated the Holy Land for over a century and supplied protection to pilgrims to the most sacred places in the Christian world. Noted among these Crusaders was the king of France, St. Louis IX (1226-1270), who won the respect of not only Christians, but of his enemies as well for his brave deeds and noble, holy life. He set the example for subsequent kings of France.

The cult of royalty, looked upon as a God-appointed duty, though at times abused as the "divine right of King" over the pope, was a moral force in France and a model followed by other countries. That model took its inspiration from the Pauline doctrine of the Mystical Body of Christ and served as the foundation of the organic structure of vocations and classes within the body politic. Obviously, when abused or attacked, the entire people suffered.

Knighthood, or soldiering at that time, was more than the profession of carrying arms for the protection of one's rights and territory. It was closely allied with and fostered by the Church. It was thus that the Church more than any other institution subdued the brutality and cruelty of the not too distant past. At the height of the Middle Ages, the Thirteenth Century, it was Catholic France which introduced the code of honor and ethics for knighthood. It was based on the beatitudes and was at the service of the defenseless, the downtrodden and the weak. Central in the chivalric code was the veneration of the perfect ideal of womanhood, the Immaculate Virgin-Mother. The concept of defending womanhood and her honor at the cost of even one's life was immortalized in the ballads of the troubadours. It was this France with which the Italian, St. Francis of Assisi, wished to be identified, especially in her devotion to the Eucharist Lord.

The Thirteenth Century could be considered the golden age of Catholic France which led the rest of Europe in introducing and developing many institutions and arts especially in the area of literature. The University of Paris was the leading institution of higher learning in Europe and hosted such luminaries and brilliant theologians as St. Thomas Aquinas, St. Bonaventure and Bl. John Duns Scotus as teachers there. It was in this age of Faith, so misnamed by the Renaissance Man "medieval," that the great architectural marvels, the Gothic Cathedrals, were conceived and built in France.

Even to this day they cover one end of France to the other. The Protestant historian, Henry Adams, wrote that in the 100 years between 1170 and 1270, the French built eighty Cathedrals and nearly 500 large churches of the cathedral class that in today's currency would have cost billions of dollars. Nearly every one of these great buildings, with their many statues and stained glass windows, are masterpieces that were dedicated to Mary and if it were not, there was sure to be a Lady Chapel in that church. Adams, who was no Catholic devotee of Mary, nonetheless wrote that the palaces of earthly queens were hovels compared with the palaces—churches and cathedrals—of the heavenly Queen.

Such a monument to the faith would be impossible in a faithless age such as ours. The Cathedral of Chartres, with its famed stained glass rose window, was built and decorated by the various guilds, assisted by theologians, nobles and common people fired by their love of the Blessed Virgin. For the most part they were named *Notre Dame.* Don Sharkey who authored two of the chapters of this book wrote the following in his book *The Woman Shall Conquer:*

"They [the people of various classes] harnessed themselves to wagons and dragged huge blocks of stone and giant tree trunks. Noble ladies helped peasant women mix mortar. All worked in silence and prayed as they worked. No one who thought himself to be in mortal sin dared volunteer. People of that time thought of the Blessed Mother in connection with everything they did. They would not venture upon the simplest undertaking without invoking her aid."

Of course, all that changed with the Protestant revolt. In their disdain of anything Catholic they struck at the two devotions that most identify one as Catholic—devotion to the Blessed Mother and the Blessed Sacrament. While the Church in France experienced the inroads of Calvinism for a time, Calvinism never gained a permanent place in France as in other nearby countries. Could it not have been largely due to the French nation's faithful devotion to the Blessed Mother?

Nonetheless, the Church in France did suffer from some very serious internal problems. Even in the Thirteenth Century, the century of St. Louis IX, St. Bonaventure and St. Thomas at Paris, the first signs of ecclesial nationalism — the exaltation of the local Church at the expense of the papacy and universal Church, later known as Gallicanism — appeared. Next came the exile of the Popes in Avignon. It was mainly engineered by the French monarchy, and eventually led to the great Western Schism, which set the stage for the Protestant repudiation of the papacy. The theoretical premises of this nationalism, so widespread even today, and typical of so much heresy and schism are commonly discussed under the headings of Gallicanism: superiority of the National Church over the Universal, and Conciliarism: superiority of a General Council over the Pope.

Jansenism is a kind of reflection of Protestant spirituality found in Catholic nations, with its corrosive effects on Catholic belief and discipline. Originating in France in the Seventeenth Century, it is still troubling the Church. It kept people away from the Sacraments, especially the Eucharist, out of a false sense of humility. At the same time in the secular world, the encyclopedists and philosophers in France opened the way to the age of the Enlightenment and rationalism. Coupled with great advances in science and technology which fostered the industrial revolution, society was in the throes of massive changes in the social order. This eventually introduced a period of revolutions throughout Europe and South America, many of which were engineered by the Masonic Lodges. All of these taken together precipitated the secularization of society, necessitating the direct intervention of heaven as illustrated in the chapter on Our Lady at La Salette (pages 47-52).

During this period when man progressively was turning away from God and religion, France not only gave to the world clever philosophers, such as Descartes and Voltaire, who precipitated the break of man from organized religion, but she also gave the Church and the world some great saints, such as St. Vincent de Paul, St. Francis de Sales, St. John Eudes, St. John Baptist de Salle and St. Louis de Montfort who would have a profound influence on succeeding centuries. Jesus singled out France to give the great revelation of His merciful love in the Sacred Heart apparitions at Paray-le-Monial to the French Visitation nun, St. Margaret Mary Alacoque.

In the Eighteenth Century, St. Louis de Montfort wrote the spiritual classic, *True Devotion to Mary*, which he predicted would be hidden for many years. When it was discovered 126 years later, it became a best seller, introducing total consecration to Mary in a simple and well organized way. It had a wide and diverse audience. One of the most famous of the followers of this spirituality of total surrender to Mary of all that we are, have and ever will have, is Pope John Paul II. The profound influence this little spiritual treatise has had in our times could be considered a catalyst in introducing the Marian Age we are living in.

The Nineteenth Century, following the bloody French revolution and its numerous martyrs, was a period of scientism and materialism: capitalism and socialism alike. The Industrial Revolution with the exploitation of the poor and all the other social injustices of laissez faire capitalism, set the stage for the further exodus of the working class from the Church. The intellectuals alienated from the Church by liberalism looked to man as the center of the universe and considered the supernatural (miracles, Divine Providence, etc.) passé. It was thought that the advances in science and new inventions would usher in an earthly paradise to mankind. All this was a consequence of the repudiation of the Christian principles upon which the civilization in France was built. And this was echoed across the globe.

If this century, during which the Church in France suffered mass attacks by the secular authorities, drew many away from the Church, it also saw great missionary initiatives among the French clergy. France was noted for its outstanding mission accomplishments in the Nineteenth Century. Many new religious congregations were founded, dedicated to Our Lady or the Sacred Heart of Jesus. One of these, founded by St. Peter Julian Eymard, was devoted to furthering devotion to the Eucharistic Christ. Interesting to relate, he had originally joined a Marian congregation, the Marists, and it was at her Shrine of La Salette that he received the inspiration to establish a new congregation to make reparation to the Eucharistic Heart of Jesus and further belief and devotion in the Eucharist.

The Nineteenth Century was noted for four outstanding French saints, St. Thérèse of the Child Jesus and the Holy Face, St. John Vianney (popularly known as the Curé of Ars), St. Catherine Labouré and St. Bernadette. The bodies of the last three are in the state of perfect preservation, which points to the sacredness of the human body, the temple of the Holy Spirit which will some day be united with the soul in eternal beatitude.

Large masses of people in France may have rejected the Church and Christianity in recent times, but obviously Mary did not reject her wayward sons and daughters, as seen in the weeping Madonna of La Salette (see page 53) and subsequent apparitions of that century. Besides the three featured in this book, there are three others that have the full approbation of Church authorities, the Green Scapular apparitions to another French Daughter of Charity, Sister Bisqueyburu in 1840 at Blangy, France and in 1871 at Pontmain, where she appeared over a barn. During the disastrous Franco-Prussion War she assured the children whom she appeared to that her "Son permits Himself to be moved" to the prayers of her afflicted children. Within ten days of her appearance an armistice was signed. Again, within a short space of time, in 1876, she appeared to a French servant at Pellevoisin, who was dying of an advanced stage of consumption. Our Lady told Estelle Faguette, "I choose the little ones and the weak for my glory." She was cured and in May, 1894, Pope Leo XIII approved the Archconfraternity of Our Mother All Merciful of Pellevoisin.

In conclusion let us return to the question posed at the beginning of this chapter, "Why should France be singled out as the recipient of the three major apparitions of Lady in the last Century?" In reviewing the Church history of France we see a people of extremes. The French have caused Holy Mother Church many crises and troubles, but at the same time great saints have arisen from their ranks. What was said in the Book of the Apocalypse can well apply to the French, "Would that you were hot or cold, but since you are mediocre I would spew you from my mouth." Yes, Our Blessed Mother, like her Son, does not settle for mediocrity and indifference when she has a message of world-shaking import. The privilege of the French to be favored with these apparitions is not without the cross. The Church in France has suffered much, both from enemies within and without, throughout the centuries, but through it all Mary herself points out how she is glorified, "through the weak and little ones." — *Franciscan Friars of the Immaculate*

Mary, Mother of the Church

Fra M. M. de Cruce, F.I.

At the close of the Second Vatican Council, Pope Paul VI proclaimed, "Mary, Mother of the Church." (Nov. 21, 1964) Though he caught many of the Council Fathers by surprise, the profound, practical consequences of his giving her this official title could not be more apparent than in her four apparitions in France during the Nineteenth Century — Rue du Bac, La Salette, Lourdes and Pontmain.

As the *Catechism of the Catholic Church* (no. 963) points out: "Mary is the Mother of the entire Christ, head and members. She joined in bringing about the spiritual rebirth of God's children." This divine plan was first made manifest at the moment of her Immaculate Conception. It was realized at the foot of the Cross when she bore all men in great suffering, in the person of St. John, as spiritual children. As Coredemptrix beside the one Redeemer, Jesus Christ, now enthroned in Heaven, she has been entrusted by her Son with the distribution of the treasury of grace as Mediatrix of All Graces.

Mary was chosen in a singular way — not to be simply another adopted child, but to be *Theotokos*, the God-bearer. In the divine plan, Mary is the one eternally predestined by the Most Holy Trinity to be the Mother of God and Mother of the Church. This extraordinary privilege required extraordinary grace, nothing less than a preservative redemption, that is, the Immaculate Conception. The apparitions mentioned above highlight the truth of her Immaculate Conception, both before and after its solemn definition in 1854.

On November 27th, 1830, when Our Lady requested of St. Catherine to have a medal struck just as she appeared, she became brighter and more beautiful and an oval frame appeared around her with these words in gold, "O Mary, conceived without sin, pray for us who have recourse to thee." Clearly, recourse to her as the Woman "conceived without sin" disposes us and enables her to exercise her role as our Mother in the order of grace.

Four years after Pope Pius IX's solemn definition, "the Lady" appeared to St. Bernadette. Although Bernadette had not claimed that the Lady was the Blessed Virgin Mary, she was pressed by the local pastor to reveal her name. On March 25th, 1858, after repeating two times her pastor's request, the Lady serenely smiled, but made no reply. After Bernadette implored her a third time, however, the Woman's face became serious and she seemed to bow in humility. Her posture resembled that on the Medal. Raising her hands to her Heart, she joined them together and looked heavenward. Slowly opening her hands she leaned forward and said, with a voice slightly trembling with emotion, "I am the Immaculate Conception."

Here we have a statement of personal identification and self-revelation. She *is* the Immaculate Conception. All of her privileges are contained and flow from this first grace of hers. It is in this mystery of the Immaculate Conception that we see not only God's supreme masterpiece in creation, not only His singular election of her, but even His choice to create at all. He foreknew that Adam and Eve would fall — yet He still created. Why? Because He saw from all eternity that the Woman designated to receive His choicest grace, the sublime vocation of being the Mother of God, would second His plan: *"Behold the handmaid of the Lord; be it done to me according to thy word."* (Lk.1:38). In her God saw the perfect fruit of a perfect Redemption, a fitting Mother for Christ and His Mystical Body, the Church. Her spotless beauty, as it were, attracted the Triune God to proceed with creation and the redemptive Incarnation.

It was St. Augustine who noted that Mary is more blessed in bearing the Word in her Immaculate Heart through faith than in her womb by the power of the Holy Spirit. In her role as Mother and Maidservant of the Redeemer she continued to second God's plan throughout her life, especially on Calvary where she, as Coredemptrix, became the Mother of the Church. It is precisely as the Immaculate, Virgin, Mother of God that Mary joined her compassion with the Passion of Christ. "On Calvary, Mary united herself to the sacrifice of her Son and made her own maternal contribution to the work of salvation, which took the form, as it were, of labor pains giving birth to the new humanity." (John Paul II, Sept. 17, 1997).

Although the emphasis at Rue du Bac, the motherhouse of the Daughters of Charity in Paris, is focused on the fruit of this coredemptive love, namely her maternal mediation of grace, nonetheless she quietly illustrates her essential, subordinate role in the Redemption in her visit on November 27, 1830. First she appeared standing on a white globe while offering to God a smaller golden globe surmounted with a tiny gold cross. Mary states that "this ball you see represents the whole world, especially France, and each person in particular." It seems that the larger globe represents the whole world with its complete history, while the smaller globe indicates that brief time in history when her Incarnate Son offered Himself on the Cross for us men and for our salvation. But she too is, as we noted above, "always living to make intercession for us." (Heb. 7:25), and continues to do so forever with Christ the great High Priest.

During this same apparition, Mary revealed the reverse side of the medal where two hearts appear. The Heart of Christ is laden with a crown of thorns which symbolizes His Passion; the Heart of Mary is pierced by a sword symbolizing her compassion; the united offering of their redeeming love for poor sinners is portrayed by the bar which connects the fire of charity burning in their Hearts. Above their Hearts we see the *M* interwoven with the base of the Cross. This teaches us that Mary was not only "the temple of God" (Rev. 11:19), where "the Word was made flesh, and dwelt among us" (Jn. 1:14), but her maternal Heart became also the altar of Christ's sacrifice as Priest and Victim. Hence her offering, though subordinate, is intrinsically part of the one offering of Jesus Crucified. Consequently, she is spiritually present at, and part of, every Holy Sacrifice of the Mass which perpetuates the "one oblation" (Heb. 10:14) of Christ.

The Magisterium recently confirmed this doctrine of Mary's union with her Son in working out our salvation saying that she "advanced in her pilgrimage of faith, and faithfully persevered in her union with her son unto the Cross. There she stood, in keeping with the divine plan, enduring with her only begotten Son the intensity of His suffering, joining herself with His sacrifice in her Mother's Heart, and lovingly consenting to the immolation of this Victim, born of her." (*Lumen Gentium,* 58).

All this illustrates the depth of meaning of the Madonna in Tears at La Salette. Her incessant weeping stopped only at the last moment when she was leaving this vale of tears to return to Heaven. She was wearing a cross which, according to the seer Maximin, "was the prettiest thing about her." Her message was one of sorrow for her poor children who desperately needed reconciliation with God and one another.

"Come to me, my children... If my people do not obey I shall be compelled to loose my Son's arm." Here we see the Mother of the whole Christ, working under and with Him to avert disaster. In her role as Coredemptrix beside her Redeemer-Son she is still in travail as Mother of the members of the Mystical Body, the Church. "How long have I suffered for you!... No matter how well you pray in the future, no matter how well you act, you will never be able to make up to me what I have endured on your behalf."

But how does our spiritual Mother, the Mediatrix of all Graces, exercise this role in Heaven? After all, St. Paul instructs us, "for there is one God, and one Mediator of God and men, the man Christ Jesus." (I Tm. 2:5). The Church interprets this passage of Sacred Scripture thus, "Mary's function as Mother of men in no way obscures or diminishes this unique mediation of Christ, but rather shows its power.... The unique mediation of the Redeemer does not exclude but rather gives rise to a manifold cooperation which is but a sharing in this one source... Taken up to Heaven she did not lay aside this saving office but by her manifold intercession continues to bring us the gifts of eternal salvation." (*Lumen Gentium,* 60,62).

It was this ongoing maternal mediation which was explicitly revealed to St. Catherine in 1830. On November 27, when Our Lady stood on a globe, offering a smaller one with a cross, brilliant rays streamed from the many rings on her fingers set with beautiful gems. "They are the symbols of the graces I shed upon those who ask for them." Noticing some gems did not emit rays, the visionary asked about them. She answered, "The gems from which rays do not fall are graces that souls forget to ask for." On the Medal itself Catherine noted that "the hands turned out and the arms were bent down under the weight of the treasures of grace obtained." The Virgin assured Sister Catherine that, "All who wear it [the Miraculous Medal] will receive great graces; they should wear it around the neck. Graces will abound for those who wear it with confidence."

As evidenced from the countless conversions and miraculous healings which have followed these apparitions in France, the Blessed Virgin Mary is truly our maternal "Mediatrix." "Mary's mediation is intimately linked with her motherhood. It possesses a specific maternal character, which distinguishes it from the mediation of other creatures." (*Redemptoris Mater,* 38). "From this point of view it is unique in its kind and singular in its effect... In truth, what is Mary's maternal mediation if not the Father's gift to humanity?" (John Paul II, Oct. 1, 1997).

Certainly, the messages given in these apparitions in the Nineteenth Century are most pertinent to our modern world. With the widespread attack on motherhood and womanhood through contraception, divorce, abortion, immodest fashions which make women out as objects of sexual pleasure, it is at once our direst need and greatest consolation to know that the spotless, sorrowful and solicitous Lady of Heaven is *our* Mother. What, then, is our response? Do we not hear our own guardian angel inviting us, "Come to the Chapel. The Holy Virgin is waiting for you"? (Angel to Catherine at Rue du Bac). And once in the 'Chapel,' the one, holy, catholic, and apostolic Church, do we not hear the voice of Mary speaking to our souls, "Come to the foot of the altar where great graces will be granted you." (Rue du Bac)

The last gift of Christ from the Cross to the apostle John was His Mother, "Behold thy Mother" (Jn 19:27); and the call of Mary, at La Salette "Come to me, my children" are addressed to all men of all times. It is our privilege and duty to respond to Jesus and Mary by consecrating ourselves as children of this most loving Mother. It was, incidentially, the French saint, St. Louis Marie Gignon de Montfort (1673-1716) who wrote the spiritual classic on total consecration, *True Devotion to Mary* which Pope John Paul II summarized and popularized on his papal coat of arms, "Totus Tuus."

In her apparitions Our Lady guides us along the way of Christian perfection: 1) the way of keeping the commandments of God and the discipline of the Church (La Salette); 2) the way of prayer — "Special graces will be given to all who ask them, but people must *pray*" (Rue du Bac and Pontmain), "Do you say your *prayers* well, my children?" (La Salette), "*Pray* for sinners" and especially the Holy Rosary (Lourdes); 3) the way of conversion of heart – "If people are *converted*... then..." (La Salette), "*Penance. Penance. Penance.*" (Lourdes).

Our Mother most amiable has one final request: "Well, my children, you will make this known to all my people." (La Salette). As we prepare to celebrate 2000 years of Christendom and enter a new millenium with the Gospel message, let us cooperate with the Holy Father's call for a "new springtime of evangelization" in the easiest, most perfect, most fruitful way: *Ad Jesum per Mariam* (to Jesus through Mary). Towards this end Mary, Mother of the Church, has given us her Medal to wear and distribute as a source of grace and a sign of consecration. Wearing it with confidence and distributing it with apostolic zeal will help to hasten the day when all may be one in Christ.

The Ballad and the Message

By Bro. Charles Madden, O.F.M. Conv.

Long time ago, said the fine old woman,
Long time ago, this proud old woman did say;
There was war and death, plundering and pillage;
My children starved, by mountain, valley, and sea,
And their wailing cries, they shook the very heavens;
My four green fields, ran red with their blood, said she.

This verse from the Irish ballad "Four Green Fields," vividly portrays in a few sentences the centuries-long suffering of the Irish people from Elizabethan times through the years of the potato famine in the mid-Nineteenth Century. The old woman is Ireland herself and the four green fields are the four provinces of Ireland. Actually, they could be a description of the sufferings of the French people and many other Europeans as well during the same time period, culminating in all the upheavals of the Nineteenth Century. It was during the Nineteenth Century that the Blessed Virgin began to manifest herself in a spectacular way to the people of Europe to lead them away from wickedness through her message of prayer, conversion and renewal of the practice of their Catholic Faith. Only in conversion to Christ could they hope to find peace and happiness.

The four major apparitions of Our Lady in the last century all occurred in France: to St. Catherine Labouré (Rue du Bac, Paris, 1830), to the children of La Salette (1846), to St. Bernadette (Lourdes, 1858) and at Pontmain (1871). They came at a time when Europe was experiencing a rapid depletion in the practice of the Faith. For example, France at the end of the Eighteenth Century and the beginning of the Nineteenth Century, had been devasted by the bloody French Revolution followed immediately by Napoleon's wars with all the nations of Europe. The Church underwent a persecution so fierce that her influence in society was severely reduced. Many new but false ideas had been springing up all over Europe prior to this time. In the aftermath of the Napoleonic wars, these false ideas continued to multiply and spread.

These ideas were popularized in newspapers and books of the day and spread like wildfire among the wealthy classes and in the great universities of Europe. Science, which was making many remarkable new discoveries, was promoted as an antidote to religion and indeed as proof that the Christian Faith was little more than a refuge for the superstitious. Why should modern man believe in miracles and foolish tales of someone rising from the dead? Science would once and for all disprove such nonsense!

During the years from 1830 to 1871, when our Lady's major apparitions occurred, materialism had begun to flourish as never before. Opportunities arose for quickly acquiring great wealth through manufacturing and banking thanks to the Industrial Revolution and the exploitation of cheap labor, as people from the countryside began flooding into the cities looking for work in the new industries. So many people came that wages could be kept extremely low, working hours were long and working conditions were of the worst sort. The new areas of the cities were often devoid of churches nearby and irreligious attitudes among the working people became rampant.

All across Europe the discontentment caused by these inhumane conditions were exploited by various political movements advocating strident nationalism, socialism or anticlericalism, and sometimes the three were commingled. Revolutions sparked by these movements occurred in France, Germany, Italy and Hungary, especially in the late 1840s. A year after our Lady's appearances at Lourdes, Charles Darwin's theory of evolution broke upon the scene. Man was now portrayed as merely a descendant of ignorant beasts rather than a special creation of God, making it easier to indulge in human exploitation. Natural selection, so necessary to Darwinian evolution, promoted the notion of the "survival of the fittest," the weeding out of the weaker members of the human species.

Some churchmen and Scripture scholars, to accommodate themselves to these new, enlightened, scientific theories, began to reinterpret the Scriptures in such a way as to undermine basic truths concerning original sin, its consequences, man's redemption, and so the need for the Redeemer, Jesus Christ.

The exploitation of workers gave rise to various forms of socialism and socialist writers such as Karl Marx and Friedrich Engels advocated class warfare in which workers would rise up to seize the means of production and other forms of wealth to be distributed to each according to his needs. Education and banking would be taken over completely by the state. The Church would be totally excluded from the public domain and from any involvement with education. From a different perspective many capitalists agreed with the socialists that the Church was an anachronism to be done away with and its influence on society to be negated. The sacredness of Sunday as a day given over to God was scoffed at and workers were compelled to work seven days a week.

At La Salette our Lady specifically singled out for condemnation the violation of Sunday as a day of rest and the resultant neglect of Divine Worship. She warned that God was so displeased with mankind that crops would begin to fail and famine would stalk the land. Within a year all across Europe the potato crop failed and vineyards died out. Famine did come. In France from 1854-1856 some 250,000 people starved. In Ireland the population declined from eight and a half million to six and a half million between 1845-1851. Some 750,000 people starved and one and a quarter million others left the country for foreign lands.

In all four of Mary's apparitions her message was the same: prayer, conversion and return to the practice of the Catholic religion. To St. Catherine Laboure she showed an image of a medal honoring her Immaculate Conception which she desired to be struck and distributed in order to help renew the faith of the people. So many miracles were wrought through it the medal was called the "Miraculous Medal." Yet when Pope Pius IX formally declared the dogma of the Immaculate Conception in 1854, it was met in many quarters with scoffing and derision. So many now assumed that the only true pathway for human progress lay through science. There simply was no room for religion; miracles simply didn't happen, all could be explained by science, and even if there was a God, He was not concerned with human affairs! In 1858, Our Lady confirmed the new dogma at Lourdes by identifying herself as the Immaculate Conception.

Although many millions in France, and throughout the world, did respond to Mary's message, many millions more did not. The wholesale reconversion of heart desired by God did not occur. Thus the stage was set for the continued descent of man in the Twentieth Century into deeper forms of barbarism while deluding himself that he was entering onto a higher plane of human evolution.

The lament of the "fine old woman" continues to ring true today and will continue to do so as long as the message of the young Virgin of Rue de Bac, La Salette, Lourdes and Pontmain is ignored.

PART II

Rue du Bac, Paris, 1830

Miraculous Medal Apparitions

"Come to the foot of the altar. Here great graces will be poured out upon all who ask for them with confidence and fervor."

Our Lady to St. Catherine Labouré

St. Catherine, the farm girl turned Saint

Whenever I go to the chapel, I put myself in the presence of our good Lord, and I say to Him, "Lord, I am here. Tell me what you would have me do." If He gives me some task, I am content and I thank Him. If He gives me nothing, I still thank Him since I do not deserve to receive anything more than that. And then, I tell God everything that is in my heart. I tell him about my pains and my joys, and then I listen. God always speaks to you when you approach Him plainly and simply.

St. Catherine Labouré

The well-to-do Labouré farm where Catherine worked so conscientiously as cook and housekeeper. However, her father opposed her vocation and wouldn't give his permission for her to enter the convent. He saw that she would lack no suitors and would make a perfect farmer's wife and wonderful mother. She sought and found consolation and help by frequenting the nearby church of Fain-les-Moutiers.

Tableau painted in 1855 by the artist Lecerf.

Top left: Statue of Our Lady of the Globe with the incorrupt body of St. Catherine under the side altar. The painting by the artist Lecerf. Note the two hearts above Our Lady. Middle left: The entrance to the Chapel of the Miraculous Medal. Past the the entrance there is an open area leading directly into the chapel. Below: Yesteryear entrance. The garden of the Enghien hospice where St. Catherine served elderly men.

Revelation of a Medal Called Miraculous

The following story is one of the most heartwarming in the history of the appearances of Our Lady in modern times. The remote preparation for Mary's appearance to Catherine Labouré occurred when her devout mother died, when the little girl was nine years old. It was a great sorrow to lose her mother whom she loved dearly. Only one could replace her and that was the Blessed Mother herself. It was related to her sister Tonine by one of the servants of the house that she found the child perched atop a table which she had pushed close to a bureau with a statue of Our Lady on it. Clasping the statue in her arms, Catherine tearfully begged the Blessed Virgin Mary to take the place of her earthly mother. That wasn't all. She even hoped and prayed from that day forward that she would be able to see the Blessed Mother even in this life.

Her desires were great and Mary honored them, beginning on the night of July 18-19, 1830, at the Motherhouse of the Sisters of Charity on Rue du Bac, Paris. The visionary, Sr. Catherine Labouré, writes: "The feast of St. Vincent was approaching. On the eve, our dear Mother Marthe, one of the novice mistresses, instructed us on devotion to the saints, and in particular on devotion to the Blessed Virgin.

"For how long a time had I wished to see the Blessed Virgin! My desire became even stronger as time went on and I went to bed that night with the thought I might see my dear Mother that very night. We had each received from Mother Marthe a little scrap of the surplice of St. Vincent. I cut mine in two and swallowed half before going to sleep, persuaded that St. Vincent would obtain for me the grace of seeing the Blessed Virgin." The seminary Sisters slept in a common dormitory, each one having her own alcove surrounded by curtains. "I was asleep," Catherine continues, "when at eleven-thirty I heard my name: 'Sister, Sister, Sister Catherine!'

"I looked toward the side from which the voice came. It was the side of the passage (on which the alcoves opened). I lifted my curtain and saw a child of about five or six, dressed completely in white. He said: ‘Come with me to the chapel; the Blessed Virgin awaits you!’ I thought at once that I would be overheard. ‘Do not be troubled,’ said the child. ‘It is half-past eleven and everyone is asleep. Come, I am waiting.’ I dressed quickly and followed after the child. He was to my left, and rays of light came from him. To my great astonishment all the lights were shining brightly along the way. My astonishment increased when at a slight touch of the child’s finger the heavy chapel door swung open. My amazement was at its height when I beheld all the candles and torches in the chapel lit reminding me of midnight Mass. However, I saw no sign of the Blessed Virgin.

“The child led me into the sanctuary on the side of the chaplain’s chair. Here I knelt down while the child remained standing. All this while I was looking to see whether the Sisters on watch would pass through the sanctuary.” What would the Sisters who were keeping the night watch say if they found Catherine in the sanctuary at such an hour?

“Then a moment later, the child said: ‘Here is the Blessed Virgin; here she is!’ I heard the rustling of a silken robe coming from the side of the sanctuary. The ‘Lady’ bowed before the tabernacle, and then she seated herself in M. Richenet’s chair.” This armchair was used by the chaplain whenever he gave a conference to the Sisters. It was similar to a chair in a painting of St. Anne in the choir. “But the ‘Lady’ did not look like St. Anne. Seeing that I did not know how to behave, the Child spoke to me again: ‘It is the Blessed Virgin!’ I am not able to say why, but it still seemed to me that it was not she whom I saw. It was then that the voice of the child changed and took on the deeper tones of a man’s voice. He spoke again, repeating strongly his words for the third time. At this moment I rushed forward and knelt before the Blessed Virgin with my hands on her knees. I cannot express what I felt, but I am sure that this was the happiest moment of my life.

“The Blessed Virgin spoke to me of the way I ought to behave toward my director, M. Aladel, and she also confided to me some things which I may not reveal. She told me how to act in times of distress. Pointing with her left hand to the altar steps, she told me to come there to refresh my heart, and she said that it was there that I would find all the solace I needed. When I asked what was the meaning of what I had seen, she explained it to me completely. I do not know how much time went by. Her leaving me was like that of a light which goes out; she disappeared as she had come. ‘She has gone,’ the child said and together we returned the way we had come. He continued to walk at my left side and to light up the way. It is my belief that this child, so resplendent in miraculous light, was my guardian angel, and that he had made himself visible in order that I might see the Blessed Virgin, whom I had prayed so hard to see in this life. When I returned

to the dormitory it was two o'clock in the morning. I went back to bed; but I could not sleep again that night."

Some months before she died in 1876, Catherine added the following lines to what she had written in 1856, Our Lady herself having then given her permission to do so: "My child, God wishes to entrust to you a mission. It will be the cause of great suffering to you, but you will surmount it with the thought that it will work to God's glory. You will know later what this mission is to be, and you will be troubled until you have told your spiritual director. You will be contradicted; but do not fear, grace will be given to help you. Tell M. Aladel of what you have seen; once more, have confidence and do not fear. Through your prayers, inspiration will be given you. The times are very evil. Great misfortune will come to France; her throne will be overthrown! The whole world will be upset by evils of every kind. The Blessed Virgin seemed very much grieved when she said this. 'But come to the foot of this altar where great grace awaits all, whether they be great or little, who ask fervently and with confidence."

The Blessed Mother then told Catherine how she was pleased to shower graces on her community for she loved it very much. However, there were great abuses and the Rule was not observed very well. Predicting that her director would some day be superior and in charge of the community, Our Lady told Catherine that he must do all in his power to restore regular observance. God will then bless the community and it will become very large, as it subsequently did. In these troubled times Our Lady predicted she and St. Vincent de Paul (their founder) would watch over the two families of men and women religious.

The Blessed Mother then added, "It will not be as well, alas, with other religious houses wherein there will be many victims." Our Lady wept when she said this: "There will also be victims among the clergy of Paris. The archbishop himself will die"—at these words she wept again. "The Cross will be insulted; blood will flow in the streets"—here the Blessed Virgin could speak no longer so great was her grief, which shown on her face. Catherine questioned in her mind when these evils would come about, and understood: "In forty years." And so it happened in 1870.

As related Our Lady had told her: "God wishes to entrust to you a mission." Four months later, on Saturday November 27, 1830, this mission was made known to her. There are two phases in this most important apparition. In the first Mary offers the world to God; in the second she offers the grace of God to the world. In the first phase, Catherine saw the traditional representation of the Immaculate Conception. "Her eyes were raised to heaven. She stood erect upon a large white sphere; her feet were standing upon a serpent. At the level of her breast she held a little golden ball surmounted by a Cross, and this she was offering to God." Both the golden orb and the white sphere represented the earth and its peoples. Although Catherine saw no more than half of the white sphere, she was happy as a French woman to behold on it her country and the name of France.

Suddenly the golden orb disappeared; and Our Lady extended her hands toward the earth. "On her fingers were precious stones of differing sizes and from them came rays of light which fell upon the sphere at her feet. But some of these stones did not cast rays. Just as I was observing this," continues Catherine, "the Blessed Virgin turned her eyes to me, and I heard a voice within me: 'The sphere which you see is the world; it includes France and every inhabitant of the earth. The rays of light which come from my hands are the graces which I shower on those who ask for them.' Our Lady gave me to understand with what generosity and great joy she dispenses graces. 'But,' the

Our Lady of the Globe: In the first phase of the Immaculata's apparitions, she is seen offering the world to God; in the second, she is offering the grace of God to the world. "Her eyes were raised to heaven. She stood erect upon a large white sphere; her feet were standing upon a serpent. At the level of her breast, she held a little golden ball surmounted by a Cross, and this she was offering to God."

Below: The Chapel of the Apparitions, 140 Rue du Bac, Paris, France, where Our Lady appeared to St. Catherine Labouré in 1830.

Blessed Virgin added sadly, 'there are graces for which I am not asked, and it is for this reason that some of the stones you see are not sending forth rays of light.'"

The second phase of the apparition immediately followed. An oval frame formed around the figure of the Mediatrix of All Graces and around the outer edge the following words were inscribed O MARY CONCEIVED WITHOUT SIN, PRAY FOR US WHO HAVE RECOURSE TO THEE.

"Once again the Voice made itself heard within my heart: 'Have a medal struck just as you see. Those who wear it with devotion around their neck and who confidently say this prayer, will receive great graces and will enjoy the special protection of the Mother of God.' Then the frame reversed itself to show me the other side of the medal." What Catherine now saw was Mary's monogram: "A large M, surmounted by a cross having a double bar under it. Beneath this M, the holy Hearts of Jesus and Mary were placed side-by-side, the first being crowned with thorns, the other pierced by a sword. And around the outer part were twelve stars." This was the end of the vision.

But it was the beginning of the mountainous problems she had to surmount to fulfill the wishes of her heavenly Mother. Her spiritual Director, M. Aladel did not at first believe she saw the Blessed Mother, much less was he ready to have a medal struck as she appeared to the Sister. The story of that and the phenomenal spreading and dissemination of millions of Miraculous Medal is found on page 41. Throughout all the time that the Miraculous Medal was spreading like wildfire she remained a hidden, silent soul. Towards the end of her life she said: "I have only been an instrument. The Blessed Virgin did not appear on my behalf. . . . If she chose me, it was so that no one could doubt her."

Could she not now feel a great sense of joy and happiness to hear about all the wonders wrought through this sacramental which she was instrumental in introducing to the world? Did she feel she had accomplished the mission entrusted to her by the Blessed Mother? There was one thing still remaining, "And," she adds, "it was this which has turned my life into a martyrdom." In the apparition of Mary clasping a golden orb to her breast which symbolized the earth, the Blessed Virgin wished to show how dear this world is to her, and how great is her love for all its people.

"It was for this reason," Catherine said, "that Mary asked me, during my prayers, to have a statue made showing her clasping the world to her heart, with a commemorative altar set up in the place where she first appeared." Little was being done over the decades in

this regard. In 1876, realizing she would not live out the year, in tears she turned to her local superior, Mother Dufès, at Enghien. Mother Dufès, who had never seen Catherine in tears before, knew something very serious was bothering her. At this point the only person who knew she was the Sister of the Miraculous Medal was M. Aladel, who had died in 1865. Catherine asked the Blessed Mother for permission to reveal the whole story of her mystical experience to Mother Dufès, which she did.

Mother Dufès was heaven's answer to Catherine's dilemma. She was both resourceful and determined, looking upon the secret that Catherine revealed to her as an order from the Mother of God. In collaboration with M. Chevalier, she had a model made of the Madonna of the Globe, but upon showing it to Catherine, the seer couldn't refrain from making a grimace declaring: "Actually, it is not bad; but the Holy Virgin is much lovelier than that." The statue was completed but it took another twenty years for Mother Dufès to succeed in having it placed on a commemorative altar in the chapel of the apparitions. There it stands today—a permanent reminder of a Mother who loves the world and all her children in it. She presses them to her Immaculate and Sorrowful Heart—sorrowful because of the ingratitude and forgetfulness of her erring ones who do not take advantage of the many graces she desires to shower upon them.

Beneath the statue of Our Lady of the Globe rests the incorrupt body of St. Catherine Labouré.

"During the first appartition, Mary said that her heavenly mission was "to give glory to the good God." She used this expression to explain to Catherine the mission she would confide to her...it is then through her intercession, and her advocacy that humanity discovers and comes to love the God who is love. Mary is thus an evangelizer par excellence.

The Triple Mission

The mission given to Catherine by Our Lady was a triple one: she was to have a medal struck, she was to spread its use, and she was to assure great favors to those who wore it with devotion. For this intention she offered up the last forty-six years of her life in service to the poor and elderly, and no one, other than her confessor, knew it was she to whom Our Lady appeared.

The Blessed Virgin returned to Catherine several times within a year to confirm this mission, notably in December of 1830 and in March and September of 1831. She showed herself during evening prayer, beneath the picture of St. Joseph and above the tabernacle during Mass. At her last visit, September 1831, she said, "After this my child you shall see me no more; but you shall hear my Voice in prayer." This Voice made itself heard whenever Catherine had need of light or of encouragement.

The Voice had already spoken to her, when Catherine was upset because her director would not take her seriously. She complained to the Blessed Mother, "You can see well enough, dear Mother, that he does not believe me." The Voice had said: "Do not be disturbed! When the time comes, he will do as I wish, for he is my servant, and he would not wish to displease me." However, her director, Father Aladel, continued to be quite skeptical. In the apparition of September 1831, Our Lady complained that nothing had been done. In writing to a friend, the priest tells how it had taken a year to make him yield: "From the day following her first vision," he wrote, "this novice tried hard to win me over; but I saw in it nothing but the work of her imagination, and I strove to convince her of this. When the vision recurred, she came again to tell me. I attached no more importance to it this time, and I dismissed her as before." But when the vision appeared again months later making the same requests, the Voice added that the Blessed Virgin was not pleased with him who had failed to have the medal struck.

"This time, fearing the displeasure of her whom the Church calls the Refuge of Sinners, I could not avoid attaching some significance to the words of the Sister, although I did not let her know this. A few weeks later I had an occasion to see and speak to the Archbishop of Paris, Msgr. Louis-Hyacinth de Quélen (1778-1838), and relate the matter to him." This prelate told the Lazarist priest that he found nothing in the account at variance with the Faith and the devotion of the faithful; that, so far as he was concerned, he saw no objection to having such a medal struck and that "he wished to be the first to be given a medal."

The archbishop's words spurred Father Aladel on, and he resolved to go ahead with the project. But it was not until May 1832 that he had the medal finally made. Toward the end of that month, he ordered the engraver, Vachette, to make an initial run of fifteen hundred medals and received these on June 30. When Catherine was given a medal, she found it conformed to the model and said, "The important thing now is to make it widely known." It was the Lazarists (today known as the Vincentians) priests and above all, the Daughters of Charity, working among their pupils and the sick, who spread the medal rapidly. The medal needed no promoting for it became so popular that the engraver was overwhelmed with orders.

At the inquiry shortly afterward, the investigator asked Vachette how many medals he had made. Between June of 1832 and February of 1836, he had made over 100,000 medals. He could not keep up with the great demand, so other engravers also supplied hundreds of thousands of medals. Vachette estimates that there were over 2,200,000 medals supplied in those early days. In less than four years in France alone over 11,000,000 medals were made. Originally the medal was known as "the Medal of the Immaculate Conception," but within two years devout souls were calling it the "Miraculous Medal," the title under which it is known by everyone today.

It seemed that nothing was able to resist the power of the Miraculous Medal. Father Aladel produced a booklet about the apparitions and miracles attributed to the Miraculous Medal. The little booklet tells of how, by contact with the medal, cures were effected from insanity, leprosy, scurvy, tuberculosis, tumors, dropsy, epilepsy, hernia, paralysis, typhoid and other fevers, canker, fractures, scrofula, palpitation of the heart and cholera. To it were also ascribed wonders "of protection and preservation in war, in shipwreck, in accidents, and even in duels."

Two journalists got into a fight which they decided to settle in a duel. The first fired but missed, the second duelist hit his target and the man, Rocheford, fell over apparently mortally wounded, but such was not the case. The bullet had struck a silver Miraculous Medal which a woman friend of Rocheford had sewed into his clothing the evening before. The contact had blunted the bullet which was thus turned from its course and made no more than a bloody scratch. "On the following day a well-known article appeared, recalling that Rocheford, when he was a young man, had written a sonnet in honor of the Immaculate Conception, and that he had received a prize for it at Toulouse. "M. Rocheford," the article read, "the Virgin owed you this, but do not presume upon it again, for she paid her debt." Not only was his life spared but possibly even his eternal salvation, for dueling has always been considered gravely wrong in the eyes of the Church.

In the spiritual order the medal was responsible for the conversion of hardened sinners, of Protestants, of Jews, of apostates, of unbelievers, of Freemasons, of evildoers and worldly persons. The conversion of Alphonse Ratisbonne, related on page 33, is a case in point. Another is the deathbed conversion of the apostate archbishop of Malines, Belgium, Baron Dominique de Pradt. His life was far from being an edifying one. It seems his only concern in life was for honors and fortune, and his attitude toward the Holy See was wanting in respect. He had written a number of articles which were giving joy to the enemies of the Church. Now that he seemed about ready to die, his irreligious friends were occupied with plans for a splendid anticlerical funeral, for no one suspected that he would die other than impenitent.

He had refused even to hear mention made of returning to religion, and on several occasions he had denied Monsignor de Quélen, the Archbishop of Paris, access to his house. However, the archbishop decided to make one final attempt. Wearing the Miraculous Medal, Bishop de Quélen went once again to see the dying de Pradt. The servants and nurses, all of whom knew of the orders which had previously been given by their master, refused to admit the archbishop and he went sadly away.

He had no more than reached home when a messenger rushed in to apologize on behalf of the Abbé de Pradt. He was very sorry at what had happened; his people had been acting on outdated orders. He begged the archbishop to return. The holy prelate hurried back. The hardened old sinner had learned of the prelate's first visit, and was so touched that he had an instantaneous change of heart. He welcomed the archbishop and begged forgiveness for the trouble he had caused him, confessed his sins and deplored the scandal he had given. He received the last Sacraments from the archbishop, and died in his arms the following night. Archbishop de Quélen himself related this conversion story which he attributed to the Miraculous Medal.

In this century, in this country there have been innumerable favors granted through the Miraculous Medal. One outstanding one took place in a southern State and was related to the editor of this book by the priest who received Claude Newman into the Church. Claude was a prisoner in a jail, sentenced unjustly to death for justified homicide, when he killed a white overseer who attempted to rape his wife. He had no religious affiliation, he was poor, couldn't read or write and he was black at a time when prejudice against the blacks was strong in the deep south. One of the four prisoners in the cell block with him wore a Miraculous Medal. Claude had never seen a medal before and asked the Catholic prisoner what it meant. The man didn't know exactly what it meant and in exasperation threw the medal to the floor of the cell. Claude picked it up and asked the guard for a string that he could wear it around his neck. That night he was awakened by "the most beautiful woman that God had ever created." Terrified at first he was reassured and told: "If you would like me to be your mother and you would like to be my child, send for a Catholic priest." With that, she disappeared.

The next day, when the priest didn't believe Claude, he told the priest an incident in the priest's life years before, that Mary had revealed to him so that the priest would believe. Claude was given instruction by the priest and at the same time Our Lady gave Claude insights into the Faith that would better prepare him for Baptism and eventual death. Minutes before his execution, Claude was granted a two weeks reprieve. He broke down. The warden and the priest thought it was in relief that he was not to die in a few minutes. Claude's reply to the *good news:* "Oh, you men don't understand. Father, you don't know. If you have ever looked into her face or looked into her eyes, you would not want to live another day. What have I done wrong in these past weeks that God would now refuse my going home?"

Claude eventually was executed on February 4, 1944. Everyone who witnessed his death was amazed to see Claude die beaming with happiness. His last words to the chaplain were, "Father, I will remember you. When you have a request, ask me, and I will ask her." The Immaculate Mother on the Medal saw another of her sons safely home.

There have been many apostles of the Miraculous Medal who have always carried a liberal supply of them to give to Catholics as well as non-Catholics, to anyone who would accept the medal. Famous among these apostles was the saintly Mother Theresa of the Missionaries of Charity. She and her sisters have given out literally millions of Miraculous Medals. Many people throughout the world today have as a cherished memento of Mother Theresa a Medal given

"If you want me to be your Mother, and if you want to become my son, ask to see a Catholic priest.

to them from her saintly hands. She may have been influenced in this by the example of St. Maximilian Kolbe, whom she greatly admired and venerated (see page 41). A year after her death Mother was given posthumously the highest award Congress can give an individual, the Congressional Gold Medal. Sister Priscilla, secretary general of the Missionaries of Charity, in accepting the medal from Sen. Sam Brownback, R, Kan., the primary sponsor of the legislation, gave him a bag of Silver Miraculous Medals and asked him to distribute them. Without hesitation, the senator assured her he would.

Through countless devotees of Our Lady, religious and lay people, religious goods stores throughout the world the Miraculous Medal is continually being distributed annually in the millions. Many graces, both spiritual (conversions) and physical are obtained through this sacramental. But even as Jesus demanded an act of Faith in encountering the physically disabled who sought a cure, so too faith and confidence in Our Lady's powerful intercession is necessary. Of itself it has no miraculous power. In the measure of the petitioner's confidence and faith, so will he/she receive.

To subscribe to the Miraculous Medal magazine put out by the Central Association of the Miraculous Medal, which relates many answers to prayers through the wearing of the Miraculous Medal, and to order a good supply of medals write to:

The Central Association of the Miraculous Medal
475 E. Chelten Avenue
Germantown, Phila, PA 19144

The actual chair in which Our Lady sat in the sanctuary of the chapel of the Daughters of Charity Motherhouse in Paris. Catherine, kneeling before her, put her hands on Mary's knees and spoke to her with the confidence and intimacy of a child to its mother, which she is indeed. Mary had answered the prayer which the small Labouré girl had directed to Our Lady when her maternal mother had died. Taking the family's statue of the Blessed Mother in her arms, she prayed: "Now you be my mother."

Rich Symbolism of the Miraculous Medal

When Our Lady gave the world her Miraculous Medal it was first known as the Medal of the Immaculate Conception. The reason is two fold. She appears on the front side of the medal crushing the head of the serpent (the devil) which is the usual way she is depicted in paintings and statues of the Immaculate Conception. This goes back to the first book of the Bible: "I will put enmities between you and the woman, and your seed and her seed. She shall crush your head, and you shall lie in wait for her heel." (Genesis 3, 15).

The second, more obvious reason is found in the lettering on the outer rim of the oval frame: "O Mary, conceived without sin, pray for us who have recourse to thee." At that time, 1830, it was already a long held Catholic belief that Mary alone out of all humanity was conceived without original sin. In the Fourteenth Century it was the Franciscan theologian, Bl. Duns Scotus, who gave the theological answer to the problem of how she could be preserved from original sin and yet be redeemed. In view of her son's redemptive death she too was redeemed from sin, but her redemption was a perfect one—a redemption that anticipated the redeeming grace of her divine Son.

Understandably, this first grace she received, in view of her divine maternity, is very dear to her and she wants her children to be aware of how much it means to her. When Catherine saw these words encircling Mary on the medal, this truth was not a dogma of the Church. No doubt it helped pave the way for the definition of this dogma in 1854 by Pope Pius IX. It was ratified by heaven itself in 1858 when Mary identified herself to St. Bernadette at Lourdes as the "Immaculate Conception."

Though Catholics for the most part have believed throughout recent centuries that Mary was conceived immaculate, this truth was reserved for the most opportune time, the Nineteenth Century, to be given special attention and defined. It was a century of great injustice and misery for the ordinary working man. Society was experiencing the industrial revolution and uncontrolled capitalism. No longer willing to accept the direction and moral restaints of the Church of Rome, powerful industrialists offered men material "progress," but at the cost of unbelievable suffering of the poor and working class. Out of their misery rose the false "paradise" of Communism. The period from 1830 to 1858 desperately needed the Mother of God to checkmate the massive onslaught of materialism, modernism and secularism so prevalent in our day. With little regard for the supernatural, our age is noted for its total disregard of sin and its consequence. In the Immaculate Conception, we are reminded that original sin does exist and its sad consequences are all around us. And so the battle goes on between "the woman" on the medal and the serpent beneath her foot.

On the medal, we see Mary's hands extended with rays coming from them. On her fingers were rings, set with precious stones that throw out luminous rays. Catherine noticed, however, there were stones that did not emit rays. Catherine understood that these represented the many graces available to men, but which were never obtained for the simple reason people neglected to ask for them. Our Lady and God never force themselves upon us.

We see in our day vast numbers of Catholics who have given up the practice of the Faith. Most of them no longer have devotion to Mary, all of which underlines the vital role Mary plays in the economy of salvation. Through the Incarnation she became the Mother of Jesus, the Head of the mystical Body (the Church). At the same time she became the mother of the members of the Church. She is the mediatrix, united and working with her Son in reconciling men with God. What wounds her motherly heart grievously is the fact that she, the Mediatrix of all Graces, wants to bestow on her children many graces from the unlimited reservoir of Graces, the Sacred Heart of Jesus—but they "would not." Our Lady makes it clear through St. Catherine Labouré that, "Graces will be bestowed abundantly on those who have confidence." In the measure we trust in her mediation we will receive.

On the opposite side of the medal, Our Lady becomes a catechist, teaching us fundamental truths of the Faith necessary to living the Faith, which is found on the front side of the medal. There she is symbolized in her role as the Immaculate Mediatrix. On the reverse side we see the large letter "M" interconnected with a bar, on which a cross is surmounted. The "M" and cross symbolize Mary standing at the foot of the cross, for one cannot separate the Immaculate Heart from her Sorrowful Heart. This is brought out again by the sword-pierced heart just below the "M." The cross and the bar intertwined with the "M" indicate the close relationship of Mary with Jesus in the plan of redemption, emphasizing her role as coredemptrix. This title when properly understood places Mary ever beside her Son, but never above or apart from Him. We see Mary's participation in every major instance of the life of Jesus: His conception, birth, hidden and public life. Remember how His mother requested His first miracle at Cana, "Do whatever He tells you" (Jn 2:5), which opened His public life? This in turn ended in His passion and death. She witnessed and participated in the paschal mysteries as no one else did, standing at the foot of His Cross, totally united with her Son's cruel death on Calvary. She viewed his Ascension into heaven and was with the apostles when the Holy Spirit descended on them at Pentecost.

Below the "M" is the symbol of perfect love, the two hearts of Jesus and Mary, both aflame with love for the other and all men—the one symbolizing the infinite love of the God-man, the other the perfection of a creature's love returning love for the infinite love of its Creator. That love of God is also a maternal love embracing all of God's children, her children by grace.

The Sacred Heart of Jesus is circled with a crown of thorns, which men place there by their sins and ingratitude. The Immaculate Heart is pierced with the sword of sorrows, as predicted by the old man Simeon when Jesus was presented in the temple. Though immaculate herself, she has taken on the sins of all men in as much as she cooperated totally with the Father's will in the redemptive passion and death of His and her Son.

The twelve stars surrounding the "M," the cross and two hearts represent the twelve tribes of Israel and the twelve apostles linking the Old and New Testaments of the Bible and representing the Church which was founded upon the twelve apostles. The twenty-first chapter of Revelations speaking of the City of God, the heavenly Jerusalem, most commentators regard as symbolic of the Church. It also symbolizes Mary, Mother of the Church in her perfection, here and now, which will be mirrored in the Church at the end of time. In the book of Revelations, we find in chapter twelve the reference to Mary and the twelve stars. "And a great sign appeared in the heaven: a woman clothed with the sun, and the moon was under her feet, and upon her head a crown of twelve stars (Rev. 12:1)."

The number twelve, as found in the number of stars, figures extensively in the twenty-first chapter of the book of Revelations. The holy city, the new Jerusalem, symbol of the Church or Mary, has twelve gates, with twelve pearls, ". . . and the foundations and the wall were adorned by all manner of precious stones." The twelve principal stones are interpreted as the twelve virtues that Mary excelled in above all other creatures including the angels. The full interpretation of the symbolism found in the medal will be finally revealed (as well as the symbolism of Revelations) only at the end of time.

The important point to remember is that when St. Catherine asked the Blessed Mother for an explanation of the various symbols she answered: “The M surmounted by the Cross and the two hearts say it all.” Surely something to meditate upon—the union of the infinite love of Jesus with the perfection of a creature’s love as found in Mary, imaged by the Hearts side by side. Their love is perfectly expressed in an obedience that embraced the Cross for the salvation and sanctification of all men.

In her first apparition to St. Catherine, Our Lady said that her mission was “to give glory to the good God.” This Medal of the Immaculate Conception in its rich symbolism, in the millions of souls and bodies it has touched, and in the many graces of which it is a channel, is an ideal means of evangelization, given to us by the apostle par excellence — the Mother of God, Mediatrix of all Graces.

The Conquest of a Rabid Anti-Catholic

Baron Theodore de Bussieres

Our Lady loves the chosen people, her people, in a special way. Nowhere is it more perfectly illustrated than in the miraculous conversion of the Jew, Alphonse Ratisbonne. This eyewitness account also illustrates the power of Our Lady's Miraculous Medal to bring about the conversion of even a most bitter opponent to the Catholic faith.

TOWARD THE CLOSE of the autumn of 1841, a young man of a well-known Strasbourg family arrived in Naples. He was on his way to the East, in search of health and pleasure. The Jew, Alphonse Ratisbonne, was destined for a brilliant position in the world. Nonetheless, he had resolved to devote himself to the great work of the regeneration of his co-religionists. His thoughts and aspirations all revolved around this one high purpose. His wrath was enkindled at everything that reminded him of the age-long sufferings of his people.

The sky of Naples, blue though it was, could not make the young Jew forget the East to where he was bound. Yet, it struck him that he had never been to Rome. When he returned to Strasbourg to be married and began to be involved in business affairs, there would be little likelihood of his ever being in Italy again. Under the influence of this sudden thought he went to a booking office and reserved a seat in the coach to Rome. Three days later he was in the Eternal City. As a tourist he began to visit the ruins, the churches, the art galleries, crowding his memory with a confused medley of impressions and excursions. He had been drawn to Rome by some unaccountable fascination rather than by any intellectual curiosity, but now he was eager to be done with this city.

The young Jewish businessman, Alphonse Ratisbonne. During his sightseeing Rome, he was given a Miraculous Medal which he reluctantly accepted and even agreed to pray the *Memorare*. She appeared to him, he converted, became a priest and the rest of his life worked for the conversion of his fellow Jews.

On the day before he was to set off for Naples he found that he had still to pay a farewell visit to an old school friend, my brother, Gustave de Bussieres, with whom he had kept up his youthful friendship in spite of differences in their religious opinions. Since Ratisbonne did not manage to see my brother who was out on a hunting trip he decided not to come into our house. He would simply leave a farewell card. Chance, or rather Providence, arranged things differently. His knock was answered by an Italian servant of mine who mistook his intention and, to his great annoyance, showed him into the drawing room. I therefore gave him a cordial welcome, chatting with him about his sightseeing and listening to him as he told me about his impressions of Rome. "A rather odd thing happened to me the other day," he said in passing, "while I was looking over the church of the Aracoeli on the Capitol, I was suddenly seized with an unaccountable and deep emotion." While Ratisbonne was telling me this, my expression must have betrayed the thought, "You will be a Catholic one day."

He read my thoughts and went on to say emphatically that his emotion had been purely spiritual and not in any way Christian! "Besides," he continued, "as I came down from the Capitol a most melancholy sight rekindled all my hatred of Catholicism. I had to pass through the ghetto, and when I saw the miserable conditions in which the Jews live there, I said to myself that after all it is a nobler thing to be one of the oppressed rather than on the side of the oppressors." Our conversation now began to take on a more controversial turn. As a recent convert, I tried to get him to share my Catholic convictions, but he only smiled at my efforts, and, in tones of good-natured pity for my "superstition," said HE HAD BEEN BORN A JEW, AND A JEW HE WOULD DIE.

At this point in our talk, there came to my mind a most extraordinary idea, doubtless suggested from Heaven, for the wise of this world would have called it foolishness. I said: "Since you are so sure of the strength and stability of your convictions, promise me that you will wear what I am going to give you." "Well, what is it?" he asked. "Only this medal," I said, and showed him a Miraculous Medal I had in my possession. At this he drew back in his chair in mingled surprise and indignation. "But," I said dryly, "since you think as you do, wearing it can mean nothing to you, whereas it would mean giving me great pleasure." "Oh, very well, then," he exclaimed with a laugh, "You will at least see that people are quite wrong when they accuse us Jews of having obstinate, insurmountable prejudices. Besides, it will give me an amusing chapter for the diary I am keeping." And he went on joking in the same way—to my great distress, for to me all that he said was blasphemous.

Meanwhile I had been fastening a ribbon around his neck: and my young daughters had attached the blessed medal to it while we were talking. But now there was something more difficult I wanted him to do—to recite St. Bernard's prayer, "Remember, O most Blessed Virgin Mary. . ." This, as I had half expected, turned out to be asking too much. He refused absolutely and in a tone which seemed to say, "Really, this man's impertinence goes beyond all bounds! But some inner force urged me on, and I struggled with his reiterated refusals with a kind of desperation. I held out the prayer to him and begged him to take it away with him, asking him if he would be kind enough to write it out, as it was the only copy I had.

At length, as if to rid himself of my importunity, he said, in a tone of good-humored irony, "All right, I'll write it out then you can have my copy and I'll keep yours," and he went off muttering to himself, "What a tactless oddity he is!" I heard him say, "I'd like to see what he would say if I were to plague him to recite some of my Jewish prayers in the same way!"

After he had gone, my wife and I looked at each other for some time without saying a word. Then, still upset by the blasphemies we had been obliged to listen to, we implored God to pardon our visitor, asking our little daughters to say the Hail Mary each night for his conversion...

Ratisbonne could not get over his astonishment at my importunity. However, he copied out the prayer which he knew I thought was so powerful—and read it again and again in an endeavor to discover what could give it such value in my eyes. After reading it so often, he almost knew it by heart: It kept coming back into his mind; he would go about saying it over and over to himself as though it was some maddening little opera tune. In the evening in accordance with a long-standing Roman custom it was my turn to watch before the Blessed Sacrament, in company with a certain prince, whom I simply call M.A.B., and some friends. I begged them to join with me in praying for the conversion of a Jew.

The following day, January 16, 1842, I dined at the Borghese palace with the Count de Laferronnays. After dinner I told him what was on my mind, earnestly commending my young Jewish friend to his prayers. In the course of our intimate conversation he told me of the confidence he always had in Our Lady's protection even in the days when a busy political life had not allowed him much time for prayer. "Have no fear," he said, "if he says the *Memorare* he is yours, and many more too."

Ratisbonne came to my house about one o'clock and we embarked on some more sightseeing. I was really grieved to notice how little impression I was making on him. He was still in the same frame of mind, still hating Catholicism intensely and making disparaging remarks about it.

That night M. de Laferronnays died suddenly at eleven o'clock, leaving to those who mourned him the memory of a life of exemplary virtue. Having loved him a long time as though he were my father, I shared not only the sorrow felt by family, but the sad duties which devolved upon them in making funeral arrangements. Yet, the thought of Ratisbonne followed me everywhere, even as I knelt beside my dead friend's coffin. I spent part of the night with the sorrowing family. I did not wish to leave my friend's remains but I could not banish from my mind the thought of the soul I was anxious to win for the Faith. When I mentioned my predicament to the abbé Gerbet he urged me by all means to carry on the work I had begun. In doing so, he said, I would best fulfill the wishes of my departed friend, who had prayed so fervently for the conversion of the young Jew.

And so there I was running after Ratisbonne and dragging him by the hand, showing him more of the city's religious antiquities, in an endeavor to impress the great truths of Catholicism upon his mind. At St. John Lateran I showed him the bas-reliefs above the statues of the Twelve Apostles. On one side the Old Testament figures, on the other their fulfillment in the person of the Messiah. He found the parallel rather clever. However, he remarked that he was more of a Jew than

Right: The painting of Our Lady as she appeared to Alphonse Ratisbonne in the church of Sant' Andrea delle Fratte. It was in the side chapel of St. Michael, special patron of the Jews, where he saw her. St. Maximilian Kolbe celebrated his first Mass here.

ever. I replied that I had perfect confidence in God's promises and was convinced that, being an honest and sincere man he would one day be a Catholic, even if it needed an angel from Heaven to enlighten him.

At about one o'clock I had to go and make some arrangements at the church of St. Andrea delle Fratte for the funeral ceremony fixed for the next day. Seeing Ratisbonne coming down the Via Condotti, I invited him to accompany me and wait a few minutes while I attended to my business and then walk on with me. We entered the church. Noticing the funeral preparations, he asked for whom were they for: "For a friend I have lost," I replied, "whom I loved very much, M. de Laferronnays." He then began to walk up and down the nave, his cold, indifferent gaze seeming to say, "What a frightful church!" I left him and went off to the convent to arrange a tribune reservation for the dead man's family. I could not have been away much more than ten minutes.

When I returned I saw nothing of Ratisbonne at first. Then I caught sight of him on his knees, in the chapel of St. Michael the Archangel. I went up to him and touched him. I had to do this three or four times before he became aware of my presence. Finally he turned towards me, face bathed in tears, clasped his hands together and said with an expression which no words can describe, "How that friend of yours must have prayed for me!"

Above: Fr. Alphonse Ratisbonne who founded a Sisterhood for the conversion of the Jews in Jerusalem. The hotel, run by his Sisters, is located over the actual pavement where Christ was condemned to death.

In the Presence of a Miracle

I was petrified with astonishment. I felt what people must feel in the presence of a miracle. I helped Ratisbonne to his feet and led him, almost carrying him, out of the church. Then I asked him what was the matter, and where did he want to go. "Take me wherever you like," he cried, "after what I have seen, I shall obey." I urged him to explain his meaning, but he was unable to do so—emotion was too strong. Instead he took hold of his Miraculous Medal and kissed it with passionate emotion. He broke into tears at the thought of all the heretics and unbelievers. Finally, he asked me if I thought him mad. "Of course I am not mad," he went on, before I had a chance to speak, "I am in my right mind. Oh God, of course I am not mad! Everyone knows that I am not mad!"

Gradually this delirious emotion subsided and he grew calmer, and now his face was radiant, almost transfigured. He begged me to take him to a priest and asked when he could receive holy Baptism, for now he was sure he could not live without it. I took him at once to the Gesú to see Father de Villefort, who invited him to explain what had happened. Ratisbonne drew out his medal, kissed it, and showed it to us, saying, "I saw her! I saw her!" and again emotion choked his words, but soon he grew calmer and spoke. I shall give his own words:

"I had only been in the church a moment when I was suddenly seized with an indescribable agitation of mind. I looked up and found that the rest of the building had disappeared. One single chapel seemed to have gathered all the light and concentrated it in itself. In the midst of this radiance I saw someone standing on the altar, a lofty shining figure, all majesty and sweetness, the Virgin Mary just as she looks on this medal. Some irresistible force drew me towards her. She motioned to me to kneel down and when I did so, she seemed to approve. Though she never said a word, I understood her perfectly."

Brief as his account was, Ratisbonne could not utter it without frequently pausing for breath and to subdue the overwhelming emotion he felt. We listened to him, awe mingled with joy and gratitude. One phrase struck us especially, so deep and mysterious was it: "She never said a word, but I understood her perfectly." From this moment on, it was enough to hear him speak, faith exhaled from his heart like a precious perfume from a casket, that holds but cannot imprison. He spoke of the Real Presence, like a man who believed in it with all his being — like a man who had experienced it.

Upon leaving Father de Villefort, we went to give thanks to God, first at St. Maria Maggiore, the basilica beloved of Our Lady, and then at St. Peter's. He prayed with great fervor at the tombs of the Holy Apostles. When I told him the account of the conversion of St. Paul all the former emotion returned.

At the altar of the Blessed Sacrament the Real Presence of Jesus so overwhelmed him that he was on the verge of fainting, and I was obliged to take him away, so terrible did it seem to him to remain before the living God stained as he was with original sin. He hastened to take refuge in the Lady Chapel. "Here," he said, "I have no fear, for I feel protected by some boundless mercy." I asked him for more details of the miraculous vision. At first he had been able to see the Queen of Heaven clearly, appearing in all splendor of her immaculate beauty; but he had not been able to bear the radiance of that divine light for long. Three times he had tried to look up to her, and three times he had found himself unable to raise his eyes higher than her hands, from which blessings and graces seemed to be falling like so many shining rays.

"Oh God," he cried, "only half an hour before I was blaspheming, and felt a deadly hatred for the Catholic religion! All my acquaintances know that humanly speaking I had the strongest reasons for remaining a Jew. My family is Jewish, my bride to be is a Jewess, my uncle is a Jew. By becoming a Catholic, I am sacrificing all my earthly hopes and interests; and yet I am not mad. So they must believe me." Surely the sincerity and good faith of such a man are beyond question — one who, at the age of twenty-eight, could sacrifice all his joys and all his hopes for the sake of his conscience. The news of this striking miracle began to spread through Rome. I was with him at Fr. de Villefort's when General Chlapouski came up to him. "So you have seen a vision of Our Lady!" he said; "Tell me . . ."

"A vision!" cried Ratisbonne, interrupting him, "I saw her herself, as she really is, in person, just as I can see you standing before me now."

Such are the facts which I submit for the consideration of all serious-minded people. I myself once wandered long—too long in the gloom and confusion of Protestantism and I shall be happy if this simple narrative may rouse some soul to cry, like the blind man in the Gospel, Lord that I may see! For if a man but pray, God will not fail to open his eyes to the light of Catholic truth.

— *Condensed from the booklet, "The Conquest of the Miraculous Medal"*

The "Bullets" Hit the Mark

St. Maximilian's involvement with the Medal of the Immaculate Conception, which the Miraculous Medal was first called, went back to his seminary days in Rome. On January 20, 1917, the rector of the Seraphic College, Fr. Stephen Ignudi, narrated to the seminarians the story of the miraculous conversion of the Jewish agnostic, Alphonse Ratisbonne (see page 33). Friar Maximilian reasoned that if Mary could conquer the heart of this rabid anti-Catholic Jew through the use of the Miraculous Medal, it would be an ideal means of conquering other souls. Moreover, as a Franciscan, this sacramental honoring Our Lady under her great prerogative of the Immaculate Conception should be given special consideration in the battle for souls. He was well aware of the fact that Franciscans were the foremost defenders and champions of this great gift Mary received at the first instance of her existence.

Moreover, on the front part of the medal she appeared with extended hands which had rings on her fingers. These rings were throwing out rays to the earth. The rays symbolized the graces that she distributes as the Mediatrix of All Graces. Having shared so intimately in her Divine Son's passion and death, she now shares in His glory and has been given the role of almoner of the graces He, the Redeemer, won for mankind. In Maximilian's battle plans Mary Immaculate, the perfect model for our imitation and the dispenser of God's merciful love, would be the commandress under whose banner he would do battle against the serpent and his minions.

Maximilian, with eyes focused on eternity, realized that this life was a continual and bitter warfare which allowed no room for compromise—too much was at stake. The concept of a spiritual warfare between the Woman of Genesis and the Serpent was the motif upon which he build his movement. Military terminology came naturally to his mind. As a young man he had first entertained the thought of a military career.

He thus looked upon the Miraculous Medal as an ideal means of conquering souls in this spiritual warfare he and his followers were engaged in. He called these medals his bullets. They would be, moreover, a perfect external symbol of the interior total consecration to Mary Immaculate of his knights (followers) through the movement, the *Militia Immaculatae,* which he founded in Rome in 1917.

St. Maximilian had unbounded confidence in the power of the Immaculate Virgin to bring about the conversion of the "tough cases." That is why he went after obdurate atheists, Communists and Freemasons. Even as a young seminarian in Rome he asked permission of his superior to visit the Grand Mason who had his headquarters in Rome, in the hopes of converting him. Impressed at the friar's zeal the Rector nonetheless prudently told him to wait a few more years and gain more experience. In the meantime he could pray for the conversion of the Masons.

In 1927, he did visit the Supreme Grand Master of the Masonic Lodges in Poland, a Mr. Stempowski. After the usual cordialities, Kolbe got right down to business. He gave the Mason who professed no religion, a Miraculous Medal, asking him to carry it with him at all times. Surprising enough, Stempowski accepted it. He left the non-praying atheist with these assuring words: We'll do the praying. The Virgin will do the rest."

Father Kolbe went on to found a Franciscan friary that was to become the largest in the world, a daily Catholic newspaper and over ten other publications. He established a mission in Japan in the 1930s and became well known throughout Poland. During the war years, he was arrested and sent to the concentration camp of Auschwitz, where he died a heroic death, giving up his life for a fellow prisoner. All during this time Mr. Stempowski carried the medal given to him by Fr. Maximilian who had become a national hero. "Yes, Fr. Kolbe is that friar who came to my house with something important to tell me and to ask me a question. Yes, I remember." A few years after the war had ended there was a sizable Catholic funeral in Warsaw. It was for a certain Mr. Stempowski who had converted on his deathbed. The *bullet* had hit the mark.

Fr. Maximilian whenever he could spread the Miraculous Medal and encouraged his followers to do likewise. He explained the ultimate purpose of his use of the Miraculous Medal: "Because conversion and sanctification are divine graces, the Miraculous Medal will be the best means for reaching our purpose. For that reason it constitutes a first rate weapon of the Knights; it is the bullet with which a faithful soldier cuts down the enemy, that is, evil, and thus rescues souls. Let us contribute all our strength in bringing about what was already foreseen by St. Catherine Labouré, to whom the Immaculata graciously revealed the Miraculous Medal, that the Immaculata be queen of the whole world and of each soul in particular as soon as possible."

The Saint of Silence

Madeline Pecora Nugent SFO

In her sixteen years as superior of this particular convent of the Sisters of Charity in the Rue de Picpus, a section of Paris known as Reuilly, Sister Jeanne Dufes had never seen Sister Catherine Labouré so upset. The seventy year old woman with the somewhat taciturn yet resigned look never made a fuss. Now, on this beautiful summer day, Sister Labouré's blue-gray eyes were streaked with tears of hidden desperation.

Today, Catherine had been disappointed about her request to switch confessors. Upon her entry into the novitiate in 1830, Catherine and the other sisters had been assigned Father Jean-Marie Aladel as spiritual director, but, upon his death eleven years ago, he had been replaced by Father Jules Chinchon. A short time ago, Father Chinchon had been made director of only male novices in these twin Orders founded by St. Vincent de Paul. Another priest had been appointed confessor to the sisters.

This switch had upset Sister Labouré so much that she had begged for an audience with the superior general of the male branch of the Order. She had just returned from that meeting, having been denied her request to continue her spiritual direction with Father Chinchon.

It was unlike Sister Labouré to question orders. With highest regard for her superiors, she even saved for them the choicest portions of meals that she cooked. Sister Dufes had never before heard Catherine discuss, much less question, an order. If told to do something disagreeable, Catherine's pale face might flush, but in silence she would obey at once. "One must obey just because Sister Superior has ordered it," she would declare. Often Catherine admonished the younger sisters, "My children, do not murmur against your superiors for they are really God's representatives." In 1872, an honorary title was assigned to one of the seven sisters who tended the old men at the Hospice d'Enghien. The honor had gone, not to Catherine, the oldest of the seven sisters, but to a much younger, inexperienced nun. Catherine had led all the sisters to Sister Dufes with the words, "Please be sure that it is enough that authority has spoken. Sister Angelique will be received among us as one sent by the Lord. We shall all obey her as we would yourself."

Catherine was clearly distraught over not being permitted to continue with Father Chinchon. "Mother, I have not much longer to live," Catherine sobbed to Sister Dufes. Since the beginning of this year of 1876, Catherine had come to believe that she would not live into 1877.

"Perhaps the time has come for me to speak. However, since I have been bidden to speak to no one but my confessor, I can say nothing to you unless I am empowered to do so. Tonight, in my prayer, I will confide the matter to the Blessed Virgin, and will seek permission to speak." Catherine had great devotion to the Blessed Virgin whom she had taken as her model. She recited her Rosary prayerfully and attentively, often chiding other sisters for praying too quickly. Frequently, as she went about her duties, she would kneel briefly before the Virgin's statue in the garden. "Should the Blessed Virgin grant my request, I will tell you all in the morning. Otherwise, I shall have to keep silence." Bowing shakily, Sister Labouré took her leave. Troubled by Catherine's distress, Sister Dufes watched Catherine disappear into the convent. Catherine had always been quiet, compliant, and obedient even when Dufes made painful, cutting remarks to the old nun to give her a chance to practice virtue.

Catherine spoke up only to defend the 1830 revelations of the Miraculous Medal to an unknown novice of their Order, revelations made public by Father Aladel. "I see that when the time comes, you can hold to your own opinion," Sister Dufes once remarked. To this, the elderly Catherine, who had been a novice herself at the time of the apparitions, had fallen to her knees, admitting, "I know very well that I am full of pride."

Why was Sister Labouré so troubled? Descended from the landed peasantry, Catherine was only minimally educated. Once, when being considered for superior of one of the minor houses, Catherine had objected. "Mother, how could such a notion ever enter your head? Are you not first among those who know me to be incompetent?" Catherine did not receive the assignment.

A hard-working country girl, Catherine for forty years had risen daily at four o'clock to care for several dozen old servants of the House of Orleans who resided in the Hospice d'Enghien. For these grouchy, rude, ill-mannered, and coarse old men, Catherine had cheerfully prepared meals, washed chamberpots, and done the most menial jobs. She had prayed for, mothered, and scolded the irascible gents, eventually reconciling every one of them to God. "I see Our Lord in them," she once revealed, "and it is too much for me."

Catherine also had been gardener, seamstress, portress, and poultry manager, caring for doves, chickens, rabbits, and cows. In her spare time, she would recite her Rosary. "After I enter the chapel, I place myself in the presence of God and I say to Him, 'Lord, here I am; give me whatever You wish,'" Catherine divulged. "If He gives me something, I am happy and I thank Him. If he does not give me anything, I thank Him nonetheless, knowing as I do that I deserve nothing. Then I begin to tell Him of all that concerns me, my joys, my thoughts, my distress, and finally I listen to Him."

Photograph of St. Catherine Labouré taken shortly before her death.

Better educated and better born sisters often treated Catherine like an incapable fool, refusing to speak to her except in mockery. Catherine countered this discourtesy with the words, "One must see God in everyone."

After what seemed an endless night to Sister Dufes, morning broke. A little before ten in the morning, Catherine asked Sister Dufes to come to the parlor. Here, without bothering to sit, Catherine revealed her heart. She was the unknown novice who, forty-six years earlier, had been given the revelation of the Miraculous Medal and told to speak of it to her confessor alone. In keeping with the Virgin's wishes, Father Aladel had related the vision without revealing Catherine's identity. Upon Father Aladel's death, Catherine had disclosed all to Father Chinchon.

As the Virgin had wished, the medal had been minted and distributed. The Association of the Children of Mary had been established. But a statue of the Virgin holding the world as a golden orb to her heart had not yet been cast. If Father Chinchon and Father Aladel before him had not seen that this was done, how could Catherine convince a new confessor to do it when she would die before the year was out? This was why the switch in confessors had so upset her. This was why she had asked the Blessed Virgin if she should reveal everything to Sister Dufes who had the authority to bring about the Lady's wish.

Sister Dufes was dumbstruck. Never had she suspected that Catherine had been the novice favored with visions of the Miraculous Medal. She felt like falling on her knees before Catherine to beg her forgiveness. Without revealing Catherine's secret, Sister Dufes made plans to have the statue cast. Of the miniature model Catherine commented, "Actually, it is not bad but the Holy Virgin is much lovelier than that." When the statue was completed, Sister Dufes began a twenty-year struggle to have it placed on the commemorative altar in the Rue du Bac as the Virgin had requested. Only in 1896, when Leo XIII granted formal approval to the statue, was the wish effected. Catherine Labouré died peacefully at 7 p.m., December 31, 1876. Then Sister Dufes broke forty-six years of silence. "Yes, it is true," Dufes said, confirming a rumor that sometimes surfaced about the old portress, poultry keeper, and cook, "she was the one who saw the Blessed Virgin."

Mary Asked for a Marian Movement for Youth

In l830, St. Catherine told her confessor, Fr. Jean-Marie Aladel, that the Blessed Mother wanted him to begin a youth organization, especially for the working class who lived in grave hardship and want, so common in those days. But it wasn't until February 2, 1840 that the Confraternity was established. The movement spread rapidly, and in less than 25 years there were more than 1,000 Associations of the Children of Mary world-wide. The movement presently is represented in thirty countries, and has more than 200,000 members. Catherine always watched over the growth of this new Marian movement with great interest.

Throughout the years, the movement has continued to take into account the signs of the times, especially with regard to the needs of youth. It desires to apply the message of the gospel to the problems of society. It assists not only its members but also those young people for whom the Church is distant, or those who find themselves in trouble or experiencing difficult situations.

The movement has always been moved to action by the spirit of Mary's Magnificat. Today as yesterday, the Marian Youth Movement encourages young people to work on behalf of the poor and the marginalized, imitating Mary's favor for the littlest ones in her life. *"It is through the movement,"* Our Lady said to Catherine, *"that 1 show my regard for the poor and those living in difficult situations."*

"A leader in the Marian Youth movement asked me one day to accompany her to a meeting... I was truck by the goals of the Movement: to live in Community, to be aware of all the factors which make life difficult for the poor, to serve others humbly as Mary, the humble servant... The goals of the Movement led me to live in this way, to listen to others, to open myself up to those who are most marginalized, and to evangelize them and be evangelized by them in turn." *—Muriel, 42 year old*

"Since I have been a member of the Marian Youth Movement, I have learned to respect each person and look at them from my heart. I have learned to discover what is beautiful within each person regardless of their external appearance. This is what I love most about Mary. She always saw the goodness and beauty of God in others. — *Sylvia, !8 year old.*

PART III

La Salette, France, 1846

The Madonna in Tears

"How long I have suffered for you! If my Son is not to cast you off, I am obliged to entreat Him without ceasing!"

"... the young shepherds are amazed by the modesty of her dress and both agree that the Christ resting on her breast seems to be the focal point of all her glory. She has identifying hallmarks: three garlands of roses recall her title of Queen of the Holy Rosary; and an apron, a headdress, a shawl are signs of her choosing to remain with the people, especially the little people. . . .We can sense that this shimmering Crucified Christ pervades all her thoughts. And the tongs to the right and the hammer to the left of the crossbar poignantly recall our choice of atonement or of sin in our ongoing role in the Lord's Passion. . . . the Lady of Compassion places before us [the challenge]: 'No matter how well you pray in the future, no matter how well you act, you will never be able to make up to me what I have endured on your behalf.'

"Finally, here we see our Mother as the angels see her in heaven, the powerful Mediatrix, always interceding for us, the generous giver of graces, the world's gentle providence, the merciful Queen, making her own all of her children's concerns, those of this life and those of eternity."

Excerpts from the book, *A Grace Called La Salette*, By Fr. Jean Jaouen

La Salette, France

Above: The actual stone which Our Lady sat upon while grieving over the sins and ingratitude of her children. Below: the mile-high sanctuary with its large hostel.

A Mother Weeps for Her Children

Msgr. John Kennedy

The parish of La Salette in the diocese of Grenoble comprises a few tiny hamlets in the French Alps. Its setting is spectacular: a series of towering mountains, majestic and mysterious, thrusting at the sky, the peaks of some glittering with snow. One could not but be impressed by the grandeur here; no more could one fail to notice the loneliness. This is a place only skimpily populated, and far from the busy world. It has the quality of a natural sanctuary, somewhat removed, austere, silent. It was the scene of an apparition of Our Lady to two rude cattle herders, Melanie Mathieu, aged 14 and Maximin Giraud, aged 11. This took place on Saturday afternoon, September 19, 1846.

The year is significant, right in the middle of the socially and politically turbulent Nineteenth Century. France was in ferment. The French Revolution was followed by the reign of Napoleon, with its further change and its constant warfare and its exactions of the people, then defeat and a succession of shifts in government. Many ties with the traditional past had been violently sundered, much that was immemorial had been sent crashing to bits, and the situation in the country was uncertain. Besides, in France and throughout the Western world, this was an age bristling with new ideas. Revolution was not confined to the political order; it affected all of life. Religion, for example, had suffered persecution or severe intellectual attack and was being countered by conceptions of man's nature and destiny radically different from those of Christianity. This had had impact even on the small, dull, isolated town of Corps, where Melanie's and Maximin's families lived.

Fewer and fewer went to Sunday Mass. The Sacraments were neglected. Once there had prevailed a Christian view of life, an awareness of God, a wholesome piety. Now, there was far more cursing than praying, and Christian attitudes and observance had given way to self-indulgence, greediness, a hard worldly spirit. We have said that Melanie and Maximin were natives of Corps. Curiously, although that town numbered hardly more than a thousand inhabitants, the pair had never met there. They first became acquainted in Ablandins, one of the hamlets in the parish of La Salette, on September 17, 1846. To Ablandins they had come as employees of two local farmers. The following day they were in sight of each other in the fields, and on Saturday, at first light, they started back for the mountain together.

At noon, as the Angelus sounded, the children drove the cows from the fields to a ravine, to water them at a spring called the fountain of the beasts. When this chore had been performed, Maximin and Melanie took from their knapsacks their lunches of bread and cheese, which they proceeded to eat with good appetite. Afterward they stretched out on the ground and napped.

Well over an hour later Melanie suddenly awoke, all solicitude for the cows. Where were they? Were they safe? She scrambled up, called to the sleeping boy, and the two ran to look for their charges. These, they soon saw, were placidly grazing.

It was getting on toward the middle of the afternoon; soon the journey down to Ablandins must be begun. Melanie turned back toward the ravine, to gather up the knapsacks and whatever scraps might be left from their meal. As she reached its lip, she suddenly halted, thunderstruck.

For below, in the ravine, she saw a large circle of brilliant light, vibrant and outshining the sun. After a moment she summoned enough voice to call to Maximin, "Come quickly. See the light down there!" He dashed to her side. "Where?" he wanted to know. She pointed. He, too, saw it. As they watched, the splendor of the dazzling light intensified, they were puzzled and fear-stricken and were about to flee when they observed that the luminous circle was opening. Gradually they could make out, ever more sharply defined, the figure of a woman. She was seated, her face in her hands, in an attitude of sorrow, weeping. Slowly, with unearthly grace, she arose. With her arms crossed on her breast and her head somewhat inclined, she confronted them.

The loveliness of her grieving face was magnetic. But they noticed as well the details of her vesture: the headdress topped by a lucent crown; the dress strewn with bursts of light; the slippers edged with roses; the golden crucifix hanging from a chain about her neck, a hammer on one side of it, a pair of pincers on the other. And all was suffused with glory. As they gazed in fascination, the children heard the woman speak in a voice both commanding and reassuring.

"Come to me, my children," she said. "Do not be afraid. I am here to tell you something of the greatest importance." She spoke in French, not in their patois. They found it hard to follow her, but grasped her meaning. They moved gingerly into the ravine, came within touching distance of her. They could now see her more closely and mark the crystalline tears upon her cheeks.

Again she addressed them, at first in French, later in their own dialect. "If my people will not obey, I shall be compelled to loose my Son's arm. It is so heavy, so pressing that I can no longer restrain it. How long I have suffered for you! If my Son is not to cast you off, I am obliged to entreat Him without ceasing. But you take not the least notice of that. No matter how well you pray in the future, no matter how well you act, you will never be able to make up to me what I have endured for your sake.

"I have appointed you six days for working. The seventh I have reserved for myself. And no one will give it to me. This it is which causes the weight of my Son's arm to be so crushing. The cart drivers cannot swear without bringing in my Son's name. These are the two things which make my Son's arm so burdensome.

"If the harvest is spoiled, it is your own fault. I warned you last year by means of the potatoes. You paid no heed. Quite the reverse, when you discovered that the potatoes had rotted, you swore, you abused my Son's name. They will continue to rot, and by Christmas this year there will be none left. If you have grain, it will do no good to sow it, for what you sow the beasts will devour, and any part of it that springs up will crumble into dust when you thresh it.

"A great famine is coming. But before that happens, the children under seven years of age will be seized with trembling and die in their parents' arms. The grownups will pay for their sins by hunger. The grapes will rot, and the walnuts will turn bad." The woman continued speaking, turning toward Maximin. She was confiding a secret to him; Melanie could not hear a word of it. Then it was Melanie's turn to have a secret entrusted to her, and of this Maximin caught nothing.

The discourse audible to both resumed. "If people are converted, the rocks will become piles of wheat, and it will be found that the potatoes have sown themselves."

A pause, and then, with a searching look, "Do you say your prayers well, my children?" "No," they murmured, shamefaced. "We say them hardly at all."

"Ah, my children, it is very important to say them, at night and in the morning. When you don't have time, at least say an Our Father and a Hail Mary. And when you can, say more." Then a reversion to the theme of reproach. "Only a few rather old women go to Mass in the summer. All the rest work every Sunday throughout the summer. And in winter, when they don't know what to do with themselves, they go to Mass only to poke fun at religion. During Lent they flock to the butcher shops, like dogs." Another question, "My children, haven't you ever seen spoiled grain?" Maximin answered, "No, never."

"But my child, you must have seen it once, near Coin, with your papa. The owner of a field said to your papa, 'Come and see my spoiled grain.' The two of you went. You took two or three ears of grain in your fingers. You rubbed them, and they crumbled to dust. Then you came back from Coin. When you were but a half hour away from Corps, your papa gave you a piece of bread and said, 'Well, my son, eat some bread this year, anyhow. I don't know who'll be eating any next year, if the grain goes on spoiling like that.' "

She was right! Just such an incident had occurred; those very words had been spoken. Maximin had clean forgotten, but, astonishingly, this woman knew all about it. "It's very true, Madame," he muttered. "Now I remember it. Until now I did not." The woman looked earnestly at them. "My children," she charged them, "you will make this known to all my people." Slowly she turned away, glided along the ravine, paused, and, without facing them, repeated the command, "You will make this known to all my people." She proceeded to higher ground. Melanie and Maximin followed.

She stood still a moment, then rose into the air. They saw her look toward heaven, joy in her face and her tears at an end. She glanced solicitously out over the world, southeast toward Rome. Her figure and the palpating circle of light about it grew more resplendent, then began to disappear. She faded into the air. The children stared at the spot where they had last seen her, and finally looked at each other. "Perhaps," Melanie said, "she was a great saint." It was the nearest either came to attributing any identity to the woman.

In the following July, Bishop de Bruillard instituted a formal juridical inquiry into the reputed apparition. This the two commissions which he had put to work the previous autumn had recommended. The inquiry lasted for many months. It involved visits to nine dioceses in which cures in some way associated with La Salette were said to have occurred. Half a dozen bishops were consulted. Once again the children were interrogated; once again they were brought to the mountain.

"Striking," said the report, "was the acceptance of the story by the people of Ablandins and La Salette." Their acceptance had been far from quick. At first they had been skeptical, had scoffed. Their assent had been hard-won and was now impervious to challenge. Attention was called to twenty-three claimed cures. Stressed, too, was the conversion to consistent Christian living both in the diocese and beyond, which was directly attributable to the message which had now been widely spread. After three years of careful study and innumerable interrogations of the children, in which they stuck to their original account without any contradictions or additions, the Bishop approved of the La Salette apparition in a formal decree, which concludes thus, "Therefore, to demonstrate our lively thanks to God and to the glorious Virgin Mary, we authorize the cult of Our Lady of La Salette."

In May of the following year, Bishop de Bruillard, though now aged, made the ascent of the mountain at La Salette to lay the cornerstone of the basilica which he was having built at the scene of the apparition. At about the same time, at his direction, a new community of priests began functioning there, called the Missionaries of La Salette. This was to grow and to establish houses in many parts of the world. The shrine of Our Lady of La Salette became ever more popular as a place of pilgrimage, drawing many thousands annually, a good proportion of these from outside of France.

There is on record the witness of many a man, rigid in indifference, who, on coming to La Salette out of curiosity, was surprised to experience recognition of his wretched state of soul, a realization of his sins and their enormity, compunction for them, a desire for release from them, the inviting prospect of a new and different life. La Salette was seen to be as a mighty font of extraordinary graces, and Our Lady of La Salette was hailed by the title "Reconciler of Sinners."

Twelve years after the apparition at La Salette the same message was reiterated at Lourdes. In our own century it has been sounded once more at Fatima. It is an indictment of man's disobedience to God, of man's forgetfulness of God, of a whole society's drift away from the life of faith and love to one of worldliness. At La Salette, Our Lady instanced abuses common in the district where Melanie and Maximin lived, abuses indicative of a turning away from religion: the serving of self rather than of God, gross irreverence toward Him and disregard for His law, the discontinuance of prayer, spurning of the Mass, contemptuous neglect of the Sacraments, an attitude of mockery toward all that is sacred.

Was all this peculiar to the district? Certainly and sadly not. The condition was generally the same across the world. Disbelief, irreligion, withdrawal from God and His Church were common. Carelessness and lukewarmness had replaced concern for religion and loving practice of it. The minds of men paid scant heed to God, their hearts had no room for Him, and in their aspirations and plans He did not figure. They were sure they were building a better world, and insuring a brighter future, without Him. They were in error, as subsequent history has proven.

Our Lady came to warn and to plead. She came to call men back, to stir up their faith, to induce them to pray and do penance. Only by prayer and penance can mankind's descent to calamity be averted. The offense of our kind is rank. Propitiation for it is possible only in Christ the Savior, His Mother and ours reminds us. In Him must we live; with Him and through Him must we pray and make sacrifice. Unless we do, divine chastisement cannot be warded off. Mary calls to us: we must attend to her words and act upon them.

—A condensation of the Chapter on La Salette, from the book "A Woman Clothed with the Sun"

How She Touched the Most Hardened Sinners

Madeline Pecora Nugent, SFO

The backward town of Corps was indistinguishable from other villages in that mountainous region of France in 1846. The piety that had made saints of King Louis IX in the 1200s, Jeanne d'Arc in the 1400's, and Jean Baptist de la Salle just a century earlier was totally absent from Corps, from most of France. Yes, there were pockets of faith. In the hamlet of Ars, Curé Jean Baptist Vianney, a shepherd's son, was, by his simple, forceful preaching and unabashed faith, converting not only Ars but people from all over Europe who flocked to his confessional sixteen hours a day. Nothing like this was happening in Corps.

In Corps, most everyone worked on Sunday as they did every other day. The few Mass attendees were women. Any man who slunk into Church became the laughingstock of the others who spent their free time and their money in the local drinking establishments and in gambling. Religious holidays, which had once spawned pious pilgrimages and processions, had become excuses for drinking, carousing and wanton dancing. With the language of the populace rife with swears, curses, and blasphemies, and days of fast and abstinence totally ignored, the parish priest Father Melin wondered if most people even prayed.

In Corps lived two children who were typical end products of this irreligion. One, eleven year old Maximin Giraud, frequently accompanied his father to drinking establishments. When his grandmother attempted to take Maximin to Mass, he would slip out of church to play with friends. The only prayers that he could stumble through were the "Our Father" and "Hail Mary." Maximin had never been to school; spontaneous, impulsive, fidgety, and inattentive, he would have been unable to sit still or learn had he been sent. A second product of faithless Corps was uneducated fourteen-year-old Melanie

Mathieu, one of eight neglected children in a destitute family. Melanie, who, as a child, had begun to work for a pittance, was sulky, silent, timid, morose. The simple prayers and snatches of catechism that her mother had laboriously taught her were no more than words. Melanie seldom attended Mass and had never made her First Communion. On Sundays, like every other day, Melanie worked.

Change began with the September 19 apparition of Our Lady in one of the wildly beautiful ravines of La Salette. Maximin and Melanie, who witnessed the tears of the Virgin and heard her pleas for reform, were the first to be moved. They would neither lie nor change their stories nor divulge the secrets entrusted to them despite assorted threats and promised rewards. At once Melanie began to pray nightly and to attend Mass. Taking longer to convert, Maximin eventually attended Mass, too, and led the Rosary along with Melanie at the site of the apparition.

Maximin and Melanie never, in this life, became saints. Yet they progressed from abject irreligion to a faith stronger than most people today have. Maximin tried to become a priest but as he readily admitted, it wasn't for him; Melanie attempted religious life but was not suited for community life and was refused. Although both later led mercurial lives, both maintained their faith and purity until death. Maximin's and Melanie's partial conversions are actually remarkable considering that, had they not heeded the Lady's message, Maximin would most likely have grown into a shiftless drunkard and Melanie become a religiously indifferent wife and cattle herder. How many young people from far more religious backgrounds even consider religious life or retain their purity?

The Lady of La Salette wrought countless other conversions, too. One of the first was Maximin's father who, after initial disbelief, accepted Maximin's story, attended daily Mass, ceased his excessive drinking, and laboriously but successfully struggled to reform his life. Following Giraud's lead and their own convictions, many other men and women of Corps and the nearby towns began to attend Mass and to keep Sunday as a day of rest. They cleaned up their degenerate language, shunned the local bars, observed religious holidays as faith filled events, and began to frequent both the confessional and the altar rail. Month after month, huge flocks of pilgrims from Corps and the surrounding environs made the four to five hour trek though mountainous terrain to the site of the apparition. The conversion of Corps was one of the greatest miracles of La Salette.

Many towns followed suit. One of the most wretched was an area near Calais called the Barracks whose inhabitants were concerned only with cheap pleasures, infidelity and immorality. With the intention of reforming the area, a priest from the Arras diocese came to the Barracks and, through evening devotions to the Lady of La Salette, brought the entire area to renewed, vibrant faith. There he built a church as a center of pilgrimage to Our Lady of La Salette. To this thousands still come.

Why these massive conversions? Some were sparked by physical healings associated with drinking the water that had sprung in an endless stream from the dried up fountain at the site of the apparition. Others, like that of Maximin's father, were birthed by the Virgin's retelling to Maximin of an incident involving spoiled wheat that had involved only Maximin and his father. Other people feared the Lady's predicted catastrophes if reform did not occur. Still more were moved to conversion by the palpable sense of God's Spirit in the ravine where the Lady had wept over humanity's ingratitude, indifference and disobedience. God alone knows the names of most whose faith was reawakened, or strengthened. Many, many of these were lay people who returned to their homes renewed and invigorated by their conversions. Yet La Salette had its profound effect on consecrated religious, too. Their conversions often had far-reaching effects.

Father Jacques Perrin, the first priest to hear of the apparition and to weep over it, revealed its message to his parish on the Sunday after the vision. In 1848 he established a confraternity in honor of Our Lady of La Salette. Its members were to pray daily the invocation, "Our Lady of La Salette, Reconciler of sinners, pray without ceasing for us who have recourse to you."

The main street in Corps, the town were the two seers were born.

Jewish brothers by the name of Lehmann not only became Catholics but also priests. A former Anglican minister William Butler became a priest and instructor at the Rondeau minor seminary. Mother Marie of Jesus, foundress of the Society of the Daughters of the Heart of Jesus, surrendered both herself and her Order to the weeping Virgin.

Marist priest St. Pierre-Julian Eymard, at the feet of the Lady of La Salette, conceived the idea of founding the Congregation of the Priests of the Blessed Sacrament whose primary purpose is to heighten devotion to the Eucharist. The priest St. John Bosco wrote a widely distributed pamphlet on the apparition and used its message to inspire and reform the poor boys for whom he built his many homes. The French Bishop Parisis, taking inspiration from the Virgin's lament, founded the Archconfraternity for the Atonement of Blasphemy and the Profanation of the Lord's Day.

St. Jean Baptist Vianney, the Curé of Ars, through a misunderstanding, came to question the apparition he had initially wholeheartedly embraced. After eight years of tortuous confusion, Vianney tested the Lady of La Salette by begging her for the exact amount of money needed for a mission. The money was given him. He concluded, "One can, and one must believe in La Salette."

The most spectacular story, however, involves a priest who was no longer functioning as such. The conversion took place six years after the apparition at the beginning of May when the bishop announced that a cornerstone would be laid in Corps for a new church dedicated to the Lady of La Salette. In preparation, Father Melin, the parish priest of Corps, urged his entire parish to pray to the Lady of La Salette during her month for a complete and enduring union of the parishioners. Without Father Melin mentioning any names, everyone knew to whom he referred, namely Father Violette and his supporters.

Father Violette was the official parish priest. But due to his gross disobedience and persistent defiance of the bishop, Father Violette had, many years earlier, been placed under interdict and deprived of his priestly functions. Father Melin had been his replacement. Father Violette and a few supporters had remained in Corps to stir up constant trouble for Father Melin. This divisive situation threatened to persist indefinitely as Father Violette adamantly maintained that he would never submit.

The day after Father Melin's plea for prayer, Father Violette walked into the empty parish church and threw himself to his knees in the shadows before the altar. He was still praying there when Father Melin came in. Following Father Melin to the sacristy, Father Violette looked his successor in the eye and gruffly and painfully said, "I wish to abandon the position I have been in. Would you please hear my confession?"

Amazed by the swift movement of grace in his predecessor's heart, Father Melin listened to the humble and complete admission of guilt and pronounced absolution. The next day, Father Violette attended Mass and received the Eucharist along with the congregation. When the bishop came to La Salette to bless the new church's cornerstone, he also restored Father Violette to his priestly functions. Father Melin was later to say that Father Violette's conversion was the greatest manifestation of grace that had occurred during his administration of the parish.

Virgin of Converts, Reconciler of Sinners are titles assigned to the Lady of La Salette. The sins that caused her to weep a hundred and fifty years ago, are, if anything, more prevalent now: Blasphemy. Working on Sunday. Swearing. Cursing. Inattendance at Mass. Disregard for fast and abstinence.

And worse today. Public immorality by prominent people. Total disregard for the Ten Commandments. Rampant atheism and secularism. A false sense of God as the benevolent Parent Who lets His children do whatever they wish without condemnation, punishment, or call to reform.

"If my people will not obey, I shall be compelled to loose my Son's arm. It is so heavy, so pressing that I can no longer restrain it. How long I have suffered for you! If my Son is not to cast you off, I am obliged to entreat Him without ceasing. But you take not the least notice of that. No matter how well you pray in the future, no matter how well you act, you will never be able to make up to me what I have endured for your sake." For our sake, for us disobedient, sinful children for whom she mediates with her Son. We have seen fathers stay punishment on wayward children because mothers pleaded for them. This, the Lady reveals, is happening on an eternal, cosmic scale. The tearful, pleading Mother holds back the just punishment of God and tries to mend the rift between Father and disobedient child.

"You will make this known to all my people," the Lady said twice, not only to convince Melanie and Maximin to be witnesses but also to convince us. How many, even among Catholics, know nothing of La Salette? "You will make this known to all my people." Let us heed her request.

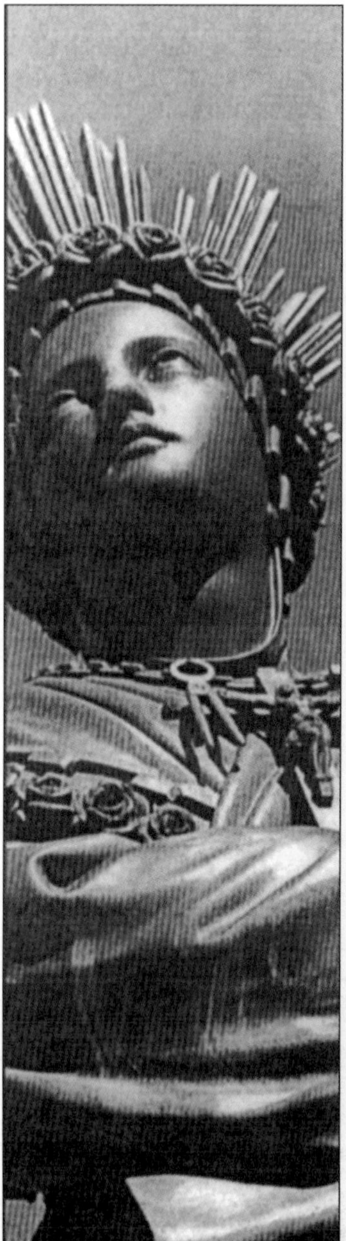

He Skied Into Mary's Arms

Roy Schoeman

My parents are German Jews who fled from the Nazi holocaust and settled here in the U.S. I was born and raised in a middle class suburb of New York City. Growing up I was quite religious, but drifted away from religion when I went to college—first to M.I.T., where I absorbed the hip scientific "we know better than to believe in God" philosophy, and then to Harvard Business School, where I eventually joined the faculty.

Then the Lord gave me perhaps the greatest grace of my life—you could say He directly revealed Himself to me. As I was walking admiring nature I "fell" into heaven—I knew that God existed, that from the first moment of my life He was loving me and watching over me with love, that everything, every event which happened in my life was exactly the best thing which could possibly happen. I knew that

The author, whom Our Lady of La Salette brought to the fulness of his Jewish Faith.

everything I did—for good or for bad—mattered, and was weighed in the scales.

I knew that heaven existed. I knew about the angelic hierarchy. I knew that this was not the picture of God that I had from the Old Testament. I prayed to know the name of my Lord and master, my God. I prayed: "Let me know your name. I don't mind if you are Buddha, and I have to become a Buddhist. I don't mind if you are Apollo, and I have to become a Roman pagan. I don't mind if you are Krishna, and I have to become a Hindu. As long as you are not Christ and I have to become a Christian!"

From that moment on I knew that the meaning and purpose of my life was to worship and serve my God. I knew that when I died I would regret two things—every hour I wasted in the eyes of heaven, and all of the energy I wasted worrying about not being loved when every moment I was held in a sea of love without knowing it. But I had no idea of who He was, of what religion this was, of "how" to worship Him.

After that experience, every night before going to sleep I said a short prayer to know the name of my Lord and Master, my God. A year later, I had a dream of Mary, in which she spoke to me and offered to answer any question I might have. When I woke, I knew that my meeting had been with Christ, and that I was to be a Christian. I still had no idea of the difference between the Catholic Church and the other forms of Christianity, and I had an aversion (based on the typical calumnies) to the Catholic Church. It took me a few more years to find my way to the Catholic Faith and to be baptized. An unintended trip to the shrine of La Salette in the French Alps proved instrumental.

In Ipswich, Massachusetts, there used to be a La Salette shrine which I would pass (without stopping) every time I went to the beach. When a local resident suggested I admire its beautiful gardens sometime, I did, and while there read a plaque which briefly described the September 1846 apparition.

The following winter I found myself in the French Alps on a ski vacation. After several days of dreary rain I decided to take a trip in my rental car to the "La Salette" shrine I had read about, simply because it sounded like a beautiful, isolated spot. There was nothing else to do because the skiing was rained out. It took longer to get there than I had expected, and it was twilight by the time I took the last bend in the winding, mountain road and saw the sanctuary glowing in a hollow, surrounded by massive mountains and deep snow. Much to my surprise, I found it would be possible to stay there, so I made arrangements to spend the night.

I was still far from being very sympathetic to Christianity or to the Catholic Church. Yet the deep peace and the palpable love which flowed from the place enveloped me and drew me into a quiet joy and contentment. A snowstorm and a mishap with my rental car prevented me from leaving when I planned, and forced me to spend most of the remainder of my vacation there.

The time was spent walking in the mountains, thinking about God and about my life, praying, and sleeping—a lot! In fact, most of my time there was spent napping. And when I would try to get up, I would feel myself gently pushed back into a delicious, healing sleep. I remember forcing myself awake after one nap, only to fall back asleep again. I had a dream in which a car was on a lift in a garage, being worked on by a dozen mechanics. I was that car and the Blessed Virgin Mary was the shop supervisor, and she reprimanded me for trying to get off the lift while I was still being worked on! And the work was done. By the end of my stay I was hopelessly in love with Mary, and committed to living the life she and her son Jesus wanted for me. I know that during those days, drifting in and out of sleep, quietly walking the spot where Mary appeared, praying at the stone on which she sat, and drinking the water from the spring which miraculously appeared at the spot of her apparition, I was healed and converted. It was the final episode of my journey into the Church, into the fullness of the faith, into true life in Christ Jesus.

"...the Seventh I Kept for Myself"

As a Jew I was struck and deeply moved when I read that Mary's words at La Salette were: "Six days I have given you to labor, the seventh I have kept for myself." For from a Jewish perspective it is very natural, almost inevitable to associate Mary in a special way with the Sabbath. In Jewish tradition the Sabbath is seen as a bride, and is referred to as the "Sabbath queen." And it is understood to be the forecourt of the Messianic Kingdom, a sort of taste of what is to come. Perhaps the clearest way to show this is to simply quote verbatim from the prayer which Jews recite at the start of every Sabbath:

"Come, my Beloved.
Let us welcome Sabbath the Bride, Queen of our days.

Come, let us all greet Sabbath, Queen sublime,
Fountain of blessings in every clime..
Annointed and regal since earliest time,
In thought she preceded Creation's six days.

Come, my Beloved.
Let us welcome Sabbath the Bride, Queen of our days.

Arise and shake off the dust of the earth.
Wear glorious garments reflecting your worth.
Messiah will lead us all soon to rebirth.
My soul now senses redemption's warm rays.

Come, my Beloved.
Let us welcome Sabbath the Bride, Queen of our days.

Awake and arise to greet the new light
For in your radiance the world will be bright.
Sing out, for darkness is hidden from sight.
The Lord through you His glory displays.

Come, my Beloved.
Let us welcome Sabbath the Bride, Queen of our days.

Then your destroyers will themselves be destroyed;
Ravagers, at great distance, will live in a void.
Your God then will celebrate you, overjoyed,
As a groom with his bride when his eyes meet her gaze.

Come, my Beloved.
Let us welcome Sabbath the Bride, Queen of our days.

[All rise and turn to the entrance in a symbolic greeting of the Bride, Sabbath]

Come in peace, soul mate, sweet gift of the Lord,
Greeted with joy and in song so adored
Amidst God's people, in faith in accord.
Come, Bride Sabbath; come, crown of the days.

Come, my Beloved.
Let us welcome Sabbath the Bride, Queen of our days."

Almost every one of these words could be sung ever so appropiately to the Queen of Heaven, the Queen of La Salette, the Blessed Virgin Mary! It seemed only natural to me that Mary should identify herself with the Sabbath, that she should say ". . .six days have I given you to labor, the seventh I have kept for myself!"

A Cautious "Mother" Investigates

Patrick McMahon

On the occasion of the 150th anniversary of Our Lady's apparition at La Salette, Pope John Paul II wrote a letter to Bishop Louis Dufaux of Grenoble, France. He proclaimed La Salette "a message of hope, for our hope is nourished by the intercession of her who is the mother of mankind." Indeed, the Church's devotion to the Blessed Virgin Mary has been greatly enriched by her merciful intercession, reflected in the name she took at La Salette, "Our Lady, Reconciler of Sinners." In preparing for the centennial year of the apparition, Pope Pius XII remarked that the Church "can only rejoice" that the canonical proceedings overseen by Bishop de Bruillard's Diocesan Commission "proved to be favorable." But how did the Church come to this favorable opinion of the famous apparition at La Salette, and what can we learn from the Church's meticulous investigation of this great "message of hope" for mankind from heaven in this current Marian age?

From the very beginning there arose an outburst of prejudice against the two seers of La Salette, Maximin and Melanie. Why would the Blessed Mother speak to these ignorant mountain children, shepherds who seemed indifferent to religion? How can the Church rely on the testimony of two children who could not even recite the Our Father or the Hail Mary, or speak proper French? Yet our Lord in His eternal wisdom has often chosen the weak to confound the proud. Did not Pope Pius IX respond "here is the openness and simplicity of a child" as he finished reading Maximin's letter? As Maximin succinctly remarked years later, "the apparition has not changed us, it has left us with all our faults." The children's shortcomings were offset by their simplicity and innocence both before and after the apparition.

It was on the fifth anniversary of the apparition that Bishop de Bruillard issued a decree in 1851, endorsing the La Salette apparition as bearing "all of the characteristics of truth" and stating that "the faithful have grounds for believing it indubitable and certain." In so doing, he was performing an act of the Church's ordinary magisterium.

(See side bar explaining the Church's teaching regarding private revelation.) Rome approved the decree and so it became the definitive judgment of the Church. Approval by such authority brings peace of mind and assurance in our beliefs. Without it, we would be overwhelmed by the plethora of miraculous phenomena. Today, with so many apparitions occurring worldwide, one can observe the climate of insecurity and confusion that can at times overwhelm the faithful, and which can cause dissension between the faithful and their bishops. The best attitude is one of patience and respect for the Church in the knowledge that the Holy Spirit will ultimately lead her to truth. A rushed judgment can cause a great deal of damage.

At the time of the apparition Bishop Philibert de Bruillard presided over the diocese of Grenoble, which includes both the hamlet of La Salette and Corps, the nearest town. The Bishop, an expert theologian and former seminary professor, steeped in mystical and ascetical theology, would not be carried away into making imprudent decisions concerning the apparition. At the ripe age of eighty-one, he would not approve or condemn La Salette until a thorough investigation took place. As a young cleric during the French revolution, he had miraculously escaped the guillotine and later he guided St. Madeline Sophie Barat, as her spiritual director. Drawing from his vast experiences, he would proceed prudently, composedly and intelligently.

As word of the apparition spread like wildfire, Father Mélin, the parish priest at Corps, sent a letter to him. This was the Bishop's first notice of the apparition. Since it fell under his jurisdiction, the Bishop instructed Father Mélin to keep him informed of events as they developed. The priest was initially skeptical, but after questioning the two children separately and visiting the site of the apparition, he became one of the apparition's strongest supporters. The parish priest of La Salette itself, Father Jacques Perrin, also gathered information for the Bishop and found "nothing that might in the least way possible point to a hoax." Later the Bishop had to remove Father Perrin from the La Salette parish and transfer him to another parish because he disobeyed the order not to preach on La Salette.

On October 9, 1846, Bishop de Bruillard took the first of five major steps. He issued a letter to his clergy warning them against improper action, such as preaching or publishing material on the apparition without his authority or that of the Holy See. Realizing that such a message of divine threats, complaints, and promises of reward could produce anxiety and distortions, he severely condemned one pamphlet on La Salette that was published without the Church's knowledge or consent. This was a prudent precaution taken before any formal investigation had even begun. Meanwhile, he was collecting reports from priests visiting La Salette in a dossier on topics ranging from the number of pilgrims to reports of miraculous cures.

The Bishop's second major step was an appeal to outside sources. Wisely, he sought a balanced and thorough preliminary investigation. He instructed the superior of a minor seminary to establish a commission and present him a detailed report on the apparition. As he quietly worked behind the scenes, the bishop released for public discussion several other reports by priests on La Salette, including news of the first known miraculous healings. Some secular newspapers ignored this gesture of goodwill. Others ridiculed the apparition or only scratched the surface in their coverage.

Bishop Philibert de Bruillard, who was bishop of the diocese of Grenoble where the apparitions took place.

Many miraculous cures were attributed to Our Lady of La Salette's intercession after a novena to her or use of the miraculous water from a dry brook which at the apparition site which suddenly began to flow. From all over France, the faithful wrote to Father Mélin. Excitement grew so swiftly that on the first anniversary of the apparition, tens of thousands of pilgrims made the difficult trip up to La Salette on foot. Even rainstorms in the afternoon lasting into night time could not dampen their enthusiastic spirit. Priests who attended were amazed at the spirit, fervor and recollection of the crowd. The chanting of the litanies, the Salve Regina, and the Ave Maria were heard the whole night, with Masses celebrated during the day. One priest reported that he had never seen such a spectacle.

Bishop de Bruillard's two commissions reported to him on December 15, 1846, just a few months after the apparition. They concluded that since nothing but good fruits had resulted, there was no need for the authorities to intervene. Since there was no danger in delay they expressed a wish for a judicial inquiry to provide a better understanding of the facts.

Over the next few months many anti-religious papers, due to Masonic influences gave distorted reports on the apparition echoing the pressure from civil authorities. The Minister of Justice and of Worship wrote a condescending letter to the bishop reminding him of his duty to suppress all questionable occurrences in his diocese. However, the wise old bishop did not need to be reminded of his serious obligations, nor did he make a cowardly retreat from hostility of the press and attempts to intimidate him. He ably defended himself, saying "my ears and eyes are open to all that is said, is done, and happens."

On July 19, 1847, the Bishop took his third major step, issuing a decree establishing a commission of inquiry entrusted to the superior of a major seminary, Father Orcel, and to Father Rousselot, a professor of theology there. After being briefed by the first commission and then conducting their own research, they concluded that La Salette had a supernatural explanation. They reported that "the disarming naïveté of the two children almost creates a bias toward the apparition in all who interrogate them." The Rousselot research team conducted inquiries in many dioceses and based the verdict on confirmed miracles. The bishop also took his fourth major step, requesting help from priests, lay people and medical doctors to arrive at the truth. The counsel of medical doctors was highlighted in this, especially those "who treated the sick who attribute their cure to the invocation of Our Lady of La Salette or the use of miraculous water."

On July 27, 1847, Fathers Orcel and Rousselot left Grenoble to travel to ten dioceses in search of testimonies and documents concerning miraculous cures. In August, they would interrogate the two children again and carefully examine the apparition site. They noted the consistent accuracy of the children's account. The first chapter of their report stated "all those who, from the very first days after the apparition, had interrogated the children and had taken notes, did indeed attest to the children's fidelity... [to] the very same account.... The children were repeating the words like a lesson." The investigators were also struck that everywhere they went people spoke of nothing but La Salette, pilgrimages and the miracles. Extraordinary graces were clearly evident. Yet interestingly, neither Father Orcel nor Father Rousselot was entirely convinced. Father Orcel wrote that "certain items raised some suspicion about the truth of the words of Our Lady...."

Father Rousselot's report published in August 1848 listed twenty-one verified cures attributed to Our Lady of La Salette. One had occurred while the commission was in session. Antoinette Bollenet rose suddenly from her death bed at the close of a novena to Our Lady of La Salette. The doctor's last words on leaving her had been "let her die in peace." Three days later the same doctor said "if I had to, I would sign my name in blood to testify that this is a miracle."

Bishop de Bruillard then established another commission, which he himself would chair, to examine the Rousselot report as well as other information obtained up to that point. This commission held eight sessions during November and December of 1848. It would re-interrogate the children as well as consult with Father Mélin and the superior of the convent where the children were staying. In the final vote of the commission, twelve of its sixteen members concluded that an apparition of the mother of God had really taken place. Three members thought the evidence inconclusive, while only one rejected the apparition outright. All sixteen members were agreed that the event was of supernatural in nature. None thought that it could be explained in purely natural terms.

Taking his fifth major step, the Bishop courageously authorized the publication of his report with the title "The Truth Concerning the Event at La Salette." He hoped to "do away with many a prejudice, to enlighten public opinion and to convince open minds." He added "those who are influenced by prejudice, who stand against everything that is outside the natural and all that is extraordinary will surely recall that the truth can sometimes appear unlikely" and that La Salette's fruits cannot be "dismissed out of hand."

Pope Pius IX received the report kindly along with the plaudits of eight archbishops and bishops. The following year Father Rousselot published "New Documents Concerning the Event of La Salette", adding further support to the cause for a doctrinal decree. Bishop de Bruillard called it "an important sequel to the report" concluding that "our hopes will have been fulfilled [when] we see a shrine worthy of Her who appeared on a holy mountain." This addendum dealt with miraculous cures in the time following the initial report, as well with spurious alleged apparitions which followed on the heels of La Salette, much like the outbreak of over fifty claimed apparitions which followed Our Lady's appearances to Bernadette at Lourdes.

During a clergy retreat in Grenoble in September 1850 over 240 signatures were gathered petitioning the Bishop to authorize pilgrimages to La Salette and to build a shrine there. A counter-petition could gather only 18 names, some of them false! With positive signals coming from Rome the Bishop took the last major step on September 19, 1851, the fifth anniversary of the famous apparition, issuing the final decree:

> ***"Having invoked anew the Holy Spirit and the help of the Immaculate Virgin [we have concluded that the apparition] bears all of the characteristics of truth and the faithful have grounds for believing it indubitable and with certainty . . . To show our heartfelt gratitude to God and to the glorious Blessed Virgin Mary, we authorize the devotion to Our Lady of La Salette....***

Reexamine yourselves seriously, do penance for your sins.... Become submissive to the voice of Mary calling you to penance and who, on behalf of her Son, threatens you with spiritual and temporal ills, if, remaining insensitive to her maternal admonitions, you should harden your hearts...."

On May 24, 1852 the eighty-seven year old Bishop de Bruillard, accompanied by another bishop, took the long torturous trip to the mountain top shrine of La Salette. The first part of his trip was by a stagecoach. He arrived during the night at the little hamlet of La Salette, where he was greeted by cheering mountaineers carrying lighted torches. Early the next morning, accompanied by a crowd of pilgrims, he mounted a horse for the last two hour tortuous trip. As the white haired Bishop in full Episcopal robes arrived, cheers went up from the large number of pilgrims with the cry, "Long live the Bishop." The bishop wept. He retired soon after and lived to the ripe age of 95.

All succeeding bishops of Grenoble have concurred with the judgment of 1851. "Miracles upon miracles" (as Father Mélin put it) have continued to occur through the intercession of Our Lady of La Salette. She appears on this deserted mountain, sitting on the shepherds' stone bench, her elbows on her knees and her face in her hands. Generations of pilgrims, seeing this statue, turn in the path as though hearing her say, "Oh, all of you who pass along the way, look and see if there is any sorrow like my sorrow" (Lam. 1:12).

Our Lady of La Salette, Reconciller of sinners pray for us who have recourse to you.

Why Believe in Private Revelations?

Catholics are obliged by their Catholic Faith to believe in all the truths which were part of the public revelations given to the Apostles. Public revelation ceased with the death of the last Apostle. Since that time any new revelation is called Private Revelation, as Pope Benedict XIV (1675-1758) stated that "no private revelation is ever to be believed with Catholic faith." This does not mean that there is not a serious obligation to believe a private revelation if one is certain that it is from God, but that there is no general obligation for all Catholics to believe all, or even some of those revelations as a condition for membership in the Church, as is the case with public revelation. The Church invites the faithful to accept its judgment on a particular apparition but not under the pain of losing membership in the Church as in the case of formal heresy. However, one is foolish in rejecting that which the Church approves and encourages. Thus, one must understand that there are two extremes in this matter of accepting or rejecting private revelation.

"We can sin by a double excess either by rash judgment, hasty commitment, sentimental enthusiasm and excessive hunger for the spectacular, or by distrust, a kind of arrogance and skepticism, maintained in spite of the encouragements of the Church. Perhaps there is reason to ask whether, under the cover of this supernatural prudence supplied by the Church, we do not harbor a kind of disdain for and lack of commitment to this type of devotion — traces perhaps, of a latent rationalism" (Fr. Lochet, *Nouvelle Revue Théologique,* Nov. 1954, pg. 953).

All that the Church is saying in approving an apparition is that the messages and experiences contain nothing contrary to the faith and are true manifestations of the supernatural and worthy of belief. Anyone, not the visionary only, who knows with certainty that God has spoken, for example, at Guadalupe, at Rue Du Bac, at La Salette, at Lourdes, at Fatima, all approved as worthy of belief by the Church and refuses to believe, or ridicules the belief of others, sins mortally against the faith. There is a certain culpability in one who would pit his will up against God's Messenger, Our Lady, and the authority of the Church in such a serious matter.

— *The Editor*

One can follow the whole sequence of events and movements of Our Lady of La Salette and the exact spots where she first appeared, weeping and sitting on a rock, to her assent to heaven at the top of a hill where she gradually "melted away," as Melanie described it.

The La Salette Seers – Faithful to Their Mission

Mary Ann Budnick

Jesus points out in Scripture, "It is not the healthy who need a physician, but they who are sick. For I have come not to call the just, but sinners (Mk 2:17)." His statement was not just for His immediate listeners but for us as well. God uses a variety of means to touch souls. In La Salette, France, He sent the Mother of God to call people to convert. Our Lady's chosen messengers at La Salette were two French children, Maximin Giraud and Melanie Mathieu, who were representative of the religious indifference prevalent in France in the mid 1800s.

While neither of these children have been canonized, they fulfilled the mission given to them by Our Lady: "You will make this known to all my people." They were not given the message because they were holy. They were given the divine assignment to call *us* to holiness. The apparition was social in purpose, not personal. As the parish priest of Corps, Father Melin, explained: "Many people would like to see the children more mystical, at least more perfect. But the Blessed Virgin has left them their own natures and there is nothing we can do about it. What has been confided to them, it seems to me, can be compared to an orange in a jar. The orange does not change the jar, will not make it crystal if it is simple glass. But the jar lets us see the orange as it is."

The children throughout their lives consistently repeated the same message without embellishments nor changing a single word. They faithfully repeated the words of the Mother of God, "If my people will not obey."

They warned the French people and Church officials that if people continued to work on Sunday and to take the name of God (Jesus) in vain than the French people would be punished severely. Their crops would be destroyed. They would endure a famine. A strange illness would kill young children. But "If they convert, the stones and rocks will change into wheat, and potatoes will be found sown in the earth."

Who were these children? Francoise Melanie and Peter Maximin were both born in Corps, a small town of not more than 1,000 inhabitants in the southern French Alps. Surprisingly, they never met until the day before the apparition. Melanie, the eldest of the two, was born November 7, 1831. Maximin, four years younger, was born August 27, 1835. Both children were born into poverty. Neither of their families was considered devout. As a young child, Melanie contributed to the support of her family by grazing cattle and shepherding for farmers in the area. This left little opportunity for her to even attend Mass on Sunday and holydays. Her contact with the Catholic church was the sound of the church bells tolling in the valley while she worked as a shepherdess on the mountains. When Our Lady asked, "Do you say your prayers well, my children?" Melanie truthfully replied, "No, Madame, hardly at all." Later in life she would muse, "Isn't justice served that I, the least of all creatures, who did not begin to pray until the age of 15, suffer more and am more humiliated than others?"

It was a lonely, frightening life for such a young child which possibly accounts for her timid, moody, sulky and introverted personality. There was no time for schooling for the little girl who spent her days out in the scorching summer heat and the frigid mountain winds of autumn. She was soaked to the skin by fierce rainstorms and chilled by sudden spring snows as she stood guard over her sheep or cows.

Her employer at the time of the apparition reported that she was "excessively timid, and so careless of herself, that on returning from the mountain, drenched with rain, she never thought of changing her clothes. Sometimes, and it was a part of her character, she would sleep in the cattle-sheds; and at others, if not observed, she would have passed the night under the stars." Baptiste Pra described Melanie as idle, disobedient, inclined to pout, and moody. He also noted that following the apparition, Melanie changed. She became more active and obedient. She began to pray. The young visionary struggled to control her moodiness.

Maximin's father was a cartwright, who by reputation was known to be undependable. In Corps, he was viewed as a spendthrift and drifter. His mother died when he was small. His stepmother disliked the high spirited little boy. Although she beat him frequently, this did not seem to affect his cheerful disposition.

Maximin preferred activity to study which explains why he could neither read nor write at the time of the apparition. In fact, his father claimed that it had taken the young boy three to four years to memorize the *Our Father* and *The Hail Mary,* prayers that toddlers today easily learn. Was it Maximin's short attention span or the fact that his father was teaching his son the prayers in the local cabaret? Like Melanie,

Maximin received no direction, no spiritual formation, had no role model, and worst of all, no training in the natural nor supernatural virtues. He was known to lie and swear previous to the apparitions.

At the time of the apparition, Melanie, fifteen, was hired out to Baptiste Pra of Les Ablandins, to watch his cows. Maximin, eleven, was similarly hired by Peter Selme to temporarily replaced a little boy who had fallen ill.

The day before the apparition the children met for the first time on the mountain in the area of La Salette. While Melanie, shy and used to the solitude, would have preferred to spend the day alone, Maximin craved companionship. Seeing her on the mountain, he hailed her, then spent the day chattering away. As they parted that day, they agreed to meet the next day on the mountain.

Saturday, September 19, 1846, began as any other day until the two children beheld the apparition of Our Lady sitting in the little hillock crying. That vision was to change their lives. As Maximin would later say to pilgrims questioning him about the apparition: "From there, she [Our Lady] rose into the air, disappeared, and left me with all my faults." At another time he emphasized: "The apparition and I are two different things. I was only an instrument. We have been only conduits, only parrots who have repeated what we have heard. We were stupid before the apparition, we were stupid after, and we will be stupid all of our lives."

When news of the apparition spread, the two children were placed for four years in Providence, a convent school in Corps to be protected, educated, and prepared to make their First Communions. Melanie's family was given a small pension by Church officials so that Melanie would no longer have to work nor her sister beg on the street for food. She was allowed to made her First Communion only after her parents made their Easter duty.

In life, whenever there is a joy, there is also the cross. Their main cross was their unsettled lives. Unlike other visionaries who entered the religious life, Maximin and Melanie never seemed to find their niche. Maximin wanted to become a priest but his years at the different seminaries proved that he was not interested in studying. The Superior of Providence explained that "Maximin has but ordinary abilities; he is sufficiently obedient, but light, fond of play, and always in motion." His attention span was limited. He tried his hand as an apprentice mechanic. He unsuccessfully tried to obtain an arts degree, to become a doctor, or a pharmacist. Nothing worked out for him. There were months that he was so poor in Paris that he went hungry. Like his father, he was unable to handle money. At the age of thirty he became a

Papal Zouave, a volunteer soldier of the Holy Father, then a French soldier. Imprudently he lent his name to a liquor venture headed by a swindler. March 1, 1875, at the age of forty, Maximin died from tuberculosis. Though of an unstable nature, he retained his innocent, childlike faith to the end of his life. When asked before his death, "Hasn't the apparition produced something special within you? I mean, hasn't it brought you a particular grace to improve you, to inspire you to live in a saintly way?" Maximin responded: "I can't say that. I never felt anything special. But the Blessed Virgin did grant me the grace of a very Christian education with the good Sisters of Corps. She surrounded me with very edifying priests. My childhood and youth were spent in a milieu that encouraged me to do good and to avoid evil. Without the apparition I could have strayed far from God and become really bad. I might even have become a member of the *Internationale,* or the *Commune*. By keeping me in this milieu and giving me the religious convictions I still have, she bestowed a wonderful gift on me."

Melanie likewise led a wandering existence. She was in and out of various convents, beginning with the Sisters of Providence in Corps. At this convent her experience brought not only acclaim but adulation, both which are deadly to spiritual growth. Comfortable with being the center of attention, Melanie began telling the sisters about her other "mystical experiences." Despite the fact that the stories were spectacular and grandiose, her mistress novice, Sister Therese de Jesus, encouraged Melanie's tales. Without a wise spiritual director or confessor working with the young woman, Bishop Ginoulhiac was unable to curb this spiritually dangerous development. When it was time for Melanie to take her vows, the bishop refused permission. Upset over that decision, she left that convent and was taken to England by Fr. Newsham where she joined the Carmelites only to leave to returned again to France. In France, she stay at the Marseille convent of Our Lady of Compassion. It was here that she became a teacher. After a year, the order sent her to work at their orphanage on the Greek isle of Cephalonia. After two years, Melanie returned to Marseille hoping to have her "secret" published. She was unsuccessful. When it was finally published it caused an explosion of controversy. To silence the ever growing controversy May 9, 1923, the Holy See placed the "secret" on the Index of Forbidden Books. The Church ruled that the "secret" was not connected to the authenticated apparition of Our Lady of La Salette (see page 76).

During this controversy disappointment and growing ill health plagued Melanie as she trekked back and forth between Italy and France. She spent the last months of her life in Altamura, Italy where she died December 14, 1904 at the age of seventy-three.

The lives of Melanie and Maximin prove that ecclesiastical approval of apparitions of Our Lady are not dependent on the sanctity of the seers. While Melanie and Maximin were devout Catholics, they were never canonized because of their lack of heroic virtues.

What lessons can we draw from their lives? Studying the lives of Saints, their formation for the most part began within the home, within the "domestic church" as the Holy Father refers to the family. If parents do not train their children at an early age, the children will have less chance to respond to God's calling. We see this so clearly in the case of the visionaries of La Salette. Their dysfunctional families produced dysfunctional children who grew up to be moral and faith-filled dysfunctional adults. We see this same situation being repeated in the United States. It is one reason for the lack of priestly and religious vocations in this country.

This message and warning from Our Lady was for the benefit of the whole Church. To be a visionary one does *not* have to possess heroic virtue. While the lives of these visionaries lacked direction and order, they never wavered in their zeal to promote the message and warning of the weeping Mother of God. To this they were singularly called and were faithful to the end of their sad lives. May we not conclude they were richly rewarded for their absolute, unquestioning fidelity, in spite of their human frailty.

What about the "Secret"?

Each child of La Salette was given a secret which the Blessed Mother forbade them to reveal. Under threat of imprisonment, death and attractive monetary reward (remember how poor they were) they were faithful in keeping their secrets. It wasn't until they were made to understand that the Pope, as the supreme head of the Church, could require them to reveal the secret to him and him alone, that they dutifully wrote out, in the presence of witnesses, the particular secret entrusted to them. These were sealed and delivered to the pope by the Bishop of Grenoble's personal envoy. Pope Pius IX took the sealed envelopes and read Maximin's first and commented, "Here is all the candor and simplicity of a child." As he read Melanie's secret, his lips became compressed and with considerable emotion he said,

" These are scourges with which France is threatened, but she is not alone culpable. Germany, Italy, all Europe is culpable and merits chastisement. I have less to fear from open impiety, than from indifference and human respect. . . . It is not without reason that the Church is called militant, and here," pointing to his breast, "you behold its captain. I must read these letters more at leisure." On the following day at an audience with Cardinal Fornari, the Pope commented again on what was uppermost in his mind "I am terrified with these prodigies; we have everything that is needed in our religion for the conversion of sinners; and when heaven employs such means, the evil must be very great."

The Holy Father chose not to reveal the Secrets. All we know with certainty is his reaction and words after reading the secrets. Unfortunately, the matter didn't rest at that. — *Editor*

* * * * * * * *

During the apparition Mary gave each child a secret. Maximin's was never revealed. About thirty years after the apparition Melanie wrote out a version of what she claimed was her secret and published it. The Church exercised her gifts of discernment and determined that the secret published by Melanie was not authentic, that it did not represent a message given by the Blessed Virgin Mary. In 1923 a newly published edition of the "secret" was placed on the Index of Forbidden Books. Yet even today some authors are not careful in distinguishing between the true message of La Salette and ideas and words coming from the spurious "secret," while some schismatic groups have openly embraced it.

— *Roy Schoeman*

The Lady Gives a Lesson in Theology

*Fr. Jean Jaouen, M.S.**

The apparition of La Salette is both a unified and a complex reality. In the history of apparitions, few have as long a message and are so varied visually. Yet, from all of this, a guiding thought emerges with the greatest of ease *"For how long a time have I been suffering for you!"* she says. What is the weeping and beseeching woman suggesting by her words and her body language? Is it not the power of her eternal cornpassion and its wonderous activation in the presence of sin?

The beautiful Lady's first sentence to the children is a preamble inspired by their own feelings, an invitation to come near and to listen without fear to the great news she has come to tell them. (We know that Mé1anie and Maximin have experienced great fear upon seeing the globe of light in the center of which the weeping Lady was sitting.) With solemn clarity and power she immediately states the basic theme of her message: "If my people will not submit, I am forced to release the arm of my Son." Everything is contained herein. Already she has expressed the meaning of her dramatic visit and has presented all its actions with their respective parts: her rebellious people, her angry Son, and herself, the Mediatrix, whose role had now become impossible to fulfill. What follows will develop this general proposition.

She now goes into detail. The situation is such that she can no longer restrain the arm of her Son. This is indeed the role long assigned to her in the economy of salvation. But people pay no heed. They should realize that nothing they can do will ever compensate for all the sorrowful Mother has suffered for them, from that distant day on Calvary.

She utters in her own vivid words, the cry of her Son: "I gave you six days to work. I have reserved the seventh for myself. And no one will give it to me." She explains: "This is what causes the weight of my Son's

* *Translated from the French by Fr. Norman Théroux, M.S.*

arm to be so crushing." She attaches the same gravity to blasphemy.

And so, she goes on, do not be surprised if the harvest is spoiled: "It is your own fault." It will punish as well as instruct you. I had warned you last year by the rotting potatoes. Since you paid no heed they will go on rotting. This coming Christmas there will be none left. You will also see diseased wheat, famine, the death of small children. All this is your penance. Understand this when you see it, when you see the walnuts turn bad and when the grapes rot.

Then come the secrets which we naturally imagine to be an extension of the preceding passages. But historical critics must admit knowing strictly nothing of them except the general sense revealed by Pope Pius IX to Bishop de Bruillard's representatives and later repeated to Father Giraud in a still more general way: "If you do not deny yourselves you will all perish."

The messenger then turns from threats to promises. "If the people are converted, the stones will become mounds of wheat." But the stipulation is that they be converted. What is now happening? First, what is the personal disposition of these innocent children? ("Do you say your prayers well, my children?") They themselves do not give to religion the place it deserves in their lives. Their countrymen even less. On the whole, they live only for their bodies. ("They work every Sunday all summer long. In winter, they go to Mass only to scoff at religion. During Lent they go to the butcher shop like dogs.") This is what must change; otherwise, people greedy for worldly pleasures will be punished in their own sin. Must they be scolded through signs such as the prophets of old gave to the princes of those days? Do they need to see in order to be convinced, that nothing escapes the eye of God?

The Lady recalls for Maximin, who had forgotten it, all the details and with the precision of an eyewitness, the rotten wheat he had seen on the farm of Coin. That is enough. She knows Maximin's story more intimately than he knows it himself. The story then becomes intelligible, within everyone's reach. The Messenger concludes by twice saying: "My children, you will make this known to all my people." No one can deny the unity and the coherence of these lines of thought. One idea follows the other logically. There are levels of thought, the universal governing the more concrete and in particular, shedding light upon them.

Addressing the people of God as a whole, the Lady of La Salette condemns the more concrete forms of its godlessness, the main beachheads opening the way to materialism. Moreover, it is quite clear that these reproaches are not isolated one from another, nor from the whole of the discourse, which has nothing in common with the dry shopping list type of conscience examination. Everything is set in a living framework. The precepts and reproaches, the threats and the promises all draw their unity and their absolute originality from the relationship first established between Messenger and people: "How long have I suffered for you!" We need only obey the rule of objectivity and every detail of the discourse becomes clear in the light of the moving and concentrated prologue wherein the Virgin describes her mediating role.

"If my people will not submit, I am forced to release my Son's arm." This is the essential, basic theme of the La Salette discourse. This is the prevailing idea, which explains everything else. The rest of the prologue develops it in moving terms. The reproaches, the threats, the promises are a concrete expression of it. When this is agreed upon, it is difficult to deny the originality of the message.

The La Salette message makes visible a facet of Catholic dogma in a new and uniquely moving light. It is not a new dogma or a new revelation. Divine Revelation ended with the last of the apostles. But there exists in the revealed teaching of the Church a specific place where all that comes to us from the apparition of La Salette can be inserted with perfect assurance. "I believe in the Communion of Saints," the Creed says. This is where we can enshrine what the beautiful Lady has told us of her suffering, of her concern, and of her power. Mary's mediation finds resonances in the Church's deep-seated intuition, although it is not defined teaching. But the Communion of Saints is an article of faith that none can set aside without ceasing to belong to the Church.

Are we able to discern how La Salette exemplifies this teaching and what new and pressing reasons we now have to let it shape our behavior? Christians know that by their solidarity with Christ, each one of their acts can strengthen or weaken the Mystical Body whose members they are. The best of them, like Saint Paul, fill up in their flesh "what is lacking in the sufferings of Christ for the sake of his body, the Church." Now the Virgin reminds us that she, the sinless one, has obeyed this law of universal solidarity. At La Salette, her tears are only a sign of this participation. What is real is that on Calvary she experienced the most unspeakable sorrow any mother has ever tasted. These real tears have a permanent value and allow her to repeat this real complaint: "How long have I been suffering for you." We do say, and rightfully, that sin *renews* the Passion of Christ.

What she tells us about withheld punishments, about blessings and rewards of conversion, is a result and an image of her spiritual mediation. Essentially, she is mediating in the supernatural sphere. But, for us human beings, the supernatural is in every way involved with the natural. A bad harvest can bring a farmer to blaspheme or to turn to

God. It is important for him to see a spiritual meaning within this natural event. This is why the beautiful Lady warns: "If the harvest is spoiled, it is your own fault." The threat of hunger is a most insuperable obstacle to the spiritual life of the poor. Thoughts of heaven have very little prominence in the mind of a man like Maximin's father, obsessed by this ever-present threat "Well, my son, eat some bread this year anyhow. I don't know who'll be eating any next year if the wheat continues to spoil like that."

The Mediatrix of all graces can therefore not be unconcerned for the "minimum well-being required for the practice of virtue." "If people are converted, the stones will become piles of wheat." We should not be misled. Promises of material prosperity following upon inner conversion are clearly meant to draw us closer to the realm of the spiritual. They recall the words of the medieval poet "Heavenly Lady, Empress of earth." Mary's concern means to drive us into the loving embrace of Jesus. "Live with my Son," she tells us, "live by my Son and in Him. Hold faithfully to the place He has assigned you in his Mystical Body. Generously fulfill the role of service and self-giving He asks of you in favor of the Body you are united to as I am who serves as go-between with Him who is Head of all the members."

Essentially, this is the message of grace that Our Lady of La Salette brings to those who want to hear it. The early commentators suggested that after the statement, "I have given you six days to work," the words "said my Son" were understood by the context. The problem would then be solved. The style of the discourse, passing immediately from the first to the third Person, stresses that the offense is directed against God — "This it is which causes the weight of my Son's arm to be so crushing" — and allows one to accept this solution. We believe that present day theologians would not be shocked to see attributed to the Virgin in person the command she voices here as Mother of God and Mother of grace, Mary is so closely associated with the work of redemption that in a unique manner, she has become one mystical person with Christ, and can assume as her own all of her Son's intentions. It might very well be that this apparition's singular purpose, more than any other, is to introduce us into the mystery of Mary's mediation and to allow Christian intuition to anticipate the thinking of theologians.

We observed how, in the beautiful Lady's discourse, the events of this world appear to be obedient to her. We noted how she attributed to herself the warning given to her people by the spoiled potatoes: "I warned you last year." It is in her role as Mediatrix of all graces that she rules over temporalities in a world where all is grace. All blessings created by God for the temporal needs of people are also made holy by her Son's redemption and ordered to eternal salvation. Mary exercises complete sovereignty over them. But if we proclaim her Queen of this world, "Empress of earth," can we refuse her the right to speak to us as Queen and to give us, in her own name, commands coinciding with her Son's will? She makes them her own in the hope of reaching us more completely, since, in a sense, she is closer to us because as the Mother she is the Mediatrix between her Son and ourselves.

To accept literally the expression she used and to give it the same obvious sense it has in the rest of the discourse would be to understand with wholehearted enthusiasm the title of Queen of the world given her by tradition. It would be to see her in the fullness of her role. Logically, this would also mean to attribute to her in the order of execution the same power of mediation that none refuses her in the realm of intercession. If we are happy to see her between her Son and ourselves to bridge the chasm caused by our evil-doing, we can also grant her the right to prevent us from doing it and the right to speak to us as Queen even when the commands she gives us are expressions of her Son's will. She who said "Do whatever he tells you" in the Gospel also said, "This it is which causes the weight of my Son's arm to be so crushing." She will not usurp her Son's place. The contrast between this last statement and the preceding one is enlightening. Even though she speaks as Queen, and makes her Son's orders her own, she does not pretend to be the offended party when these orders are violated. It is the arm of her Son that we are making heavier. As if she were telling us: my Son has the supreme authority, to Him alone belong vengeance and justice.

Nothing here suggests conflict between Mother and Son. The beautiful Lady of La Salette embraces the cause of justice as much as the most exacting theologian would hope. In the end, she is only claiming the rights of her Son. She is only asking the children to make this plea known to all her people. Would we want her to abstain from making us understand in the only way we can that her mercy also pleads for us? We can understand divine realities only in human terms. We even distinguish between mercy and justice in God. We acknowledge a host of saintly intercessors between God and ourselves, leading to the person of Christ. We would have to hold guilty of anthropomorphism every Christian invoking Mary as advocate. Fortunately, we realize that all of these apparent conflicts are resolved in the unity of God. A careful reading of the discourses clearly shows that Mary's maternal intercession is subordinated to her Son's justice. "If my Son is not to abandon you, I am obliged to entreat Him without ceasing." We could not find more appropriate or more admirable terms in any course of theological study.

She appears on this deserted mountain sitting on the shepherds' stone bench, her elbows on her knees and her face in her hands. Generations of pilgrims, seeing this statue of her at a turn in the path, believed that they were hearing the prophet: "Come, all you who pass this way, look and see whether there is any suffering like unto mine." In the central scene of the conversation, as she tells of her mediation and the limits imposed upon it by our sin, the young shepherds see her tears flow.

They are amazed by the modesty of her dress and of her demeanor, but both agree that the Christ resting on her breast seems to be the focal point of all her glory. She has identifyng hallmarks: three garlands of roses recall her title of Queen of the Holy Rosary; and an apron, a headdress, a shawl are signs of her choosing to remain with the people, especially the little people whose misfortune touches her. We can sense that this shimmering Crucified Christ pervades all her thoughts, her tears, and her entire penitential demeanor. And the tongs to the right and the hammer to the left of the crossbar poignantly recall our choice of atonement or of sin in our ongoing role in the Lord's Passion. Facing this scene we can better understand the challenge the Lady of Compassion places before us: "No matter how well you pray in the future, no matter how well you act, you will never be able to make up to me what I have endured on your behalf."

Excerpts taken from chapter eight, "The Seal of God," of the book, A Grace Called La Salette: a Story for the World*, by Fr. Jean Jaouen, M.S., translated from the French by Fr. Norman Théroux, M.S. (see bibliography, page 180).*

The Woman of La Salette is the same as the "Woman" of the Gospel

"Consider this holy apparition for a moment. First, we note the Virgin hidden from the eyes of the public, a humble, modest, Mary of Nazareth speaking a people-language, wearing a simple dress, preferring the company of humble, helpless and poor people. We also recognize, in this weeping Mother wearing the cross of Jesus praying without ceasing for her guilty children, the afflicted Mother of Calvary. Finally, here we see our Mother as the angels see her in heaven, the powerful Mediatrix, always interceding for us, the divine keeper of heavenly gifts, the generous giver of graces, . . . making her own all of her children's concerns, those of this life and those of eternity."

—A Grace Called La Salette

The Ars Incident

Msgr. John S. Kennedy

Any coverage of the La Salette apparitions would be incomplete without some explanation of why the saintly Curé of Ars questioned the authenticity of La Salette for a time. His doubting the authenticity of La Salette was due to a misunderstanding that arose when the Curé met with Maximin for the first and only time. Maximin had came to Ars to see the saintly Curé about his vocation. The Curé was interested in meeting Maximin as he believed in the apparitions, but his assistant priest, Father Raymond, was convinced that the whole thing was a fraud, and he had the special mission to expose it. The following explanation taken from "Light On the Mountain" *by Msgr. Kennedy is a slightly condensed version of what happened on September 25, 1850, to throw completely the whole authenticity of La Salette under a cloud of doubt.*

— The Editor

Father Raymond had now been in Ars for five years, five years which were terrible for the Curé and those closest to him. The assistant was forty years of age when assigned to the parish, some twenty years the junior of Father Vianney. The latter was by then famous all over the world, and to the town and to his confessional there flocked people from many countries. He was held in veneration by great churchmen in France and elsewhere. But the new assistant approached him with no awe at all.

Father Raymond was vigorous and good-looking. He fancied himself as an exceptional preacher and administrator. He was sure that in intelligence, learning, and wisdom he far surpassed the pastor so fortunate as to have him around. Ars, he believed, needed someone like him to bring order out of the perpetual tumult. And the Curé, he felt, needed someone like him (could there be another?) to direct and correct him.

Although the Curé had paid Father Raymond's way through the seminary, the young man did not hesitate to sign himself on the parish books and on any documents as "pastor," as if the Curé had been officially superseded. He kept a close check on the Curé, demanding an account of his day as well as an outline of anything he might have in mind to do. If he found the account not to his taste, he called the Curé down. If the Curé's plans did not meet his approval, he forbade their execution. He would listen critically to the Curé's sermons, and when the preacher who moved more hearts and fired more souls than almost anyone in history had finished, Father Raymond would ponderously mount the pulpit to contradict whatever displeased him. The Curé never objected; his humility and meekness were such that he took no offense.

As in most other things, Father Raymond disagreed with the Curé's attitude toward La Salette. The Curé believed in the apparition. He had a lithographed picture of it in his house. He blessed religious articles representing the beautiful lady's meeting with the children. He used water from La Salette. He encouraged people to go there on pilgrimage. Father Raymond, on the other hand, would not grant that there was any truth to the story. His reason seems to have been, according to his own word, that when he once went to La Salette and met Maximin, the boy refused to answer his questions. If, on that occasion, the priest had shown his accustomed brusque and choleric manner, it may have alienated Maximin and caused him to refuse to be interrogated. In any case, Father Raymond was unfavorably disposed to the lad,

When the boy arrived in Ars, the Curé was not available. He was in the confessional, where he spent most of the time. And now, on the evening of September 24, 1850, it was to Father Raymond that Maximin was brought. The Curé's assistant made no attempt to hide his feelings. He pitched into Maximin, pelting him with questions bristling with animus. The substance of what he had to say was, not to put too fine a point on it, that La Salette was a fiction and Maximin a liar. At length, Maximin said, "You'll have it your way. If you suppose that I actually saw nothing, then you'll call me a liar." The heated interview ended on that note and Father Raymond informed the Curé that the boy had as much as admitted that he was a liar.

The next morning, before seven o'clock, Maximin was brought to see the Curé in the sacristy.

The boy asked the pastor of Ars about entering to the Marists and was strongly advised to return to his own diocese and do as his bishop thought best. When the Curé asked him whether he had seen the Blessed Virgin, as reported, Maximin replied that he had seen a beautiful lady, but whether or not it was the Blessed Virgin he did not know. It appears that the Curé, already having had to listen to Father Raymond's diatribe, misconstrued this answer. What Maximin had said was, in fact, exquisitely right: he had, indeed, seen a beautiful lady, but it was necessary to await the doctrinal decision of the Bishop of Grenoble before one could properly assert that the lady was the Blessed Virgin.

But the Curé interpreted his words as a denial that he had seen anyone at all, an admission that there was no apparition. The Curé wanted to know whether the boy had told lies in the past. Yes, was Maximin's answer, he had occasionally lied to Father Mélin, his pastor in Corps. This, too, was a truthful reply which cast no shadow on the apparition, for Maximin referred to lies which he had told Father Mélin when, as he put it, "I did not wish to tell him where I was going, or when I did not want to learn my lessons." But the Curé concluded that La Salette was a fraud, and this caused him bitter suffering.

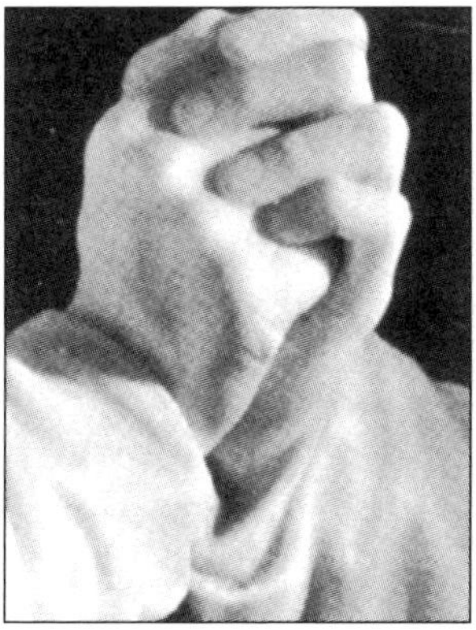

Some weeks later, the bumptious Father Raymond took it on himself to write a long letter to his ordinary, Bishop Devie, and sent copies to the Cardinal Archbishop of Lyon and the Bishop of Gap, both of whom he had reason to believe doubted the authenticity of the apparition. He asserted flatly that Maximin had made a retraction to the Curé, admitting that he was a liar and that the apparition story was a falsehood. Moreover, the Curé had stopped speaking of La Salette, refused to bless religious articles in any way connected with it, and said of Maximin, "I was dissatisfied with him, and he was dissatisfied with me."

Bishop de Bruillard was thunderstruck. A retraction by Maximin after all the grilling he had been put through for four years without ever being shaken? But Bishop de Bruillard did not retreat. He had Maximin examined by a commission composed of priests and layfolk. The boy reaffirmed the actuality of the apparition, insisted that he had made no denial of it to Father Vianney, and explained the misunderstanding. A letter from Bishop de Bruillard to the Curé drew a noncommittal reply. An appeal to the Curé's own bishop brought a letter in which Bishop Devie said that the Curé had no competence to judge the truth or falsity of La Salette, that Father Raymond had undoubtedly handled the boy roughly, and that any decision as to the authenticity of the apparition was Bishop de Bruillard's province and no one else's. He added that two other bishops, then his guests, joined him in the opinion that everything pointed to the reality of an appearance of the Blessed Virgin to the children.

The storm over what was to become known as "the Ars incident," blew for years. In 1851, Bishop de Bruillard would indicate that in his considered judgment, it had not in the least overthrown the fact of the apparition. Backing for this would be supplied later by none other than the Curé of Ars himself. Father Vianney said that his abandonment of credence in La Salette caused him protracted torment. He grieved over it, and for eight years the subject kept coming up in his mind and disturbing him. "You will never know," he told a friend, "what agonies my soul has endured because of this. I suffered in a way that defies description. To get some idea, imagine a man in a desert, in the midst of a fierce sand storm, not knowing where to turn."

This torture of heart ceased only when, after some years, he made a firm act of faith in Our Lady of La Salette. "I was at peace once more," he said, "I was as light as a bird, I could fly!" He had put Our Lady of La Salette to the test in this wise. He was in need of money for the foundation of a mission. He prayed to the Blessed Virgin, under the title of Our Lady of La Salette, to procure it for him, naming the exact amount required. That exact amount was promptly given him. "I firmly believe in La Salette," he now told everyone he could reach. "I have been represented as not believing in it. On the contrary, I am a firm believer in it. That boy and I did not understand each other. But I have asked heaven for signs to shore up my faith, and I have had them. I tell you, one can and one *must* believe in La Salette."

The saintly Curé of Ars met the visionary of La Salette, Maximin Giraud, in the sacristy of his church, but through a misunderstanding, he went through a long period of agonizing doubt of whether the apparitions were authentic or not. In the end, he accepted them wholeheartedly. Left: The confessional where he met with Maximin.

PART IV

Feb. 11, and April 7, 1854

Lourdes, Southern France

"Pray for sinners. . . . Penitence, Penitence, Penitence"

Our Lady of Lourdes

We greet you, Daughter
of God the Father!
We greet you, Mother
of the Son of God!
We greet you, Spouse
of the Holy Spirit!
We greet you, dwelling-
place of the Most Holy
Trinity!

We greet you, Immaculate
Mother of God!
Virgin most prudent!
Pray for us,
intercede for us, Immaculate
Virgin, our merciful
and powerful Mother,
Mary!

John Paul II

Excerpts taken from a prayer to Mary given publicly on December 8, 1997

SVPER
RIVOS AQVARVM

Above: The statue which Bernadette prayed before at the Mother House in Nevers, saying it was the statue that most closely resembled Our Lady. Below: A room in the Bartrés farm and the sheepfold.

Lourdes, France 1858

The Lady of the Grotto

Don Sharkey

The Nineteenth-Century revolt against God was led by some of the most brilliant men the world had ever known. God had given them their wonderful minds that they might better serve Him. Instead, they turned against Him. He permitted them to make astounding discoveries in the field of science and to make great progress in a material way. Instead of thanking Him, they took all the credit to themselves.

"The sovereign majesty of God has tumbled," said Cauchy, the great mathematician who died in 1857. "Only the material exists. . . . Reason alone can and has the right to explain everything.

"The supernatural order is impossible. Religion and faith are superfluous; they are burdens which encumber the human spirit. . . Science . . . .alone reigns victorious; it alone emancipates man, releases him from his chains, permits him to reach his full height and to search all horizons."

The ordinary people of the world read statements such as this and decided these great men knew what they were talking about. The peasants of La Salette cursed and swore and defiled the Sabbath because the men they respected said there was no longer a need for God. There were probably no intellectuals in the mob that stabbed Count Rossi and drove the Pope from Rome in 1848, but the writers, the scientists, the college professors were as much responsible for these actions as if they themselves had paraded through the streets with the bloody knife. And the anti-God movement was growing. There is no telling where it might have ended if it had been allowed to go unchecked.

But Our Lady had no intention of letting it go unchecked. Her appearances in Paris and at La Salette and the definition of her Immaculate Conception had started a countermovement in the world. In 1858, the movement was spurred on by the most challenging series of apparitions that had taken place up to that time. Since the revolt against God was led by such brilliant men, we might expect Mary to combat it by raising up a saint of great intellectual powers — a saint who would lead

A good likeness of St. Bernardette capturing the gentle strength of her face.

people back to God by the very brilliance of his arguments. Instead, Mary chose Bernadette Soubirous, a poor, sickly, uneducated peasant girl, who at the age of fourteen did not even know her catechism.

On February 11, 1858, Bernadette had gone with her sister and a friend to gather wood. The other two girls had run on, leaving her to follow as best she could. Suddenly as she stooped over to take off her shoes before crossing a little millstream, there was a noise like a violent wind. Startled, Bernadette looked up and saw a golden cloud emerge from a grotto on the other side of the stream. This was followed by a beautiful Lady. "She looked at me immediately," said Bernadette later, "smiled at me and motioned me to advance, as if she had been my mother. All fear left me; I seemed to know no longer where I was. I rubbed my eyes; I shut them; I opened them. But the Lady was still there, continuing to smile at me and making me understand that I was not mistaken. Without thinking of what I was doing, I took my rosary in my hands and went to my knees. The Lady made a sign of approval with her head and took into her hands her own rosary which hung on her right arm."

As Bernadette recited the Rosary, the Lady allowed her own beads to glide through her fingers. She joined only in the recital of the Gloria at the end of each mystery. When the recitation of the Rosary was finished, the Lady returned to the interior of the rock, and the cloud went with her.

This happened near the town of Lourdes in the southwestern corner of France on February 11, 1858. It was the first of nineteen appearances which our Lady was to make to Bernadette Soubirous.

The people of Lourdes had never wavered in their faith from the time they were first converted. They had endured the persecutions of the Roman emperors, the Vandals, the Arians and the Albigensians. When many other people in southern France succumbed to the Protestant Revolt, they held fast. They did not fall prey to the madness that swept most of France at the time of the French Revolution. Nor did they join the revolt against God which was led by the Nineteenth Century intellectuals and liberals. They were especially devoted to the Blessed

Virgin. Perhaps it was because of all this that Mary chose Lourdes as the scene of her apparitions in 1858.

As news of the apparitions spread throughout the countryside, larger and ever larger crowds were attracted to the Grotto. Only Bernadette saw the Lady. The others saw nothing but a big black hole in the rocks. But the people saw Bernadette in her ecstasy and knew when our Lady was there. Most of the people believed Bernadette's story. A minority, including the government officials and other members of the "intelligentsia," scoffed at it. This minority was to cause trouble. During the third apparition, on Thursday, February 18, Mary said to Bernadette: "Will you do me the kindness of coming here every day for two weeks?" Bernadette said she would come. Then the Lady said, "I do not promise to make you happy in this world but in the next." Bernadette was to have many occasions to recall these words before she died. At the sixth visit the Lady looked sad and said, "Pray for sinners." Very quickly, however, she smiled again.

At La Salette, Mary had wept the entire time. At Lourdes, she looked sad part of the time, but she frequently smiled. Could it be that the increased devotion to her and the definition of the doctrine of the Immaculate Conception had caused this change? It seems possible, but we cannot be sure.

During the eighth apparition, the crowd saw the girl move on her knees to the rosebush upon which the Lady had been standing. She prostrated herself at each step. Then turning to the people, she cried,

One of the oldest photographs of the grotto Massabielle where on Feb. 11, 1858, Our Lady appeared to Bernadette Soubirous.

"Penitence! Penitence!" Our Lady revealed a spring of water during the ninth apparition. This water was to become world famous for the miraculous cures worked through it. On Friday, February 26, the Lady said, "Bend low and kiss the ground for the sake of sinners." Bernadette did, and so did most of the spectators. On March 2, the Lady requested that a chapel be built at the place of her appearance. She also said that she wished processions to come there.

On March 25, the feast of the Annunciation, Bernadette had an uncontrollable desire to ask her visitor her name. Others had freely been calling her the Blessed Virgin, but to Bernadette she had been "the Lady." The girl made her request, and the Lady merely smiled. Bernadette repeated the question, and then she asked it a third time. "The Lady was standing above the rosebush," Bernadette tells us, "in a position very similar to that shown on the Miraculous Medal. At my third request, her face became very serious, and she seemed to bow down in an attitude of humility. Then she joined her hands and raised them to her breast. She looked up to heaven. Then slowly opening her hands and leaning toward me, she said to me in a voice vibrating with emotion: 'I am the Immaculate Conception.' "

These momentous words meant nothing to the ignorant peasant girl. She repeated them to her pastor, Abbé Peyramale. This priest had been very skeptical about the apparitions, but now his skepticism began to fade. She could not have made up those words! Thus our Lady put heaven's approval on Pope Pius IX's solemn definition of the Immaculate Conception of just a little more than three years before. The whole story of the Fall of man, the Incarnation, and the Redemption are implicit in her words: "I am the Immaculate Conception." So we have a new summary of Christian revelation in our own day. It came at a time when the world had almost forgotten the original revelation.

The local politicians watched the proceedings at Lourdes with uneasiness. They saw that the crowds were getting larger and larger, and crowds made them nervous. Mobs in Paris had overthrown the government in 1789, in 1830, and in 1848. Who could tell what a crowd in Lourdes might do in 1858? Conditions in the Third Empire were none too stable anyway. Most of these local politicians called themselves Catholics. They attended Mass every Sunday and made their Easter duty. But they scoffed at the idea that the Blessed Virgin might really be appearing. Such things just did not happen in the enlightened Nineteenth Century. The officials questioned Bernadette and threatened her, but they could get nowhere. They even threatened her father who had once been in jail on an unwarranted charge of theft. This did no good either.

When all else failed, they put a fence around the grotto. Then they placed police on guard to see that no one broke through the fence. This, they were sure, would end the nonsense. The fence did not prevent the Blessed Mother from appearing once more. Bernadette had to kneel on the other side of the river, but that made no difference. "I saw neither the river nor the barrier. The distance between the Lady and me appeared no greater than usual. I saw nothing but the Blessed Virgin, and never had I seen her so beautiful." Mary smiled a tender farewell. After that, Bernadette saw her no more.

A commission appointed by the Bishop of Tarbes, the diocese in which Lourdes was located, investigated Bernadette's story thoroughly. Every witness was questioned again and again. Bernadette told her story over and over and answered the same questions so many times that she would surely have lost her patience if she had been less of a saint. On January 18, 1862, the Bishop gave his approval to the devotion which had sprung up at Lourdes.

Bernadette later entered the convent. As our Lady had warned her, she found little happiness in this world. She suffered from the curiosity of visitors who wished to see "the saint," from the strictness of her superior who was of the mistaken opinion that Bernadette needed humbling, and from the tuberculosis that racked her body. Hundreds of pilgrims were being cured at Lourdes, but for Bernadette there was no cure. She died on the afternoon of April 16, 1879. On her lips was a final prayer to her Lady of the grotto: "Holy Mary, Mother of God, pray for me, a poor sinner, a poor sinner." She was canonized on December 8, 1933.

The Blessed Mother is very much present at Lourdes today even though no one sees her. The people there are forcibly reminded of her presence when a person thought to have been incurably afflicted is suddenly cured. And this is still happening with amazing frequency in our own day. At the beginning of this century a group of doctors tried to close Lourdes on the grounds that it was unsanitary. Their attempt failed because they could not find a single case of infection resulting from a visit to the shrine. "At Lourdes," an English nurse once said, "we find our Lady putting microbes and bacilli firmly in their place." This flouting of the microbe, the suspension of the usual laws of nature, has been going on for well over a century.

What do men of "science" have to say about all this? Most of them simply refuse to recognize Lourdes. "Miracles are impossible," they say. And that is that. The late Dr. Alexis Carrel was asked to leave the University of Lyons because he said that one of his patients had been cured at

Lourdes. When Dr. Carrel's book, *Man the Unknown,* appeared, the *New York Times* carried letters from other doctors who seemed to think that Carrel was the victim of superstition or that he had lost his mind.

The amazing thing about this is that Dr. Carrel had visited Lourdes several times and had personally examined pilgrims before and after their cures, while his adversaries were not even acquainted with the story of the shrine. Ordinarily, the rule of the scientist is: investigate, investigate, investigate. In the case of Lourdes, however, they refuse to investigate. Lourdes causes the scientists to act in a strangely unscientific manner.

Our Lady's challenge to the irreligious intellectuals still stands. "Come to Lourdes and see for yourselves," she seems to say. But most of them refuse the invitation. In refusing, they make themselves look ridiculous in the eyes of all fair-minded people. This refusal is probably one reason why these intellectuals do not have the following today that they did in 1858. Our Lady has held in check a movement that was threatening to sweep the world.

Why did our Lady make her nineteen appearances at Lourdes in 1858? The obvious and most certain answer is to save souls. That is always her purpose. As to more specific aims, there was her request, repeated by Bernadette, for "Penitence! Penitence!" These words em-

Many of the miracles occur in the baths of Lourdes where the sick line up to be immersed in the cold spring water (see illustration on pg. 131) which has no curative properties.

phasized the sinful state of the world and the need for penance. This was a repetition of the message of La Salette. Very much the same idea was expressed when she said, "Pray for sinners!" This was also to be an essential part of the Fatima message some years later.

Our Lady emphasized the value of the Rosary by allowing the beads to slip through her fingers at each apparition while Bernadette said the prayers. She joined in the Gloria at the end of each decade, but she could not say the Hail Mary, because she could not pray to herself. She told us that she is the Immaculate Conception and thus emphasized this important doctrine while confirming the action of Pius IX who had defined the dogma. In the marvelous cures at Lourdes, she confounds those who say there is no such thing as the supernatural.

Last, but not least, she has left us the great shrine that is visited by at least a million and a half pilgrirms every year — a great powerhouse of prayer. The number of spiritual cures that have taken place there cannot be estimated. The degree of religious fervor that has been generated cannot be computed. The shrine has had a profound effect upon France and upon the world. Although visited by many pilgrims each year, until World War II Lourdes was virtually unknown in many parts of the world. Millions of non-Catholics in the United States, for example, had never heard of the shrine. To other millions, Lourdes was merely a name. Then an amazing thing happened.

Franz Werfel, a Bohemian Jew, found himself in Lourdes in 1940. The French army had collapsed, and Werfel knew he was a marked man with the Nazis. He and his wife fled toward the border of Spain, but they found the border closed. Forced to reside in Lourdes, in hourly danger of being apprehended, Werfel listened with wonder to the story of Bernadette and the apparitions. "One day in my great distress," said Werfel, a professional writer, "I made a vow. I vowed that if I escaped from this desperate situation and reached the saving shore of America, I would put off all other tasks and sing, as best I could, the song of Bernadette."

When he made this promise, it seemed impossible that he should escape the Nazi net that was closing in on him. Yet, escape he did. He made good his promise and wrote the novel, *The Song of Bernadette*. Amazingly, the book became a best seller overnight although the usual best seller in America was a novel of lust and illicit sex. Even more amazing, a movie was made from the book, and millions of people in America and in other parts of the world sat in darkened theaters and watched the wondrous story of Bernadette unfold before their eyes.

The majority of people who read the book and saw the movie were not Catholics. A fair proportion of them were probably "moderns" who did not believe in miracles. What did these people

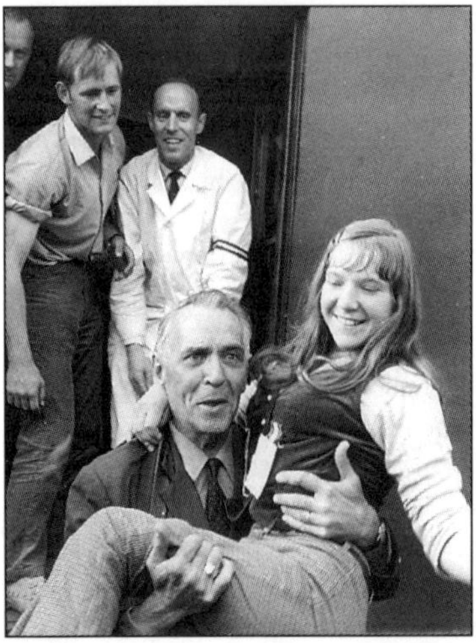

Whether they arrive at Lourdes by train, plane or any other mode of modern transportation, the sick are always greeted with much tender care.

think? It seems certain that the novel and the motion picture made a tremendous impression. For one thing, they prepared Americans for the story of Fatima which they were to hear soon afterward.

One cannot help but see the hand of God in all this. Of all the places in the world Franz Werfel might have chosen to visit, Lourdes would have been close to the bottom of the list. Although not a Christian, he was moved to write a story about the Mother of Christ. How could a nonbeliever write such a story with so much reverence? One searches in vain for an answer unless it is the one given by St. Louis Marie de Montfort: "God wishes that His holy Mother should be at present more known, more loved, more honored, than she has ever been."

The above chapter is a slight condensation of a chapter from the book, The Woman Shall Conquer, *by Don Sharkey*

Miracles — Who Is Unreasonable?

"My belief that miracles have happened in human history is not a mystical belief at all; I believe in them upon human evidence as I do in the discovery of America. Somehow or other an extraordinary idea has risen that disbelieves in miracles consider them coldly and fairly, while believers in miracles accept them only in connection with some dogma. The fact is quite the other way. The believers in miracles accept them (rightly or wrongly) only because they have evidence for them. The disbelievers in miracles deny them (rightly or wrongly) because they have a doctrine against them." —G. K. Chesterton

The Brave Little Heroine

M. Jacomet was a first-rate police officer. He rose rapidly and ended his career in Paris. A tall, fine, manly figure, he knew how to overawe others and, when he wished, gain their confidence. He was a ready public speaker, which rendered him formidable even to the barristers. He was observant and his penetrating glance could detect the slightest subterfuges by reading the countenances of the speakers. "As a police officer," writes one of his most familiar friends, "no one knew better than he how to unmask a rogue and make him confess his guilt." It has been also said that he "put Bernadette through it" according to all the rules of his art.

When the Lourdes congregation came out from Vespers, he had the constable, Pierre Gallet, point out Bernadette. Then he came forward, put his hand on her shoulder and said: "You must come along with me." Surprisingly calm and self-possessed, she replied: "Yes, sir; wherever you like," and followed the Superintendent, escorted by the constable. The onlookers were saying, "Poor Bernadette! They are going to put you in prison," but she answered, smiling, "I am not afraid. If they put me there, they will soon take me out again." Any other little girl under such circumstances would have been upset and begin to cry.

Later on, her cousin, Jeanne Vedere, told her that she intended to go to the grotto when access to it was forbidden. "Don't go," Bernadette said, "the grotto is barricaded, entrance is forbidden, and if the Superintendent or those employed to watch it, saw you, they would arrest you and you would die. You are too frightened." At this time, Jeanne Vedere was over twenty years of age. Bernadette knew how afraid girls were of being taken up and sent to jail; the very thought of it was enough make them panic. A woman of Lourdes howled when cited before the court at Pau and admitted she was terrified when she saw the police behind her. "I imagined they were going to take us to prison!" At the thought of it alone, she lost her head. With still greater reason, the girls of the simple folk at Lourdes shared this dread.

The more we consider this question, the more astounded we are at Bernadette's coolness and composure. When the Superintendent made her enter his office, he began by questioning her with assumed a good-natured sympathy. "Bernadette," writes M. Estrade, who was present at the examination, "remained seated in a perfectly natural attitude, her hands folded on her lap and her head slightly bent. Her face showed great seriousness and simplicity." When the Superintendent had taken down her name and age, and had made her give an account of the apparitions, "he took his page of notes and began to cross-examine the visionary, trying to entrap her into contradicting herself." All the witnesses agree in acknowledging that when made to relate the story of the visions Bernadette was rather taciturn, answered the questions put to her very shortly, and disconcerted her visitors by her lack of imagination and of aptitude for conversation.

The expression of her face seemed dull, and to some she seemed insignificant; but if anyone expressed doubts concerning the possibility of the apparitions, or of her sincerity, she was transformed, her eyes shone and her retorts could be devastating. "If anyone tried to oppose Bernadette," writes Fr. Duboé, who long knew her intimately at Lourdes and was the first to write her story, "if they pronounced her statements to be impossible, then it was her chance to triumph. An astounding change took place in that child. Contradiction rendered her interesting. She amazed and put to silence the well-informed men who fought against her, with all their advantages of easy speech and experience, just by the sallies of her common sense and wit. At ceremonious meetings, there were some who clapped their hands at her unexpected and decisive retorts."

Accustomed as he was to battles of words, the Superintendent was to experience the sudden metamorphosis of the little peasant. In his notes, he had purposely made alterations in Bernadette's account. He had written that the Lady was nineteen years old, wore a blue dress and a white girdle. With an assurance equally tranquil and imperturbable, Bernadette replied: "On the contrary, sir, you, must put a white dress and a blue girdle. I did not say nineteen, but sixteen or seventeen. I did not say her hair hung down behind. You did not understand. It was the veil that hung down behind."

It was in vain that he insisted. Bernadette only persisted in her previous statements, more firmly and serenely. M. Jacomet, on the contrary, began to grow annoyed. "Bernadette," writes Estrade, "corrected, without insolence but also without timidity, all the variants which he had purposely introduced into his report." After his fatherly approach, it was a veritable duel that took place, and one in which all the feints of the policeman were immediately parried, and accompanied by replies which, however innocent they might be, did not fail to wound his self-importance. Judging that he stood to gain nothing on the ground he had taken up, M. Jacomet changed his tactics.

"Becoming grave," Estrade tells us, and looking fixedly at the child, in a slightly ironical tone, he said: "My dear Bernadette, I must tell you that I already know the story of your pretended visions. This tale is a pure invention and I know who has taught it to you." At these words, Bernadette raised her great, shining, soft, black eyes to the Superintendent — those eyes her contemporaries so admired — looking straight at him, "I do not understand you."

Beaten again, and compelled to lower his own eyes, M. Jacomet resolved to play his last card. Suddenly showing great anger, he declared: "I do not demand a confession, but I require of you a simple promise. Will you assure me that you will not return to the cave."

"Sir," Bernadette replied, "I do not promise you. I told the Lady that I would return there."

"Oh, indeed!" cried the Superintendent, rising to his feet, "so you think that we shall still humor you by listening to your fairy tales?" Subsequently Bernadette asserted, that before getting up, he was so furious and flustered that, when he was trying to take some ink, he could not manage to find the hole in the inkwell. Obviously, the girl had retained all her coolness and presence of mind. The Superintendent felt that he was virtually powerless and defeated.

On Sunday, February 28, a week after the examinations by the public prosecutor and the police superintendent these representatives of public authority arranged with the local magistrate that he should summon Bernadette to appear before him. This enquiry before M. Rives, with the superintendent of police also present, was more important and still more intimidating than those of the previous Sunday. Had not the magistrate sufficient authority to send Bernadette to prison, and was he not prepared to do so? Moreover, in this case the Superintendent was acting on the instructions of the public prosecutor.

After High Mass, M. Jacomet, having arranged with the district road surveyor, Lèon Latapie, to accompany him, said to the latter, as the schoolgirls emerged from church in charge of the Sisters: "Go and fetch Bernadette." The surveyor obeyed and took her by the arm. He tells us himself that the Sisters began to cry. Bernadette, on the contrary, after the experiences of the last Sunday, felt more sure of herself than ever. "What do you want with me?" she asked. "I answered, "Little one, you must come with us." She began to laugh and said, "Hold me tight, or I shall run away!" She was taken to M. Rives, the magistrate. He addressed the child in patois, without showing her the slightest consideration. "So you're here, you gadabout?" "Yes sir. I'm here," she replied.

"Why are you making so many people run after you like this? We are going to put you in prison." "I am ready," was her reply. "Put me there, but see that it is strong and firmly shut, or I shall escape."

"I will make you die in prison."

"I am not giving up going. Next Thursday is the last day."

At that moment, the sister superior of the hospice entered and, in tears, besought them: "Gentlemen, I beg of you, leave the child to us. Don't kill her." Bernadette remained impassive and calm. Her confidence, tinged with gallantry, and recalling the last days of Joan of Arc, did not amount to insolence. She withdrew without having renounced her mission.

The particular characteristic which proves Bemadette's gift of fortitude, which was really inspired and supernatural, is that, however strong it might be it never in her case carried with it, as happens only too frequently, a want of discipline and obedience to lawful authority. Those who are strong and energetic only by nature too often end by laughing at laws, and transgressing the prohibitions of constituted authorities. In Bernadette's case, on the contrary, we observe an unfailing obedience to her parents and her confessor.

During the retreat preparatory to her first Communion, a strange lady, who was talking to Bernadette, asked her: "If M. le Curé Feast were to forbid you to go to the grotto and the Blessed Virgin were to order you to go, what would you do?" Bernadette replied, without either embarrassment or hesitation: "I would come and ask permission from M. le Curé."

When we see in Bernadette this resolute attitude to obey before all else, even though she might hear the Lady order her to go to the grotto, we cannot doubt that the indomitable strength that animated her, united to an interior sense of submissison towards lawful authority, despite all else, was inspired by God.

— *The True Story of St. Bernadette,* Newman Press

"Won't they be caught, these artists"

"My dear Mother, how they slander you!" she would say. "Won't they be caught, these artists, when they see you!" "Was she so very beautiful then?" "So beautiful that when once one has seen her it is impossible to love anything else on earth." Nevertheless she did venerate pictures of Our Lady and would hold them lovingly in her hands and kiss them. But once she abruptly asked a Sister of Nevers why, while praying, she looked at a statue. "To have fewer distractions," she answered. "It would be the opposite for me," Bernadette whispered, and her eyes closed on the vision she vividly saw in her memory.

Lady Poverty Finds a Home

It would seem that if there was one characteristic that foreshadowed the heroic sanctity of the little shepherdess of Lourdes it was her love of "Lady Poverty." When the rich young man, Francis of Assisi, lost the attraction he had to worldly amusements, his Assisian companions accused him of having fallen in love. He told them yes, indeed he found his lady love, at the same time not disclosing that his love was none other than evangelical poverty, the poverty exemplified in the lives of Jesus and His holy Mother Mary. But in the case of the little poor girl of Lourdes, Bernadette Soubirous, her early years were quite different. They were marked by a crushing poverty that no human being should have to live through. It was a poverty that was not freely embraced. But the final end was the same for both — a total love of God and disdain for money and all that money could buy.

Through many seemingly uncontrollable circumstances the parents of Bernadette, François and Louise Soubirous lost everything when she was but a small girl. They did retain a certain personal dignity, however, which never allowed them to beg even when the situation was so critical that they had little or no food to give their children. Not able to meet their debts to creditors, they finally ended up in the former Lourdes jail, called the "Cachot," or the "Dungeon," which no one else wanted to rent, in which they were allowed to live rent free. Utter poverty could be quite demoralizing, but François and his young wife never gave up hope. Their positive attitude in dealing with poverty was passed on to their children.

As one neighbor remarked, "Never," testified André Sajous, "would you have heard them complain that they were hungry. But how often have I seen Bernadette, Jean-Marie and little Justin laugh and skip on an empty stomach!" On one occasion a woman visiting in the parish church was distracted by one of the Soubirous boys who was making a scraping noise on the pavement of the church. Upon close investigation she found him scraping wax off the flagstones and eating the spilled wax. At her invitation she fed the starving boy each day. He sat on the step of her house which he used as a table, but would not enter her home nor give her his name.

With such a tragic situation, one would think that the immediate result of the Lady's apparitions to their oldest child and all the notoriety accompanying it, would be that Bernadette and her parents would accept something at least to stave off the crushing poverty of their hungry children. In fact her mother, Louise Soubirous, in a moment of understandable weakness remarked to a woman who was pitying her for the "more than frugal meal" which Louise was putting on the table "in which there was nothing but water:" "We would surely be well off if my daughter was willing to accept the rolls of money offered her, often with insistence."

Bernadette refused to accept any sort of recompense for the many times she was asked to relate the story of the apparitions. Gifts were offered to her in all sincerity. She had only to accept them and her parents, who were so poor and living from day to day on God's Providence (which was pretty lean in their case), would no longer need to worry where the next meal would come from, and work so hard for so little. Bernadette with wisdom and prudence beyond her years adored the designs of Providence, which had preordained both the rich and the poor, understanding how readily something so sacred as the apparitions could be compromised by the world by accepting money, and how readily scandal could arise from profiting of so sacred a thing as Mary's apparitions.

Bernadette viewed without envy the money of the rich and the things that the rich so readily enjoyed. She had no bitterness, as many poor would have under the same circumstances, at the injustice of it all and the fact that in many instances the rich looked down on the poor while offering little help. In fact, for some Christians, riches were looked upon as God's benevolence and a blessing. As Sergeant d'Angla of Lourdes noted, Bernadette looked upon money with no feeling, neither contempt nor aversion, but she never accepted it. It was a disinterestedness that seemed simple at first glance, but actually was heroic under the dire circumstances under which the Soubirous family were forced to live. Several instances have been recorded for us.

A lady once slipped into the pocket of Bernadette's apron one of those rolls of money mentioned by her mother. Bernadette pulled it out at once and returned it to the visitor as if the money "might have burned her fingers." A gold coin in the palm of a priest's hand drew an immediate reaction by Bernadette, "Monsieur l'Abbé" she said hastily before he offered it to her, "give it to the poor."

But while the young visionary was obstinate in refusing every gift, her brother and sister were more accommodating. For instance a lady slipped a two-franc piece to Toinette. "No, no," exclaimed Bernadette authoritatively, "no money." Jean-Marie was more unlucky. He came in one day triumphantly bringing home two francs. He explained that some ladies and gentlemen whom he had taken to the grotto, and for whom he had drawn water from the miraculous spring, had rewarded him with this. But reward or not, hadn't he been given orders never to accept anything? Poor little Jean-Marie! Bernadette was very annoyed, we are told, and she gave him a box on the ear, the soundest he ever had in his life. She ordered him to return the two francs. After he returned, Bernadette searched him to make sure he had given the money back.

"No money!" No presents in disguise either. Some wealthy people begged Abbé Peyramale to use the gold refused by Bernadette to buy some white bread for her and her family. It was a useless stratagem. The twelve-pound loaf delivered by the bakery was returned to him untouched, and the Curé sent the money back to the donors. Some rich farmers asked the chaplains of Bétharram if they could "without offending Bernadette and her family, offer them some provisions." The Fathers, who did not suspect the lengths to which the Soubirous carried their disinterestedness, approved of their generous scheme. But in the evening they were amazed to see these worthy people bringing back from Lourdes their baskets of foodstuffs. To their offers the visionary's parents had given an absolute refusal.

If the love of "Lady Poverty" of St. Bernadette went well beyond the self respect of her parents, who though poor never begged, could we not say she must have learned the value and the virtue of evangelical poverty from another? Certainly it was no merely natural virtue but the work of the Holy Spirit. Apart from supernatural grace, it seems certain that the virtue of evangelical poverty and humility, which Francis called the "Sister" of "Lady Poverty," would have been part of the secrets that the blessed Mother imparted to her personally. No doubt the three times that Our Lady Immaculate gave secrets to Bernadette for herself alone had to do with spiritual direction.

This would explain how tenacious she was in the defense of "Lady Poverty." This, as well as all private revelations, if true, are a reiteration of the Gospel message. Money and attachment to material

The home of the Soubirous. The parents of Bernadette were so poor they had to reside in the former city jail where they did not have to pay rent.

things are two of the most insidious and successful ways that Satan and his followers have to gain control over souls. Is he not the Prince of the world and did he not promise Christ when he was tempted in the desert to give him the kingdoms of the world? Jesus Himself was born in a stable, and buried in another's tomb. He admitted that "Foxes have holes, and birds nests, but the Son of Man has no where to rest His head." On another occasion He said, "No man can serve two masters. You cannot serve God and Mammon."

Can we not say that Our Lady is actually the "Lady Poverty" St. Francis had in mind, she who was the personification of utter detachment from the material world, but totally given to love of God and the things of God? She said in her hymn of praise in greeting her cousin Elizabeth, "The hungry He fills with good things, the rich he has sent away empty." (Luke 1:53). The "hungry" in her *Magnificat* are the poor. Christ and His Mother in word and deed made it clear that poverty is in no way shameful, that, "For a Christian" as one Franciscan wrote, "money should remain in the place assigned it in the Gospel, namely at the lowest rung in the scale of human values."

At Lourdes in 1858, and La Salette in 1846 Our Lady appeared to extremely poor children. Though Catherine Labouré came from a wealthy family, her father wouldn't pay for her dowry, he was so bitter at her entering the convent. She left behind nothing but her prayer books. When Our Lady appeared in, Banneux, Belgium, in 1933 at the height of the Depression years, she identified with the poor. When the visionary, Mariette, asked her who she was, she replied: "I am the Virgin of the poor."

Only in the next world will we know the secrets Our Lady imparted to St. Bernadette. What we do know is that the **Little Poor One of Lourdes,** through her espousal to "Lady Poverty" in the same manner as the **Little Poor Man of Assisi,** points back to the Gospel and reminds us how shallow and spiritually bankrupt our consumerist, materialistic society really is. *"Blessed are the poor in spirit for the Kingdom of God is theirs."*

City of the Poor

It is indeed strange that up to 1956 the poor were inadvertently excluded from Lourdes because of their poverty. The city itself has a flourishing business in accommodating and feeding pilgrims who come to Lourdes, for the most part, from affluent countries. The many religious goods stores selling every imaginable religious article are lined up for blocks and do a thriving business. This inevitable commercialism of the shrine would exclude any modern Soubirous family coming any distance.

Experiencing first-hand the lot of the poor, Bernadette desired some sort of lodging to be provided for the poor who would come to the Lourdes on pilgrimage. At first a small wooden structure was erected in 1872, but this burned down in the early part of the century and interest seemed to wane. The poor had to fend for themselves. In the early 1950s, Bishop Pierre Maria Theas, the bishop of Lourdes at that time, could not forget the humble circumstances of the first family

Msgr. Jean Rodham who wholeheartedly supported Bishop Pierre Maria Theas' plans of building a center for the poor in his diocese at Lourdes. This project, which the saintly bishop (see pg. 167) called "dear to my heart," is called *The City of the Poor of St. Peter.* Below: the spacious, attractive dinning room, where meals are served at a nominal price.

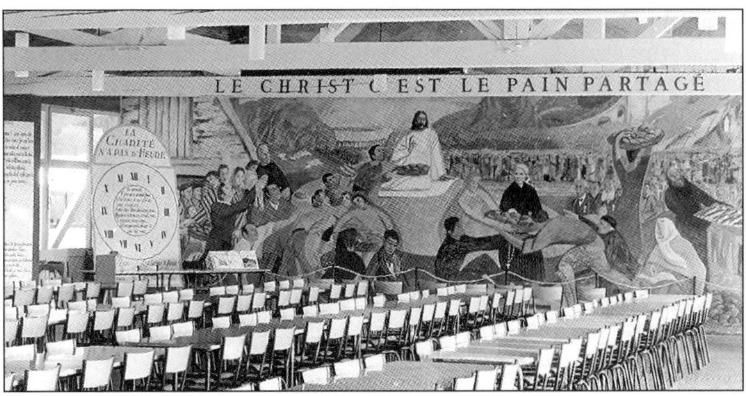

of Lourdes and Bernadette's desire. He appealed to the *Secours Catholique,* an organization comparable to the Catholic Relief Service.

Monsignor Jean Rodham, the dynamic Secretary General of *Secours Catholique* at that time, gave his wholehearted support to the venture. A forty-five acre piece of land overlooking the city of Lourdes was selected as an ideal location. The project which Bishop Theas called "dear to my heart" came to be called *Cité-Secours Saint Pierre,* the City of the Poor of St. Peter. Its purpose was to make possible pilgrimages to Lourdes for thousands of people who otherwise would never be able to fulfill Our Lady's wish: "Let the people come in procession." Since May 1, 1956, when the "City" first opened its doors many thousands of pilgrims have been treated with the greatest consideration by the staff, which is largely made up of volunteers.

The over a dozen building "City" is within easy walking distance of the Grotto. A large cafeteria-style dining room serves meals at a nominal cost. The chapel is the most unique and appropriate of the buildings. It is an exact copy of Bernadette's sheepfold at Bartres. "I wanted to build a chapel in which a poor person could feel at home," Msgr. Rodham said, "a chapel in which Bernadette would have a place." Bernadette, who was small (only 4′7″) would have loved the small, rustic chapel. It was never intended to accommodate large crowds since the pilgrims assist at daily Mass at either the Lourdes Basilica or the Grotto. It is a fitting place for meditating on the poverty of the God-man. There in the Presence of the Eucharistic Lord who has divested Himself of even His visible human body one learns poverty of spirit. There is no commercialism, nor discordant noise in this "City." As the pilgrim enters a sign "Peace - Silence - Peace" greets him. The atmosphere is of peace and quiet.

Who are the poor that take advantage of these facilities at *Cité-Secours?* They might be pensioners, or people from large families, sometimes sick persons who have depleted their financial reserves by medical bills. A typical diocesan pilgrimage would be somewhere between fifty and seventy pilgrims. Some of these may have been accompanying the sick. Others were elderly folks. In one instance the train fare for several pilgrims was paid with money which parish children had collected. This is the kind of charity on which the *Cité-Secours* is built.

There are also the individual pilgrims who walk to Lourdes and seek lodging, like Jacques. He arrived late one night after walking from Bordeaux. "I can't afford a night in a hotel," he said. "I've got a blanket with me if you can give me some shelter." For him and all like Jacques there is always room. Poverty entitles one to a bed in one of the dozen pavilions and to meals in an up-to-date cafeteria. There is even free transportation to and from the Grotto. Where else are the poor so privileged?

A School of Evangelical Penance

*Aloys de Moulins, O.F.M. Cap.**

It is a fact, a moving and serious fact, that the Most Blessed Virgin Mary formally preached at Lourdes that which our Lord Jesus Christ Himself insisted upon many times in His sermons, namely, together with prayer, the great need of penance; from her most pure, loving and sweet lips there fell that most austere of sermons.

At the grotto of Massabielle the radiant face of the Immaculate was at certain times covered with an indescribable sadness. Tears ran down her cheeks. When she taught penance to Bernadette she prepared her for the future with these words: "I do not promise to make you happy in this world." And at the same time as Bernadette watched Mary directed and demanded she do certain penitential things. She required Bernadette to remain for a long time on her knees, to drag herself on her knees, kiss the ground, to try to find water where there seemed to be none, to drink from the still muddy water, to be saddened and weep over sin and all sinners.

Finally, Mary pronounced the terrible word, the word which causes one to fear. She pronounced it three times, "penitence, penitence, penitence." If this merciful mother, who is sweetness itself, most amiable, the smile and the grace of Christianity, interjects in the midst of an ecstasy of a child of fourteen a demand so difficult, it is to make us understand there is no one in the world, even among the best persons, who can pretend to escape from this law or be dispensed from it.

There, on the lips of His mother, is the profound teaching of her Son. The first words which Christ as a preacher used were: "Repent, for the Kingdom of heaven is at hand" (Mt. 4:17). This was the theme of a great number of his sermons, and in truth the conclusion of all of them. "If you do not do penance you will all perish." Before He left them to go up to heaven, this was the mandate given to the apostles the day He gave them His power and sent them on their mission. They were commanded (they and their successors) to preach to all nations

**Translated from the French by Fr. John J. Richetta*

even to the end of time — "penance and the remission of sin" (Lk. 24:47).

Putting aside the question of personal sin, penance is of the essence of the Christian profession. "He who wishes to come after me, let him deny himself, take up his cross daily and follow me." If the Immaculate Conception, who knew neither sin nor concupiscence, does not herself need penance, as in our case (as a necessary preservative, or an indispensable remedy), nevertheless she practiced it, because she belonged to Christ. Following the spirit of Jesus himself, she was the greatest of penitent souls.

To refuse the call of Mary to penance would mean being totally opposed to the Gospel of Jesus. Penance then is not just beating the breast. Persecution, contradiction, betrayal, ingratitude, blasphemy, the agony of the vision of souls lost forever, physical trials, toil, poverty, destitution, fastings, days without rest, nights without sleep, made of Christ's entire life a continuous cross and martyrdom. He became a man of sorrows, bruised by beatings, a leper, a worm of the earth, reviled, rebuffed, mistreated by the people, abandoned by his friends, abandoned by heaven itself.

The appeal for the necessity of penance came at Lourdes at the right time. A picture of naturalism and sensualism of our times in not necessary here. It is apparent all around us. Our century of secularization and naturalization is becoming more and more materialistic. The complete possession of all good things here below is the perverted, uto-

There are many forms of penance at Lourdes — from penitential practices to the Sacrament of Reconciliation (formally called the Sacrament of Penance). The Chapel of Reconciliation, where confessions are heard in many languages, has this moving statue of the Curé of Ars.

pian ideal of communism. Modern civilization must have no other goal but to suppress pain and substitute pleasure. A government is worth nothing if it does not stem the difficulties of life. It is considered doing nothing, if it does not multiply material well-being.

However, a man does not live wisely if he simply avoids difficulties and fills his existence and those of his own with satisfactions of every sort. Science and discoveries should not merely tend to advance a sweet and easy life. Literature does not uplift or inspire if it only describes troubled passion. Art does not call attention merely to foolish spectacles filled with confusion which evokes laughter. And medicine itself has other aims than lessening pain to the point of euthanasia [assisted suicide] in which there is no other hope than to sleep forever. Being comfortably lodged, carefully nourished, luxuriously dressed, lead easily to a refined, sensual life. The one ambition of pagan Rome during its decline, expressed in the words "*Panem et circenses*" (bread and circuses), has been revived by our century which has returned to the paganism of Rome. In a spirit of obedience to the Gospel, Lourdes sets up a violent reaction against the present day current of sensuality.

Poor soul, soiled and disfigured by sin, you are irredeemably lost if you do not at least do this: confess your sins, weep over them, let your conscience reproach you, repent in this sacrament of penance which is the sacrament of mercy and forgiveness. The Blessed Virgin said: "Go to the spring and drink and wash yourself." At the miraculous fountain one can drink the clear water in long draughts. Sick bodies are washed there and leave, cured of their sickness and of their wounds. But, that souls may go to the holy pool cleansed and radiant with grace, they must be washed by the blood of Christ the Redeemer, and not merely by the water from the rock. The great miracles of Lourdes are found particularly in the penitents' confessions which tear apart and purify souls. God does not resist the cry of a soul even the most hideous, who confesses and repents. He Himself assures us He cannot resist. "Even if your sins be as scarlet they will be made as white as snow" (Is. 1:18). "And though you may have been drawn to the farthest corners of the world, even from there will the Lord your God, gather you, even from there will he bring you back" (Dt. 30:4). But there is something better — the penance of love.

It is the penance of those who seek to be Christ-like, the penance of those who suffer at the thought that their God is so much offended. Theirs is the penance of reparation for the sins of the world. They desire to console the Divine Heart with their inexhaustible tears in the measure that their love becomes stronger. They live by the words of a great thinker, "He who increases in love, grows also in suffering." And

God who is so good accepts the sacrifices dictated by this love. He desires these penances. He Himself inspires them, to use them as an opportunity to unleash torrents of grace on the throng of sinners who owe their repentance, their conversion, their health to the prayers, tears and penances of the saints.

For that reason Mary made the little soul whom she instructed and formed a penitent, a great penitent. That which touched those present during Bernadette's ecstasy was seeing this child, so calm and recollected losing this calm, when she carried out the penances commanded by the Holy Virgin. There was in her a sort of excessive agitation as she kissed the ground or walked on her knees or ate the bitter grass. She did this with such great courage that in seeing her one could not help but weep. This was love which one could not doubt that filled her childlike heart. This love would make of her life a martyrdom to the very end.

Penance of love! That is, the penance of accepted suffering, suffering searched for, suffering desired. The worldly rejoice, but the world also has thousands who are friends of redemptive suffering. It is the triumph of the cross. The cross in which Mary taught Bernadette how to seek from Christ the greatest tenderness. A tenderness the world would never know, with all its enjoyments, as it creates among its followers such a spirit of enthusiasm and gift of self. And if a seraphic mouth can translate into human syllables a superhuman heroism, she/he would cry out with the fervor of ecstasy: "Always to suffer, never to die, that Love may be love." This is not a passing exaltation and the cry of an isolated soul, but, rather the great voice which comes from the bosom of the Church, where thousands of penitents, virgins, martyrs and saints, known or unknown, belonging to all nations and all generations, have immolated their hearts, bodies, all their being, their whole lives out of love for the Divine Crucified One.

There is still the penance of holy joy. This penance is created by love; it is the purest love. Nothing is farther removed from worldly joy and enjoyment. Joy is not found in orgies and reprehensible foolishness. It is found in sacrifices. To receive the cross as a gift, to embrace it lovingly, to bear it happily, to kiss with smiling lips the hand that chastises us, to say "thank you" with a joyful heart to the Providence which tests us, is at the same time to have a superabundance of the most loving joy in our hearts. The Lord Himself assures us that his yoke is sweet and his burden light.

The apostles are said to have found joy in having suffered for the name of Jesus. St. Paul affirms his superabundant joy in the midst of tribulations. All the saints spoke the same language — from St. Ignatius of Antioch who cried in the name of the millions of martyrs, "I hope to be ground by the teeth of lions to become bread worthy to be offered to Jesus Christ," to one of the most modern saints, the Curé of Ars, who cried, "When one courageously embraces the cross and presses it strongly to his heart he distills its nectar and becomes drunk by its sweetness." St. Thérèse of the Child Jesus, with a smile, cries out: "I do not want merely one suffering, I want them all." The holy Mother Barat follows this advice: "To suffer everything and never to give suffering to anyone." Blessed Javouhey cries out with conviction, "If suffering were sold at the market, I would quickly go and buy it."

The sick at Lourdes are, finally, filled with joy at their involuntary penances. They rejoice in seeing others cured of their illness while their own must still remain. The penance of the little consumptive who smiles and considers it good fortune to be able to continue her suffering when one of her little sisters is suddenly cured. The penance of the blind man who resigns himself to seeing nothing of the earth, who will however see, tomorrow, the beautiful face of the Virgin in Paradise. All these sick tortured by suffering are happy, they may return to endure the same sufferings, but they carry, in eyes filled with fever, the most beautiful flame of love!

All the penance of Lourdes ends in an overpowering joy. Everything ends with songs and acclamations after the innumerable Masses where the sacrifice of Christ calms all sadness, leading to the hosannas of the processions and the interminable repetition of Ave's. If it is correct to say that Lourdes is the Capital of Prayer, Lourdes has also become and it must be the great School of Penance! The two powerful messages of the Gospel are joined together. We must also keep them together in order to preserve their twofold lesson.

The question is sometimes posed as to which should be more important in our Christian life, prayer or penance. To this question we answer that they must march together and must be equally developed in souls. We cannot say then that prayer has precedence over penance nor that penance has precedence over prayer! Both are equally instruments of purification, of love, of holiness. They are in the souls as two scales — a balance which must always be preserved, and which marks the progress of the Christian life and the life of greatest perfection. — *MARIE*

The Penetrating Sweetness of that Smile

"I was an atheist! I breathed atheism! I labored for it! I was proud of it! I loved it and I boasted of it! God? Bosh! Just so much myth! Good for the weak minds of women, children, the naive and the unlettered! Gives them something to talk about! But for strong minds like mine, God belongs to the realm of fairy tales!" So snorted Count de Bruissard as he scanned the daily paper over a demitasse on the boulevard.

Suddenly, his eye lighted on a news item telling of the apparition of the Blessed Virgin at Lourdes to a little girl named Bernadette Soubirous. What was even more incredible was the fact that the Apparition was said to have smiled! Sheer nonsense, thought the Count! "Whatever the case might be, I'm ready for a leisurely trip to Lourdes! I'll go there as a tourist, and expose the lying fraud."

"I arrived at the home of the Soubirous," wrote Bruissard many years later, "and found Bernadette sitting on the threshold, busy knitting a stocking. As I studied her she appeared to be a very ordinary girl. The features of her little face bore the traces of a hidden sickness, however, shining through them appeared unmistakable evidence of a strange sweetness. In response to my request, she narrated the story of the apparitions with straightforward simplicity, but with a certitude I have not often met with before. This struck me deeply.

"'Very well,' I said when she finished. 'But how did that nice lady smile?'

"The little girl looked up at me with marked surprise, and after a moment of silence, answered: 'Oh, Sir, one would have to come down from Heaven to imitate that smile!'

"'Couldn't you attempt to imitate it for me? You see, I'm an unbeliever and haven't the least faith in apparitions.'

"Her countenance darkened and took on an expression of severity. 'Then sir, you must think I'm a liar?' she said knitting her brow. 'Very well, even though you are an unbeliever, I'll try to imitate the smile of the Virgin for you.'

"As she raised her eyes to Heaven, her little face began to glow with indescribable sweetness. I had my answer! I will never forget that smile! Some time after, I lost my wife and my two darling daughters, however, I don't feel abandoned; that smile of penetrating sweetness is ever with me!"

— From IL CAVALIERE DELL'IMMACOLATA

Pope Pius XII Remembers Lourdes

The Lourdes pilgrimage, which We had the pleasure of making when We went to preside in the name of Our predecessor Pius XI at the Eucharistic and Marian celebrations closing the Jubilee of the Redemption, left in Our soul deep and sweet memories. We are firmly confident that in this jubilee year Our Lady will want to respond again with liberality to the expectations of her children. But We are especially convinced that she urges Us to recall the spiritual lessons of the apparitions and set them upon the path which she so clearly traced for us.

These lessons, the faithful echo of the teachings of the Gospel message, throw particular light on the contrasts which oppose the judgment of God to the vain wisdom of this world. In a society, barely conscious of the ills which assail it, which conceals its miseries and injustices under an outward appearance of bright and carefree prosperity, the Immaculate Virgin, never touched by sin, showed herself to an innocent child.

With maternal compassion she looks upon this world which has been redeemed by the blood of her Divine Son, but in which sin sows so much ruin. And on three occasions she made her urgent appeal: "Penitence, penitence, penitence!" She even appealed for outward manifestations: "Go and kiss the earth in penance for sinners." And to this gesture must be added a prayer: "You must pray to God for sinners." This same injunction was made in the time of John the Baptist, and at the beginning of Jesus' ministry, showing men the way to return to God: "Repent!" And who would dare say that this appeal for the conversion of hearts is not applicable to our times?

But how could the Mother of God come to her children except as the messenger of forgiveness and hope? The water already flows from beneath her feet: "Omnes sitientes, venite ad aquas, et haurietis salutem a Domino." (All ye who thirst, come to the waters and ye shall draw health from the Lord.). At this spring, where gentle Bernadette was the first to go and drink and wash, there will flow away all the miseries of the soul and body. "And I went and washed and I see," the blind of the Gospel and the grateful pilgrim will be able to respond.

But, as it was with the crowds which pressed around Jesus, the healing of physical wounds remains as a gesture of mercy and a sign of that power which the Son of Man has to remit sins. The Virgin invites us to the blessed grotto on behalf of her Divine Son, for the conversion of the heart and in hope of pardon. Will we heed her? In this humble response of man who admits himself to be a sinner there resides the true greatness of this jubilee year.

The Church would have a right to expect great good, if each pilgrim to Lourdes — and even all Christians united in heart with the centenary celebrations — realized in the first place this action of sanctification within himself "not in word, neither with the tongue, but in deed and in truth." There is everything to invite the Christian to this action of sanctification, for nowhere except, perhaps, at Lourdes does one feel so moved to prayer, to the forgetting of oneself and to charity.

For instance, the sight of the stretcher-bearers and the serene peace of the invalids; of the fraternity which assembles faithful of all origins in one single invocation; the sight of the spontaneity of helping each other and the fervor with which without affectation the pilgrims kneel in front of the grotto. At seeing all these things, the best persons are compelled by the attraction of a life more completely dedicated to the service of God and to their brothers; the less fervent become conscious of their lukewarmness and once again return to the road of prayer; the more hardened and incredulous sinners themselves are often touched by grace, or at least if they are honest, do not remain unmoved by the testimony of this "multitude of believers with only one heart and one soul."

But this experience of a few brief days of pilgrimage does not in itself generally suffice to engrave in indelible letters the appeal of Mary for a genuine spiritual conversion. A return to a regular reception of the sacraments, to the respect of Christian morals in everyday life, and the rallying to the ranks of Catholic Action and to the various institutions recommended by the Church: is it not true that only on these conditions can the great crowds expected to gather at Lourdes in 1958 yield, according to the expectations of the Immaculate Virgin herself, the fruits of salvation so necessary to mankind today?

The world, which in our days offers so many legitimate motives for pride and security, knows also nowadays a terrible temptation to materialism, often denounced by Our predecessors and Ourselves. This materialism is not to be found only in the condemned philosophy which rules the politics and economic life of a segment of humanity. It rages also in the love of money, the ruin of which increases according to the dimensions of modern enterprises, and which unfortunately determines so many decisions which weigh on the life of the people. It expresses itself in the cult of the body, in the excessive search for comforts and the flight from all the austerities of life. It prompts one to despise human life, the life itself which is destroyed before it is able to see the light of day.

It resides in the unrestrained search for pleasure which exhibits itself without modesty and even attempts to seduce souls which are still pure with reading matter and entertainments. It shows itself in the lack of interest of one's brother, in the selfishness which crushes man with injustice and deprives him of his rights, in a word, in that concept of life which regulates all things only in terms of material prosperity and earthly satisfactions. "And I will say to my soul, the rich man said, Soul, thou has many good things laid up for many years; take thy ease, eat, drink, be merry. But God said to him, Thou fool, this night do they demand thy soul of thee.'" (Lk.12: 19-20)

To a society which in its public life often contests the supreme rights of God, which would conquer the universe at the expense of its soul and has hastened to its own ruin, the Virgin Mother sent out a cry of alarm. Christians of every class and every nation will seek to meet one another in truth and in charity, and to banish misunderstanding and suspicion. The weight of social structures and economic pressures burdening the good will of men is undoubtedly enormous and often paralyzes it.

But if it is true as Our predecessors and We Ourselves have insistently stressed, that the question of man's social and political peace is

above all a moral question, no reform can be fruitful, no agreement can be stable without a change and purification of hearts. The Virgin of Lourdes, in this jubilee year, recalls this to all men! And if in this solicitude Mary looks upon certain of her children with special predilection, is it not, beloved sons and venerable brethren, toward the small, the poor and the afflicted whom Jesus loved so much?

"Come to me, all you who labor and are burdened, and I will give you rest" she seems to say together with her Divine Son. Go to her, you who are crushed by material misery, defenseless against the hardships of life and the indifference of men. Go to her, you who are in mourning and assailed by moral trials. Go to her, beloved invalids and infirm, you who are truly welcomed and honored at Lourdes as the suffering members of Our Lord. Go to her and receive peace of heart, strength for your daily duty, the joy of sacrifice offered.

The Immaculate Virgin who knows the secret ways of grace in souls and the silent work of the supernatural leaven in this world, knows the great price which God attaches to your sufferings united to those of the Saviour. They can greatly contribute, We have no doubt, to this Christian renewal of society which We implore of God through the powerful intercession of His Mother. May there be added to the prayers of the sick, of the humble, of all the pilgrims to Lourdes, that prayer to Mary that she may also turn her maternal look toward those who are still outside the limits of the only fold, the Church, so that they may come together in unity. May she look upon those who seek and are thirsty for truth, and lead them to the source of living waters.

May she cast her glance upon the immense continents and their vast human areas where Christ is unfortunately so little known, so little loved; and may she obtain for the Church the freedom and joy to be able to respond everywhere, always youthful, holy and apostolic, to the expectations of men.

"Kindly come . . .," said the Virgin to Bernadette.

This discreet invitation which does not compel, which is addressed to the heart, and requests with delicacy a free and generous response, the Mother of God puts forward again to her sons of France and of the world. Christians will not remain deaf to this appeal; they will go to Mary.

The above inspiring words of the saintly Pope Pius XII were excerpted from his Encyclical Letter, "A Pilgrimage to Lourdes" given during the centenary year of the apparitions of Our Lady of Lourdes.

A Most Astounding Miracle

When people hear of Lourdes, they quite naturally think first of the many astounding miracles Mary works there. One of the most celebrated of these took place, not at Lourdes itself, but at a replica of the shrine in Oostacker, Belgium.

ON FEBRUARY 16, 1867, a laborer by the name of Pierre de Rudder from the town of Jabbeke near Ostend, Belgium, had a leg crushed by a fallen tree. The doctor found that the fracture of both bones, the tibia and the fibula, just below the knee was a complete one. Complications soon set in. Purulent and gangrenous ulcers appeared with a large ulcer spreading over the top of the foot. Many physicians were called in to treat the patient, but all without exception declared the case hopeless. Each one proposed the only solution, amputation of the limb. However, de Rudder steadfastly refused.

After a short period of time, a fragment of bone was loosened in the wound and it became necessary to remove it with the result that the two extremities, held together only by flesh and muscle, were separated by at least one inch. This situation continued for eight years causing the unfortunate man constant, and at times intolerable pain.

On April 7, 1875, Pierre, accompanied by his wife, undertook a pilgrimage to the sanctuary of Our Lady of Lourdes which had been established for some time at Oostacker which had become a popular Marian shrine in Belgium. The trip, partly by rail and partly by coach was a most distressing one. The poor cripple, dragging himself along on two crutches, finally reached the Grotto. He was a pitiful sight. When he walked, his afflicted limb, to which no device had been attached, swung freely back and forth. After he took a little Lourdes water from the Grotto, he circled the rustic sanctuary twice while praying, then sat down facing the statue of the Blessed Virgin.

Suddenly he rose, and as one who had lost his mind and without any help whatsoever he went and knelt before the venerated image. He rose and walked easily and without pain. He was miraculously cured! Many witnesses certify that the bones had indeed been reunited. There were two scars indicating the place of the ulcers. The sudden fusion of the bones produced a tremendous sensation in Belgium and it was soon brought to the attention of the medical profession. For a great number of freethinkers, including one of the physicians who had treated de Rudder, it became an occasion of a sincere and public conversion.

Pierre de Rudder lived twenty-three years after his cure. He died of pneumonia, March 22, 1898, at the age of seventy-five. The following year, at the prompting of many physicians, the body was exhumed and the legs amputated at the knees. The two bones of the left leg showed clearly where the fractures had occurred and they were found similar in length to those of the right leg not-withstanding the extraction of a fragment of the tibia before the cure. They have been preserved as a mute testimony. Pilgrims can examine at Lourdes an exact reproduction in bronze of these miraculously reconstructed bones.

Nontheless, after de Rudder died, from 1911 to 1913 the *Bibliothèque Nationale de Propagande,* a virulently anti-Catholic publication, carried on a fight to discredit the miracle. A desperate effort was made in a series of eight articles which were not only ineffectual but positively ludicrous, to discredit de Rudder as well as the witnesses and doctors who testified to the authenticity of the miracle. The first article tried to prove that, after his return from Oostacker, de Rudder showed his right leg as the one that had been cured rather than the broken left one. The incredulity of it all brings to mind the Pharisees in the Gospel story about Our Lord's cure of the man born blind.

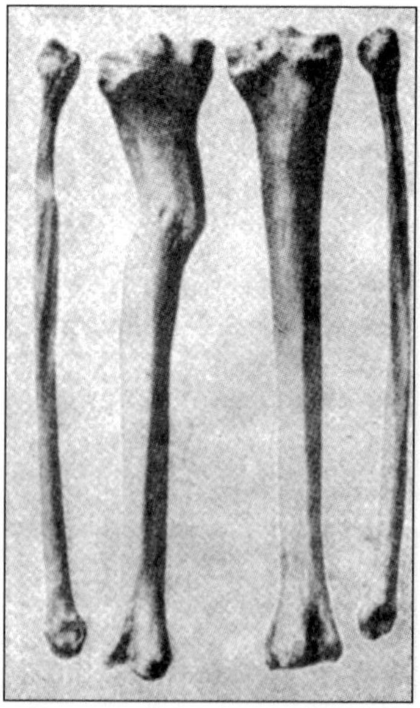

Photographs of the bones of de Rudder. The bones of the right leg are reproduced for comparison with those of the fractured limb. Before the miraculous cure, the fractured leg bones of his left leg were completely separated by an inch when the limb was extended. The leg could be twisted, turning the heel forward, and could make the osseous extremities stand out in the wound where pus and blood oozed out quite freely. A fragment of the bone 3 centimeters in length was removed, yet, after the miraculous fusion of bones, de Rudder walked without even a limp.

I Met a Miracle

Rev. Patrick O'Connor

Friday morning, September 10, 1937, I came face to face with a miracle. The name of the miracle was John Traynor. I first beheld him at a bustling railway station as I came along the platform. A powerfully built man, about five feet ten inches in height, with a strong, wholesome, ruddy face, dressed in a rather rumpled gray suit. Two of his little boys were with him, and eight or ten Irish and English pilgrims on their way home from Lourdes.

Now John Traynor was a miracle because, by all the laws of nature, he should not have been standing there, hefty and healthy. He should have been, if alive at all, paralyzed, epileptic, a mass of sores, shrunken, with a shriveled useless right arm and a gaping hole in his skull. That is what he had been. That is the way medical skill had to leave him, after making its best efforts. That is the way medical science had certified that he must remain. Only a miracle could cure him. . . . A miracle did.

I rode with him for about ten hours on the train that day, and when I said good-by to him it was with a certainty that I could never forget him. He was a delightful character, that big Liverpool Irishman, with his manly faith and piety, a fearless militant Catholic with only a primary grade education. I was bound to remember him for his story, which he told me on our long journey that day. He told it simply, exactly, a narrative that it was a grace to hear and a duty to recall.

When the first world war broke out in 1914, Jack Traynor was mobilized with the Royal Naval Reserve. He was in the naval brigade that took part in the unsuccessful Antwerp expedition of October 1914, and was in the last battalion to retreat. While carrying one of his officers to safety, he was hit in the head by shrapnel. He lost consciousness for five weeks. When he woke in England, after an operation he recovered rapidly and went back into service in April 1915 as member of the expeditionary force sent to Gallipoli, Egypt.

He was in charge of the first boat to leave the ship and was one of the few to reach the shore that day. From their positions in the steep banks above the beach the Turks raked the ship and the boats with deadly gunfire. The casualties were so heavy that the operation was suspended until nightfall. For days the bitter fighting continued. On May 8 he was hit by machine-gun fire during a bayonet charge. He seems to have been literally sprayed with bullets. He was wounded in the head and chest, while a bullet tore through the inner side of his upper right arm and lodged under the collar-bone.

He was shipped to the base hospital at Alexandria, Egypt. Now began his long years as an invalid and as a patient of many unsuccessful surgical operations. A well-known English surgeon operated on him in an attempt to sew together the severed nerves in the upper arm, which the bullet wound had left paralyzed and useless. The attempt failed, as did another made by another surgeon. In the naval hospital in England a third operation was performed with the same result. While on the hospital ship Traynor suffered his first epileptic attack. These attacks became frequent. The surgeon general of the navy now advised amputation of the paralyzed arm, as there seemed to be no hope of ever joining the torn and shrunken nerves. Traynor would not consent. In November, 1916, another doctor tried to suture the nerves, bringing the number of unsuccessful operations to four.

John Traynor, years after his miraculous cure, volunteered as a Brancardier at Lourdes.

By this time Traynor had been discharged from the service, on 100% pension as being permanently and completely disabled. He had to spend months in various hospitals as an epileptic patient. In April, 1920 a doctor realized that the epilepsy was probably the result of the head wounds and operated on the skull. The operation left Traynor with an open hole about an inch wide in his skull. Through this opening the pulsation of the brain could be observed. A silver plate was inserted to shield the brain. The epileptic condition was no better and the seizures were as frequent as three a day. Both legs were partly paralyzed, and nearly every organ in Traynor's body was impaired.

An ambulance brought him back to Liverpool, where he lived with his wife and children. By the year 1923, Traynor had passed through the hands of ten doctors. The result of all their efforts and examinations was to prove that he was completely incapacitated and incurable. Unable to stand or walk, subject to frequent epileptic fits, with three open wounds, one of them in his head, without the power of feeling or movement in his torn and shriveled right arm, he was indeed a human wreck. What follows is his own narrative, as I wrote it down and as he checked it out.

John Traynor's Narrative

I had always had a great devotion to our Blessed Lady, having acquired it from my mother especially. I felt that if Our Lady's shrine at Lourdes was in England, I would go there often. But it seemed to be a far-away place that I could never reach. In the month of July 1923, I was at home, helpless as usual, when a neighbor woman came into the house and spoke of an announcement that had been made in our parish. A Liverpool diocesan pilgrimage was being organized to Lourdes. It would cost thirteen pounds (about $54.00) to go. A down payment of one pound reserved a place for me.

I called my wife. I found afterwards that she had already heard about the pilgrimage but had decided not to tell me, fearing that I'd want to go. I told her to go upstairs and get a certain box in which was a gold sovereign (about $5.00) which my brother had given me and which we were treasuring for some special emergency. She asked me what I wanted to do with it. I said that I wanted to give it to Mrs. Cunningham, as a first payment on a ticket to Lourdes. My wife was very disturbed but finally did as I told her, and the neighbor went off to make the booking for me.

A few days later, one of the priests in charge of the pilgrimage came to see me. He was upset at the thought of my going and wanted me to cancel my booking. "You cannot make the trip," he said. "You will die on the way and bring trouble and grief to everybody." My answer was that I had made my first payment, I had booked my place and I was going to Lourdes! After much talking, he said, finally: "Well, you won't be allowed to travel unless the doctor gives his approval. If you get a medical certificate, we'll take you." Clearly he seemed to think that it was impossible. I thought that my doctor would approve of the trip, but he refused. We called in several doctors and every one of them said that it would be suicide. Later, when the government ministry of pensions learned that I had gone to Lourdes, they protested very strongly.

The priest came again to visit me, begging me to give up the idea. I would not, and finally succeeded in going without a medical certificate. To raise the twelve pounds, the balance due on my ticket, we sold some of our belongings and my wife pawned even her few bits of jewelry. By this time it had got around Liverpool that this crippled and paralyzed ex-serviceman wanted to go to Lourdes, and the papers began to write about it. I was the center of more attention than I liked.

The day for leaving Liverpool came. The pilgrims were to travel on two trains. It was a terrible task to prepare me. My brother Francis got me into my invalid chair and they raced me down through all the back streets of Liverpool to the station. People began to fuss around us, making it still more difficult for me to get to the platform. I did reach it — just too late. The first train was about to leave. The priest-director came up to me in great agitation and said: "Traynor, you're too late! We can't get you on the train now. In Heaven's name, take this as a sign that you are not to come. You will only die on the journey." I said: "Father, I have paid for my ticket to Lourdes and I'm going to Lourdes." He said: "You'll die on the way." I said: "Then I'll die in a good cause." There was another train, and I said that they could put me in the coal tender or anywhere they liked, as long as they put me on the train. By being obstinate about it, I won my point, was placed on the second train amid scenes of excitement and confusion, and began my journey to Lourdes.

I remember practically nothing of the journey, except seeing a number of sick people on stretchers beside me on platforms and docks, some of them bleeding, all of them suffering. I believe that I was very sick on the way. Three times they tried to take me off the train in France to bring me to a hospital, as I seemed to be dying. Each time there was no hospital where they stopped, and the only thing to do was to go on again, with me still on board.

We reached Lourdes on July 22, and I was transferred with the rest of the sick to the Asile hospital in the domain of the Grotto. We spent six days in Lourdes. During that time I was desperately ill. I had several hemorrhages as well as epileptic fits. In fact, one woman took it on herself to write to my wife, saying that there was no hope for me and that I'd be buried in Lourdes. In spite of my condition, however, I succeeded in being bathed nine times in the water from the Grotto spring. I was brought to the different devotions in which the sick could join. On the morning of the second day I had a bad epileptic fit, as I was being wheeled to the baths. Blood flowed from my mouth and the doctors were very much alarmed. As I came to, I could hear them saying: "Better take him back to the Asile at once." I protested, saying: "No, you won't. I've come to be bathed and I'm not going back."

"You'll die in the bath," they told me.

"Very well," I said. "If I do, I'll die in a good place." I put the brake on the wheelchair by holding the wheel with my good left hand, and the brancardiers (volunteer stretcher-bearers) had to give in. They brought me into the bath and bathed me in the usual way. I never had an epileptic fit after that. We were to leave on the morning of July 27. The afternoon of July 25 came and I seemed to be as bad as ever. Then it was time to get ready for the baths. I was wheeled down to wait my turn. There were many to be bathed and we all wanted to be finished before the afternoon procession of the Blessed Sacrament, which began at four o'clock. My turn came, and when I was in the bath, my paralyzed legs became violently agitated. The brancardiers became alarmed once more, thinking that I was in another fit. I struggled to get on my feet, feeling that I could easily do so, and wondered why everybody seemed to be against me. When I was taken out of the bath, I cried from sheer weakness and exhaustion.

Well-wishers see John Traynor, the totally disabled World War I veteran, off to Lourdes.

The brancardiers threw my clothes on hurriedly, put me back on the stretcher and rushed me down to the square in front of the Rosary Church to await the procession. Practically all the other sick were already lined up. The procession came winding its way back, as usual, to the church and at the end walked the Archbishop of Rheims, carrying the Blessed Sacrament. He blessed the two ahead of me, came to me, made the sign of the cross with the monstrance and moved on to the next. He had just passed by, when I realized that a great change had taken place in me. My right arm, which had been dead since 1915, was violently agitated. I burst its bandages and blessed myself — for the first time in years. I had no sudden pain that I can recall and certainly had no vision. I simply realized that something momentous had happened.

I attempted to rise from my stretcher, but the brancardiers were watching me. I suppose I had a bad name for my obstinacy. They held me down and a doctor or a nurse gave me a hypo. Apparently they thought that I was hysterical and about to create a scene. Immediately after the final Benediction they rushed me back to Asile. I told them that I could walk and proved it by taking seven steps. I was very tired and in pain. They put me back in bed and gave me another hypo. They had me in a small ward on the ground floor. As I was such a troublesome case, they stationed brancardiers in relays to watch me and keep me from doing anything foolish. Late that night they placed a brancardier on guard outside the door of the ward. The effect of the hypos began to wear off during the night, but I had no realization that I was cured. I was awake for most of the night.

Traynor ran the whole three hundred yards to the Grotto over graveled ground in his bare feet without getting a single mark or cut on his feet.

The chimes in the big basilica of the Rosary rang the hours and half-hours as usual through the night, playing the Lourdes Ave Maria. Early in the morning I heard them ringing, and it seemed to me that I fell asleep at the beginning of the Ave. It could have been a matter of only a few seconds, but at the last stroke I opened my eyes and jumped out of bed. First, I knelt on the floor to finish the Rosary I had been saying. Then I dashed for the door, pushed aside the two brancardiers and ran out into the passage and the open air. Previously I had been watching the brancardiers and planning to evade them. I may say here that I had not walked since 1915 and my weight was down to 112 pounds.

Dr. Marley was outside the door. When he saw the man over whom he had been watching during the pilgrimage and whose death he had expected, push two brancardiers aside and run out of the ward, he fell back in amazement. Out in the open now, I ran towards the Grotto, which is about two or three hundred yards from the Asile. This stretch of ground was graveled then, not paved, and I was barefoot. I ran the whole way to the Grotto without getting the least mark or cut on my bare feet. The brancardiers were running after me but they could not catch up with me. When they reached the Grotto, there I was on my knees, still in my night clothes, praying to Our Lady and thanking her. All I knew was that I should thank her and the Grotto was the place to do it. The brancardiers stood back, afraid to touch me.

The news was beginning to spread, even though it was still early in the morning. After I had prayed for about twenty minutes, I got up surprised and not pleased to find a crowd of people gathered around, watching me as I walked back toward the Asile. They drew aside to let me pass. At the far end of Rosary Square stands a crowned statue of Our Lady. My mother had always taught me that when you ask a favor from Our Lady or wish to show her some special veneration, you should make a sacrifice. I had no money to offer, as I had spent my last few shillings on rosaries and medals for my wife and children, but kneeling there before the Blessed Mother, I made the only sacrifice I could think of, I resolved to give up cigarettes. All this time, while knowing that I had received a great favor from Our Lady, I had no clear recollection of all the illness that had gone before. By now a crowd of excited people had gathered in front of the Asile. As I went in to dress, I couldn't understand what they were doing there.

I put my clothes on in a hurry, but kept away from the bed, for fear the doctors and brancardlers would tackle me again and treat me as a sick man once more. I went to the washroom to wash and shave. Other men were there before me. I bade them all good morning, but none of them answered me -— they just looked at me in a scared way. I wondered why. It was still pretty early in the morning when a priest, Father Gray, who knew nothing about my cure, entered the ward where I was and asked if anybody there could serve Mass. I answered that I would be glad to, and went off and served Mass in the chapel of the Asile. It did not seem strange to me then that I could do this, after being unable to stand or walk for eight years.

I went in to breakfast in the dining room of the Asile. The other men drew back, as if they were afraid of me. I could not grasp the situation nor could I understand why people were staring at me so hard. After breakfast, when I tried to walk out from the Asile, I found a large crowd outside. They made a rush for me, and I had to retreat, going into the little enclosure, feeling rather upset.

A Mr. Cunningham came out to talk to me. I could see that he found it hard to control his excitement.

He said: "Good morning, Jack. Are you feeling all right?" Yes, Mr. Cunningham," I answered. "Quite all right. Are you feeling all right?"

Then I asked: "What are all those people doing outside?" "They're there, Jack, because they're glad to see you." "Well, it's very nice of them and I'm glad to see them but I wish they'd leave me alone." He told me that one of the priests on the pilgrimage — the one who had opposed my coming — was anxious to speak to me. He was at his hotel in the town, and the problem was how to get me through the crowd. Finally, after appeals to the crowd, I got through to the hotel where I found the priest. He, too, asked me if I was all right. I was quite surprised by the question. I told him that I felt quite well, thanks, and that I hoped he did, too. He broke down and began to cry.

That day was a nightmare of excitement and crowds. I was the center of attraction for all the people in Lourdes it seemed. We left on the nine o'clock train next morning, July 27. I found that a first-class compartment had been set aside for me. I protested against taking it but I had to give in. At one of the stops, the door of my compartment opened and to my amazement I saw the skullcap of Archbishop Keating. He came into the compartment and I knelt to get his blessing. He raised me up saying: "John, I think I should be getting your blessing." I could not understand why he said that. Then he led me over and we both sat down on the bed. Looking at me, he said:

"John, do you realize how ill you have been and that you have been miraculously cured by the Blessed Virgin?" Then everything came back to me, the memory of my years of illness and the sufferings of the journey to Lourdes and how ill I had been in Lourdes itself. I began to cry and the Archbishop began to cry, and we both sat there, crying like two children. After a little talk with him, I felt composed. Now I realized fully what had happened.

Meanwhile the news of the miracle had been telegraphed to the Liverpool papers, but my wife had not heard of it. Somebody on the train — Father Quinlan or Father McKinley said to me that I should send her a wire. I did not care to make a fuss in a telegram; so I just sent her this message: "Am better — Jack." Arriving home, my wife went down to the station with her friend, Mrs. Reitdyk. It seemed as if all Liverpool had gathered there. The people had seen the news of the miracle in the evening papers and had come down to see me. There were extra police on duty to handle the crowd, while railway officials stood at the entrance to the platform to keep the people from rushing the train.

With difficulty, my wife and her friend reached the platform gate, where she told the official that she was Mrs. Traynor and asked to be allowed through.

"Well," replied the man, "all I can say is that Mr. Traynor must be a Mohammedan, because there are seventy or eighty Mrs. Traynors on the platform already!" Anyhow he let them through, and they waited on the platform. Meanwhile the railway company had decided that the only safe thing was to stop the train outside the station. They did this, and then the Archbishop walked towards the crowd, now a huge one, and addressed it. He asked the people to be orderly and asked them to promise that if they just saw Traynor walk down the platform, they would be satisfied and would disperse. They assured him that they would. But when I did appear on the platform, there was a stampede. The police had to draw their batons to force a passage for my wife and myself to a taxi. My brother got a blow on the side of the head before he could fight his way into the taxi with me. As we drove home, I cannot describe the joy of my wife and children.

I am in the coal and haulage business now. I have four trucks and about a dozen men working for me. I lift sacks of coal weighing around 200 pounds. with the best of them. I can do any thing the other workers do, but I am officially classified still as 100% disabled and permanently incapacitated!

I never accepted a penny from anybody at the time of my cure or after it. I came back from Lourdes penniless, except for my war pension. I have never permitted any money to come to my family in connection with my cure or the publicity that has followed it. Nevertheless Our Lady has improved my temporal affairs too, and thanks be to God and to her, I am now comfortably situated, and my children are all well provided for. Three of them have been born since my cure, one a girl whom I have named Bernadette. The two non-Catholic girls who looked after me when I came to Lourdes joined the Church as a result of my cure. Their family at home in Liverpool followed their example and so did the Anglican (Episcopalian) minister of the church they had been attending.

Addendum of Fr. O'Conner

At the Medical Bureau at Lourdes and again in Liverpool where five doctors examined him before and after his cure, they found no trace of epilepsy or paralysis. His right arm was completely free from atrophy. The pectoral and shoulder muscles were fully restored. His wrist worked normally and he could use his right hand. As often happens in Lourdes cures, he had a souvenir of the injuries from which he had been miraculously liberated. The right hand does not hang quite normally. The right forearm is less thick than the left. The only trace of the hole in his skull was the slight depression that could be felt in the bone. The official report issued by the Medical Bureau at Lourdes on October 2, 1926, declared that "this extraordinary cure is absolutely beyond and above the powers of nature."

The most striking part of this multiple miracle is the instantaneous cure of the right arm. The nerves had been severed for eight years. Four surgical operations had revealed that they were truly severed and had failed to reunite them. If mended the shrunken nerves would need to go through a long process of regeneration. A feat that four surgeries and slow restoration had failed to do was achieved instantaneously as the Blessed Sacrament was raised over John Traynor.

The doctors and officials of the British War Pensions Ministry, certified that John Traynor was incurable, and they showed the strength of their conviction by never revoking that decision, awarding him full disability. John Traynor died on the eve of the Feast of the Immaculate Conception 1942. The cause of his death was hernia, in no way related to the illness and wounds of which he was cured in Lourdes. For more than twenty years he lived a vigorous life, every moment of which he owed to the miracle of July 1923. He is a standing stalwart testimony of the power of Almighty God and the efficacy of the intercessory prayer to Mary Immaculate. Miracles such as the cure of John Traynor are rare and point the way not to a wide-open exit from all physical suffering but rather to the spiritual recoveries and triumphs that are certain to come from unhesitating faith and a childlike approach to Jesus Christ, through Mary, His Mother and ours.

—The above chapter is edited and condensed from a booklet by the same title, published by the Columban's Foreign Mission Society.

The Miraculous Confronts the Science-skeptics

Almost a hundred and fifty years have elapsed since the Blessed Mother appeared to St. Bernadette at the Grotto of Massabielle, and the miracles at Lourdes continue to challenge a scientific world which has abandoned long since the scientific method for the "dogma" that science has all the answers. "Science, not religion has the last word, and the two can not be reconciled," so it goes. Faith and metaphysics cannot compete with the so called rational approach — it matters little how irrational it may be. If something can not be examined under a microscope, it is not worth considering. Nor was there any shortage of sociologists and philosophy professors from state universities who were willing to air the same views.

It was in the middle of the Nineteenth Century, when the Enlightenment had not yet been exposed for what it is, a bust, that an illiterate, poor, little French shepherd girl claimed she saw a woman from another world. This was so much medieval superstition according to the rationalists, freemasons, modernists and such like. Those who were aware of Lourdes among the nonbelievers looked upon it as a last desperate attempt of the churchmen to save a moribund Catholic Church.

The scientific community could scoff at the "illusions" of an illiterate peasant in a backwater of France, and ignore or explain them away. But the skeptics could hardly dismiss the miracles of Lourdes so easily. These incontestable happenings were totally outside of the experiences of the scientists and inexplicable by known physical laws.

They might ask: what purpose would there be for miracles in our enlightened modern times? It is true Our Lord performed many miracles, recorded in the Gospels — raising the dead to life, restoring sight, curing leprosy, etc., to reinforce His message and make credible what He preached, but that was twenty centuries ago. Who among the enlightened intelligentsia still believed in those miracles? It was easy to dismiss something that happened twenty centuries ago, but what about miracles in modern times?

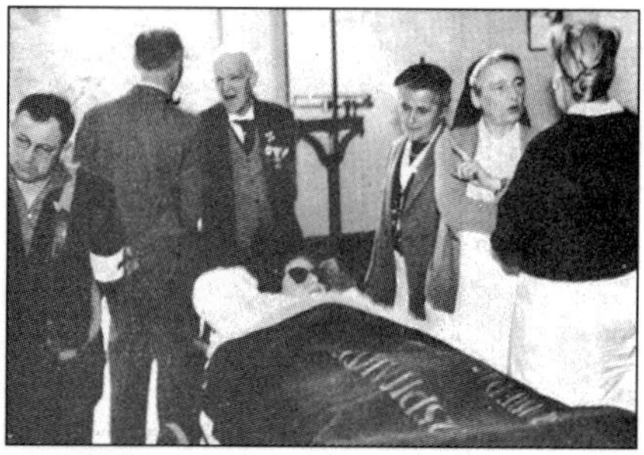

Above: Visiting doctors discuss the case of a sick pilgrim at the Medical Bureau. The president of the Medical Bureau at that time, Dr. Leuret, was a remarkable man: Legion of Honor, Croix de Guerre and professor of medicine and head of a large clinic in the worst section of Bordeaux.

It is a fact, beyond question, that miracles do occur at Lourdes. God, the Creator of all things, if He wishes, may suspend the laws He uses to govern the universe. A thoughtful reading of *The Miracle of Lourdes* by Ruth Cranston, a non-Catholic who spent a whole year at Lourdes interviewing doctors, nurses, stretcher-bearers, and patients, besides studying documentary evidence, will convince one that what happens at the Grotto and the baths at Lourdes has no natural explanation. At first, the medical profession, particularly the professors of medicine in the French universities by and large were adamant in denying miracles at Lourdes. In 1905, a young research doctor by the name of Alexis Carrel related a miraculous cure at Lourdes he personally observed and examined. He reported merely what he saw — a tubercular girl at the point of dying, cured instantaneously in some unexplainable way. He was dismissed from the University of Lyons. "With such views, sir," the dean coldly remarked, "you can hardly expect to be received as a member of our faculty!" "In that case," the young physician said, "I must look elsewhere." He was accepted by the Rockefeller Institute in 1912 and eventually received the Nobel Prize for his research in joining blood vessels and transplanting organs.

Not satisfied with attempting to discredit one man, the opposition through the anti-religious press mounted a campaign to close the shrine on trumped-up charges of unsanitary conditions, endangering public health. This time, however, it was the medical profession that came to the defense of Lourdes. Ironically, it was Dr. Vincent of Lyons who gathered over threethousand signatures of doctors attesting that there was not a single case of contagion being passed on among the sick and that there were cures among the sick which "we doctors were powerless to save."

Perhaps the main reason the doctors began to support Lourdes was the establishment of the Bureau for Medical Verification (BMV) at the sanctuary in 1883. With no hidden agenda, the BMV rigorously investigated purported miracles using the latest methods of scientific investigation. Doctors were invited to examine the miraculous cures and were given all the pertinent information regarding the case. All was done with the most rigorous scientific care, excluding all consideration of the religious affiliation. The work continues today in the Medical Bureau, the successor of the BMV, which is made up of Catholics and non-Catholics, believers and non-believers — all of which underlines the objectivity of these doctors' reports. It has its own laboratory and conference rooms, the latest equipment for examinations and an extensive library and archives. A full-time staff of professionals are in contact with medical research centers in France and other countries.

Of the fairly complete records of 1,200 cures which it recognizes as being "inexplicable under scientific and natural laws," only 64 are registered by the Bureau as beyond medical explanation. In addition there are notations and material on some 4,000 other probable cures. It would seem that the Church is even more "skeptical" than the medical profession, since in the over hundred and forty years of the existence of the shrine only fifty-odd cases have been pronounced miraculous by the Church.

The first recorded miracles were from the water of a miraculous spring that Bernadette "found" at the direction of Mary herself. She was told to drink muddy water, which had first come out of the ground in a trickle, just enough to make a little mud which she smeared on her face. The people thought she was out of her mind. But the trickle soon became a steady stream in an area that had previously been bone dry. It would eventually flow at a rate of 30,000 gallons a day. The first miracle was dramatically screened in the award-winning film, "The Song of Bernadette." Little Louis-Justin Bouhorts was slowly dying of consumption with endless seizures. He was a pitiful sight; all he could do was moan and gasp for air in his crib. His doctor didn't believe he could live out the night when his mother, with the deep faith typical of the people in that area of France, bundled up the boy and ran to the grotto plunging him up to his neck in the small reservoir collecting the spring water.

Upon the mother's return home with the boy having turned blue after the fifteen minute exposure to the icy water, the father remonstrated, "Well, are you happy now? Have you finished killing him?" The mother prayed and the child began breathing normally for the first time in two years. The next morning the doctor couldn't believe his eyes, seeing the child running and playing as if he had never been sick a day in his life. This was the first in the long series of miracles at Lourdes, which caught the attention of a world that thought that the day of miracles was something of the past. And little Louis-Justin? He was the guest of honor seventy-five years later at the canonization of St. Bernadette.

The miraculous cures of the sick are not the only miracle of Lourdes. It seems, as one invalid pilgrim put it, that germs are powerless there. The fact that countless sick with contagious diseases pass through Lourdes yearly, yet the city has never had an epidemic; that the water where the sick are bathed is polluted with germs at the end of the day, yet no infection is passed on, is a continuous miracle which no amount of medical science can explain. When the Medical Bureau took samples of the water in which patients were bathed and had them analyzed, they discovered extreme pollution from germs of the most deadly type. Guinea pigs were inoculated with this polluted water and suffered no ill effects. Yet when these guinea pigs were later inoculated with water from the Seine River with the same amount of bacteria, two out of three died.

Then there are those doctors who come to Lourdes unbelieving, even hostile to religion. One such doctor, after he saw his patient cured of tubercular peritonitis, left the room speechless and was so overcome with deep emotion that when he returned a few minutes later, the tears were still running down his cheeks. Now his former patient, who is a volunteer nurse at Lourdes, points out with humor that she has been a terrible blow to her doctor's "scientific self-respect." Yet it was his precise and honest report that established the case as a miraculous cure. Then, there are those doctors who are so overcome by the supernatural, and moved by the grace of God, that they return to the faith they once scorned. Doctor Alexis Carrel, mentioned earlier, is a striking example of such a conversion. However, there are other rationalist doctors, who will not concede that the miracles are of a supernatural origin. They are forced into the rather pat, but unscientific, viewpoint that the cures are produced by "unknown natural forces," which may be discovered some day in the future.

Every imaginable ailment has been cured at Lourdes in the baths, at the Eucharistic procession, or thousand of miles away using the Lourdes water or at a replica of the Lourdes Grotto. The various ways and circumstances are too many to be counted. But faith definitely

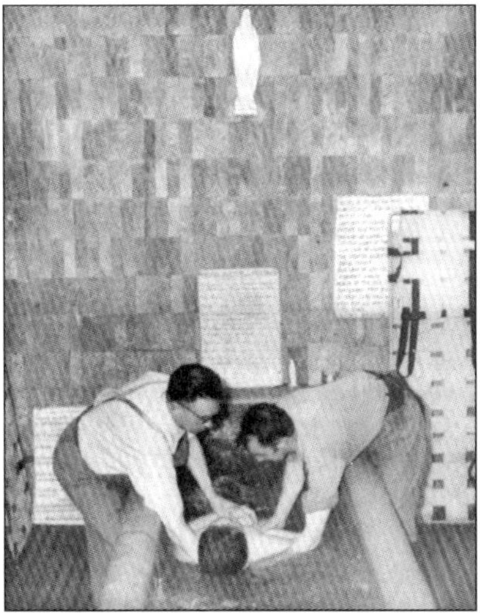

The trickling spring which St. Bernadette "discovered," produces over 1,400 gallons an hour. Thousands of cures are recorded at the baths (left). The baths become extremely polluted with germs of people with every conceivable disease, but there has never been a case of contagion. At Lourdes microbes are powerless.

enters into all the cures. When Our Lord met along the roadside those who begged him to be cured of blindness, of leprosy or of lameness, He asked them "Do you believe?" If they had faith, they were granted their petition. Millions have come to Lourdes over almost 150 years having great faith but were not cured, though many were. This all points to the fact that the miracles, as spectacular as they are, at Marian Shrines such as Lourdes simply aren't an end in themselves. One has to look deeper into the mystery of human suffering, which above all has meaning and purpose when united to that of the crucified Savior. An American journalist, J.B. McAllister asked an English-speaking man at the desk of the Hospitalité, "What about the uncured?"

"True," he said, "only a few are cured, but many are helped. Of the uncured, none despairs. I often interview patients before they leave. I have never seen a case, even the worst, downcast. They go away filled with hope." A man crippled from birth came to Lourdes to be cured. On the second day, nothing had happened; but sitting among the sick during Benediction, he noticed on his right a blind woman and on his left a consumptive. "I looked around at all those sufferers and then up to the green mountains and higher up to the sky. I could see and I could move about, having the free use of my ears and tongue and arms. I had not known sickness or disease — and I was praying for my cure! Since that moment, I have felt that I ought to think of others and not myself."

One outstanding case which received much news coverage was that of "the man in the iron lung," the rich young American, Frank Snite. He contracted infantile paralysis on a trip to China in 1936 and lay flat on his back in a respirator, unable to live outside of the "iron lung" for more than a few moments at a time. Portable respirators were not available in the thirties and it took a great deal of ingenuity to transfer the big cumbersome iron lung with Snite in it to Lourdes. The trip was covered in major newspapers in this country as well as in newsreels. It would seem that if he were cured, there would not be enough ships going to Europe, bringing sick pilgrims to be cured at Lourdes. But nothing happened. He returned to the United States in the iron lung. There was a general feeling that Snite must have been disappointed, on the verge of dispair, that his trip was in vain. Snite didn't think so.

He wrote a diary and the following are a few extracts from his writings: "Life here at Lourdes is so wonderful, such a series of unending thrills that I find it difficult to record my reactions. Everyone is happy, happy because they are in a place apart from the world — a place seemingly halfway to heaven. Here there is no talk of war, of politics, of business; life here is a prayer. Is it any wonder we are happy?" He was advised by his doctors not to bathe in the *piscines.* Leaving the life sustaining lung and going into the cold water could be fatal. He ignored the doctors, as so many have at Lourdes, and afterwards told friends that while bathing, a wonderful feeling of peace came over him, a feeling he had never experienced before.

The Friday before he was to return to the United States, he wrote in his diary, "Sunday the last day. I have not in any way given up or lost hope. I am praying very, very fervently, and if nothing happens, as I have often said before, God certainly knows what is best for me, and for the world in general." He concludes his diary entry with two short sentences. "Our Pilgrimage is at an end. God's will be done." He lived for a number of years, married and had his own children, one whom he named Bernadette. Everyone who knew him marveled that he could be so cheerful despite his affliction. But it is no wonder as it is one of the graces that Our Lady of Lourdes gives to those who have faith and confidence in God's loving care.

The big mystery at Lourdes is not why some are cured while the great majority are not.

The big mystery is the mystery of iniquity — that in the face of such supernatural power there are skeptics, who still cry, "I don't believe!" With all the evidence to the contrary, verified incontestably by science, rather should it not be "I **won't** believe?"

Interview with Doctor of the International Medical Committee

Dr. Bernard Colvin, has been an orthopedic surgeon at the Royal Infirmary Hospital in Dundee, Scotland, for many years. Since 1976 he has served as a member of the International Medical Committee for the study and verification of Lourdes cures. The Committee of doctors from many countries reviews the findings of the Lourdes Medical Bureau and has the final word to say if a cure is beyond medical explanation.

Crusade: Could you give us an idea of how cures are authenticated?

Dr. Colvin: The process is elaborate and exhaustive. A sick person who is cured at Lourdes is invited to the Medical Bureau for a thorough examination, both physically and psychologically. This begins with the study of their medical history. Witnesses are questioned. A report is made. If the Medical Bureau is satisfied that an extraordinary cure may have taken place, the patient is invited to return one year later with all his documents, test reports, X-rays, and so on, for another thorough examination. This is to see if the cure is permanent. At this stage the case has only a file. There is as yet no decision.

During that year, a sort of probation period, a doctor who lives near the patient is appointed by the Medical Bureau to make a local investigation. The patient's GP is consulted, medical records are cross-checked, the clinic or hospital where the diagnosis was made is visited. Family and friends are interviewed. Above all, the patient is monitored. After this process, the patient returns to the Medical Bureau for the re-examination. Visiting doctors, often non-Catholics and even atheists, are asked to examine the case objectively as scientists, whatever their religious beliefs, thus safeguarding the Bureau from accusations of bias.

By this stage most cases have been dropped for one reason or another, not necessarily because they are fraudulent, but because some link in the chain of evidence is faulty. If the Bureau people are still satisfied that an extraordinary cure has really happened, they pass the case on to us, the International Committee. We now have the job of reviewing all the evidence. We get about two cases a week from the Medical Bureau. Most of these we sift out, leaving about five to seven a year that we seriously consider. Then comes the final stage when the cure is declared to have no medical explanation. And this is all we doctors are asked to do. We are to stick to hard medical facts. All this takes time. Some cases take years to get to this point. Most never get this far.

If the International Committee finds the cure to be extraordinary it sends the case to the patient's local bishop. He appoints a team of canon lawyers to examine all the facts from the point of view of their particular specialties. They are interested in the moral life of the cured person, if, for instance, the patient is using the cure for gain or notoriety. A team of five doctors advises the canonists on medical matters. Finally, the bishop has the responsibility to say whether or not the cure is a miracle. I should add that the medical end of this is all done by doctors and paid for by doctors. The Church does not fund any of it. This keeps the Bureau autonomous and free from any kind of pressure or influence.

Crusade: What criteria do you follow during hearings?

Dr. Colvin: What we have to decide is whether the case can or cannot be explained according to the laws of biology. It boils down to deciding if there really was an illness to begin with; if the illness was actually cured; if the cure is permanent or at least stable, since diseases can temporarily decline only to rebound later; if there had ever been any treatment which could explain the cure. We must make a distinction between a treatment that is aimed at eliminating a disease and one that is only intended to ameliorate it. In the latter case, obviously, treatment could not have cured the patient. We follow a questionnaire, giving a yes or a no to eighteen questions. Then a yes or a no to whether it is scientifically explainable. A majority vote decides.

Crusade: Do you consult individuals or organizations outside the Committee?

Dr. Colvin: Oh yes, and not all Catholic resources either. But you do like to know who you are sending things to reasonably well, because some people might say "Lourdes? I'm sure its a miracle," while others would say "Lourdes? No way!" What you want is impartiality.

We have had very good cases that have fallen through because X-rays mysteriously got lost. We had a child with an autogenic sarcoma of the skull. The mother was told that the child was going to die. They went to Lourdes where the child recovered. Back at the pediatric unit, more X-rays were taken. But the originals mysteriously got lost, so we had nothing to compare the new ones to. The case had to be dropped.

Crusade: It has been claimed that the number of cures has been dropping recently. Would you have a comment on that?

Dr. Colvin: I wouldn't necessarily agree that the number of cures is declining, but the number of registered cures may be. Remember, in the early days of the Bureau there were no X-rays and other technologies. Diagnosis was by examination and history. A lot of the early cases were tuberculosis and relatively easy to diagnose. As medical procedures became more sophisticated, verification became more elaborate and rigorous. This may mean that we are missing a lot of miracles. But a miracle doesn't have to be labeled one by us for it to be true. It's really between God and the patient.

Our Lady of Lourdes, Health of the sick. Pray for us!

It is during the blessing of the sick with the Blessed Sacrament that many cures take place (see story about one of these cures on pg. 176).

No where are there so many hopeful sick gathered in one place as at Lourdes; yet if not cured, never disappointed.

Pilgrims drawing Lourdes water. How many miracles have been worked through its use and the faith of petitioners.

The incorupt body of St. Bernadette lies in the chapel of St. Joseph at the Mother House of the Sisters of Charity and Christian Instruction of Nevers.

The Untiring, Heroic Service of the Brancardiers

The brancardiers (stretcher-bearers) come from all walks of life generals, mechanics, judges, clerks, civil servants, college students, etc. The more than 2,000 members of the brancardiers association pledge a certain amount of time each year to care for the sick. They are on duty from dawn to midnight. Their tasks are heavy, their meals uncertain, their rest is slight and often broken by emergency calls, especially during the busy season, the hottest months of the year. They ask nothing for themselves but to serve the sick and handicapped. A past president of their order of over thirty years proudly points out, "I have never once been refused by a brother Brancardier, or even heard a murmur from him, when I asked him to perform one more hard job at the end of the day."

“Come to the foot of the Altar, here great graces will be granted to all who ask with confidence.”

Our Lady to St. Catherine Labouré

If someone is declared miraculously cured the Bureau publicizes it fully. But we have to be totally rigorous. The last thing we want is to have any discredited because the moment we do the Church has many enemies who will blow it up. Only 64 cures have been declared miraculous to date.

Crusade: Finally, your work has enabled you to see a lot of suffering over the years. Has Lourdes influenced your views on suffering?

Dr. Colvin: Yes, as a doctor one is bound to think a bit about the purpose of suffering. Why does God allow it? It gives us a chance to atone for our sins. And why shouldn't we? We inherited suffering as we inherited the sin of Adam. But on a higher level, suffering lets us share in Our Lord's crucifixion. The Psalmist asks why evil men seem to do so well. They live a life of luxury, never suffer, that sort of thing. But with the good men, like Job, everything goes wrong.

Above all it is the Faith that makes sense of suffering. I often wonder, what's the point of living if you don't have the Faith? We live to die, and if we live well we die well. That is the important thing. —*Crusade Magazine*

Human Interest Side of Medical Bureau

*Winifred A. Feely**

One must not imagine that the Medical Bureau is a dull sort of place. It is a remarkably cheerful and interesting center where doctors from all parts of the world, of all nationalities and creeds, meet to study and investigate. It is, in fact, run *by* doctors *for* doctors. Pilgrimage doctors are encouraged to bring in their most interesting or rare cases. Special cards are issued enabling the recipients to be seated during the processions and to enter the piscines (baths) with the minimum of standing and waiting.

Besides the sick there are others who come to visit us in the Medical Bureau: journalists, writers, dignitaries of the Church, parish groups, and distinguished visitors from various countries. I met Ruth Cranston, a non-Catholic American, who wrote the beautiful book *The Miracle of Lourdes.* I was able to help her in the research work for that book. When I saw her in the States a short time before her death, her last words to me were: "Please give my love to Our Lady when you kneel at her Grotto, and be sure to tell her of the pain I have in my back."

Not only Christians of other denominations, but non-Christians as well find great comfort and inspiration at Lourdes. In one year I was astonished to have so many Jewish people calling upon us. A young woman, lonely and fearful, faced with a serious operation for which she had neither courage nor acceptance, cried "I would rather kill myself." A little later, when calm, she added, "Do you think the Lady I have heard about will help me even if I am not a Christian?" She left Lourdes uncured, but she did not go away empty-handed. She was given courage and strength to face what lay before her. The operation was successful. Now my little Jewish friend is a happy woman who spends her time visiting cancer patients in various hospitals. In her last letter to me she wrote: "I have so much now to share with others, all those lovely things the Lady taught me when I was at Lourdes!"

One terribly wet day a Ceylonese couple came into the Medical Bureau, he a lawyer and blind, she in her drenched sari and bare feet — an unforgettable pair. They were Anglo-Catholics and had come all that great distance because they had read of Our Lady's gracious healings at her Shrine. To pay for their voyage they had been obliged to sell their only piece of land. Ten days they spent in Lourdes fasting, bathing in the piscine, doing penances which they offered up that his eyesight might be restored. He left Lourdes still blind. On leaving they gave me a generous offering for the new Basilica. I did not wish to take this, knowing they could ill afford to part with such a sum. Nothing would dissuade them. They kept repeating that "the only gifts worth giving are those which mean a real sacrifice, which are given with love."

An English woman came to see me with an introduction from a priest in London. She could not believe. She did not love Our Lady and rejected the idea of miracles taking place through Our Lady's intercession. For the week she was in Lourdes nothing seemed to touch her heart, nothing impressed her. She much preferred visiting the local market to praying at the Grotto. I found her indifference and lack of Faith most disconcerting. And finally came the last day of her stay. I felt despairing and helpless so I hurried to the Grotto and begged Our Lady to let me say, or do, the right thing to help my friend find belief and peace of soul. Right after that prayer something prompted me to invite my friend to come into the Medical Bureau to see me before she left.

Afterwards I was to wonder why I had ever suggested that particular hour; it was our busiest time, no time for visitors. And then what a wonderful thing happened! A young French woman was brought in to be examined and X-rayed. She had just been cured in the piscine of a cancer of the spine. My doubting friend and the cured woman arrived simultaneously at the Medical Bureau. Something urged me to introduce them to each other. Radiantly well and overjoyed, the young Frenchwoman flung her arms impulsively about my friend. "Let me embrace you," she said, "let me share my great grace and happiness with you!" They wept in each other's arms. It was enough. Mrs. L. left Lourdes believing and loving. "I cannot explain it," she said, "but it was as if Our Lady shared her gift with me too. I am cured and well!"

Now these are but a few examples. No, the Medical Bureau is no dull place and certainly no sad place. We who are privileged to work there see all the miracles and share the radiance of Our Lady's mercies towards her suffering children.

— ***MARIANIST***

**The author, the late Winifred Feely, came to Lourdes in 1950 to prepare, as she put it, "for a good, holy death." Instead she was cured in the baths. In gratitude, she volunteered to work at the Medical Bureau during the pilgrimage season.*

Two Novelists Went to Lourdes

Don Sharky

Two novelists went to Lourdes. One was Émile Zola; the other was Franz Werfel. Both had achieved no small amount of fame as writers. Neither was a Christian. Each wrote a novel which was based upon his visit. The novels were in direct contradiction to each other. The one author was firmly convinced that the events which take place at Lourdes are miraculous. The other reported that they are due entirely to natural causes, that the claims of miracles are so much humbug. The facts were there for both to examine. Why such conflicting reports?

Which of the novelists was right? Which was wrong? Let us examine the facts in each case.

Many remarkable events have taken place at Lourdes in the past ninety years, and the story of Franz Werfel and *The Song of Bernadette* is not the least remarkable of them. Franz Werfel, a Bohemian Jew, as one of the earliest opponents of Nazism. In 1922, eleven years before the Nazis came to power in Germany, he wrote a play entitled *Schweiger.* This play, he tells us, "depicted the Nazi type in the naked frightfulness of its consistency." It appeared in Berlin and a number of other German cities. The Nazis, who never forgave an enemy, marked Werfel for punishment. He was sure that this punishment would be death.

After Hitler's rise to power, Werfel dared not set foot in Germany. Later Austria fell to the Nazis, and that country also was closed to him. Next Czechoslovakia fell, and his own native city of Prague was in the hands of the enemy. He was a man without a country. Werfel fled to France and was living there in 1940 when that country was locked in mortal combat with Nazi Germany. When the French army collapsed the Nazis were free to overrun all of France. All those who had any reason to fear personal reprisals from the Nazis — and there were thousands of such unhappy souls — fled toward the Spanish border. Werfel and his wife were among those who found themselves in the French Pyrenees with all means of escape cut off. He describes the situation thus:

"Crowded together in the southwest corner of France, the confused throng of fugitive peoples, Poles, Czechs, Dutch, Belgians, French — soldiers and civilians, men, women, and children — moved about in aimless circles without food and shelter in heavily laden, sometimes bullet-ridden cars. The frontiers were relentlessly closed; the consuls pitilessly bureaucratic! And in all the crowds lurked the spying forces of the Gestapo, calmly spotting their victims."

The district around Lourdes was an island of charity in the tumultuous, pitiless sea. The Church and even the government officials did everything they could to help the refugees. They provided them with rooms in the hotels, food, clothing, even a little money. They steadfastly refused to turn the fugitives over to the Germans, an act of incredible courage. No wonder the refugees flocked to Lourdes. There were 80,000 of them there at one time.

Although this was a time of terrible dread and uncertainty, it was also a time of great spiritual consolation. Carla Zawish, M.D., an old friend of Werfel from Austria, was in Lourdes at the same time. She noticed how greatly affected Werfel was by Lourdes. Dr. Zawish says of him, "I saw the deep emotion of Franz Werfel, the future author of *The Song of Bernadette;* never before had he been so profoundly shaken in all his being. A new world had opened before him, and he plunged into it with all his eagerness. I liked to answer his questions because I saw what was going on was much more than merely the enthusiasm of a poet."

Even though the net of the Nazis was closing in on him, this was a time of great significance for Werfel. He listened to the story of Bernadette over and over again and was thrilled by it. He became acquainted with the wondrous healings that take place at Lourdes. He tells us, "One day in my great distress I made a vow. I vowed that if I escaped from this desperate situation and reached the saving shore of America, I would put off all other tasks and sing, as best I could, the song of Bernadette."

Werfel did escape, and he made good his promise. After thousands and thousands of persons had read the book, millions more became familiar with the story of Bernadette by seeing the movie based on it.

Émile Zola was a French novelist who enjoyed great popularity in certain circles toward the end of the Nineteenth Century. Zola denied the existence of the supernatural. To him, man was nothing but an animal. Nobility, spiritual greatness, self-sacrifice were of no account. He looked upon himself as a scientist who collected "human documents." Science, he said, left no room for the spiritual.

In 1892, Zola announced that he intended to visit Lourdes and investigate the cures reported to have taken place there. He would examine the facts very thoroughly and scientifically and then make his report; he would let the world know the truth about Lourdes. The announcement was widely hailed. Newspapers sent reporters to accompany him on his trip. The officials of Lourdes said they would be more than happy to cooperate with him in any way possible. Several Catholic publications said that the announcement was no doubt an indication that Zola had seen the error of his ways and would soon do an about face.

After a two weeks' visit to Lourdes, Zola returned and prepared his report in the form of a novel.

Two characters stand out in Zola's novel *Lourdes.* They are Elise Rouquet and La Grivotte. The former was described as having a horrible lupus which had gnawed away at her nose and mouth, "almost obliterating the traces of what once were pleasing womanly lineaments." La Grivotte was a consumptive whose lungs were almost eaten away by tuberculosis.

In the novel, Elise Rouquet bathed her face with Lourdes water for a whole morning and gradually the sore seemed to grow paler in

Charity is ever linked with faith at Lourdes. Right: A nurse volunteer assists a young man. Below: The large square between the statue of Our Lady of Lourdes (see pg. 175) and the basilica is the center of much activity in the summer months. The great candlelight processions where the "Credo" in Latin is sung by thousands of pilgrims.

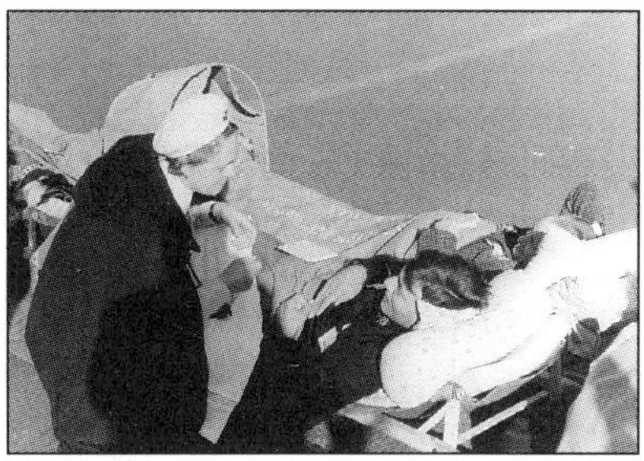

color. Dr. Bonamy of the Medical Bureau advised Elise to continue using the water as a lotion and return each day for further examination. To the other doctors he said, "At all events, gentlemen, there are signs of improvement in this case — that is beyond doubt." La Grivotte, according to Zola, came dancing into the office of the Medical Bureau shouting, "I am cured! I am cured!" She had not been bathed in the icy water of the baths for longer than three minutes before she felt her strength return to her body. But alas, the cure proved to be temporary. La Grivotte died on the train on her way home.

That was Zola's report on Lourdes. The one patient was cured slowly and imperfectly. The other seemed for a short time to be completely cured, but she died soon afterwards. Clearly her cure had been due to autosuggestion. Zola attributed all the cures of Lourdes to hypnotism, the shock caused by the cold water, the "healing inspiration of the crowd," and the curative effect on disordered nerves of the monotonous roll of the Litanies and the Aves. Zola's book was enthusiastically applauded by those who did not believe in the supernatural. Zola, they said, had gone to Lourdes with an open mind, ready to accept or reject miracles according to the evidence which he found. He came away convinced that all cures were due to purely natural causes. This book, they said, should end forever the superstition of Lourdes.

Werfel or Zola? Whom is one to believe? Werfel was in danger of his life and was perhaps overwrought emotionally. Zola looked at the situation coolly and dispassionately from a scientific point of view. Isn't there a good chance that Zola was right, Werfel wrong? It is very easy to check Zola's story, for his characters were based on real persons. Elise Rouquet was in reality Marie Lemarchand, and her disease was just as terrible as Zola described it. La Grivotte was Marie Lebranchu. She was so racked with consumption that the doctors begged her not to make the trip to Lourdes. Both of these women were on the train that brought Zola to Lourdes, and he studied their cases very carefully.

Marie Lemarchand, the Elise Rouquet of the novel, arrived at Lourdes on August 20. She was cured the next morning while bathing in the *piscine.* There was no continued washing as Zola had reported. Her cure was immediate and complete, not slow and imperfect. She lived for many more years, married, and eventually became the mother of five children. The old disease never returned. Marie Lebranchu, Zola's La Grivotte, was cured just as completely as the novelist recorded, but there was a slight difference in the sequel. Zola had her die on the way home from Lourdes. In reality, she lived for many years and never had a return of the consumption of which she had been cured. When she finally died, it was of an entirely different cause.

The fact that La Grivotte continued to live, despite the fact that he had her die, became embarrassing to Zola. In 1895 he went to see Marie Lebranchu. Later, in an interview, she told the story of Zola's visit. "He told me that if I wanted to leave Paris and go to Belgium with my husband, he would see to it that we should not want for anything."

"Then he suggested that you go to Brussels?"

"No, not to Brussels nor to any other large city. We would have to live in a country place which he would get for us himself. Then he pulled out his pocketbook and took a bundle of notes from it. I do not know how much it was, for he did not count them. He held them out to me saying, 'Here, this will do for your first needs. It will be enough for a month. In that time, I will look for what you want and I will myself secure you a place.'" "Did you accept the offer?" "For a moment I was tempted to do so, for we were destitute. But my husband, making up his mind quite suddenly, went up to Mr. Zola, took him by the arm, and put him out. Mr. Zola left, and I never saw him again."

Dr. Boissarie was head of the Lourdes Medical Bureau at the time of Zola's visit. He appears in the novel as Dr. Bonamy. He was, naturally enough, indignant at Zola's "report" of the cures. Some years later, he met the novelist and demanded to know why he had made La Grivotte die when in reality she was quite well. Zola replied, "I am the absolute master of my characters. I make them live or die to suit my pleasure. Madame Lebranchu, being healed, has no ground to complain. I don't believe in miracles, anyhow; *should I see all the sick in Lourdes get well in a moment, I still would not believe.*"

Zola is typical of a certain type of mind which is determined not to believe despite any evidence it may behold, no matter how convincing. Persons of his type have tried to discredit Lourdes ever since the Virgin first appeared to Bernadette. They closed the grotto while the apparitions were still taking place and tried to prevent the crowds from going there. Later, they wrote untrue articles in the newspapers to convince people that the whole thing was a fraud. At the beginning of this century, they tried to close Lourdes in the name of hygiene. All these attempts have ended in failure and have succeeded only in swelling the number of pilgrims flocking to Lourdes.

The conflict is not between Werfel and Zola, just as it was not between Bernadette and the police commissioner who tried to keep her from going to the grotto. It is a conflict between good and evil. It is a conflict between the Blessed Virgin and Satan. After Satan, in the form of a serpent, caused Adam and Eve to be cast out of the Garden of Eden, God promised that the Woman would crush the serpent with her heel. The Woman appeared on earth after several thousand years and became the Mother of the Savior. She is always trying to guide people into heaven; Satan is trying to lure them into the lowest depths of hell.

During the fourth appearance of the Blessed Virgin to Bernadette, the girl, according to J. B. Estrade who lived in Lourdes at the time, heard a great outburst of sinister voices which seemed to come from the bowels of the earth. The voices questioned, contradicted, interrupted each other, like the shouts of a quarrelsome crowd. One voice, louder than the others, cried, "Escape! Escape for your life." The Lady raised her head and frowned in the direction of the river. The voices seemed to be seized with fear, then to be scattering in all directions, and finally they died away.

When Satan himself was unable to prevent the processions at Lourdes — the processions for which the Blessed Virgin had asked — he tried working through human beings. This is not to say that Zola or any other individual was consciously obeying the devil's wishes. Zola did not believe in the supernatural at all; he did not, therefore, believe in Satan any more than he did in the Virgin. Nevertheless, Satan must have been pleased, indeed, when Zola made his report about Lourdes. Zola sought to discredit Lourdes and succeeded only in discrediting himself. Angered by Zola's attack, a number of prominent persons, including the brilliant French novelist Huysmans, sprang to its defense. Lourdes was again given widespread attention. The number of pilgrims increased at once. The Virgin had defeated Satan.

World War II came and stopped the great pilgrimages to Lourdes. Satan had a few moments of triumph, but they were brief indeed. Lourdes was crowded with refugees, and a great number of conversions took place. Franz Werfel was driven there by the war, learned the story of Lourdes, and went forth to sing the song of Bernadette to all the world. Even though people in distant places could no longer visit Lourdes, they learned its story, and devotion to the Blessed Virgin increased immeasurably. If it had not been for the war, this particular song of Bernadette would never have been sung. Once again the Woman had crushed the Serpent — as she will until the end of time.

In all the world, there is no other place like Lourdes. Million of pilgrims go there every year to pay their homage to the Blessed Virgin. Wonderful cures take place, cures which cannot be explained away by natural means despite the efforts of Zola and others to do so. And more wonderful than the cures of bodies are the cures of souls. It is a fascinating story and a consoling one, the story of this Miracle City in the High Pyrenees.

—From the book After Bernadette

The Real Bernadette

Bernadette, the eldest daughter of François and Louise Soubirous was petite in the dictionary meaning of the word — small, (less than 5 feet tall), pretty with dainty, well formed hands and features, yet nothing outstanding that would attract attention. Due to her size, childlike face and modest demeanor, shunning any particular attention to herself, she looked much younger than she actually was. Shy with strangers, naturally humble, fully aware (as if she needed to be reminded) of her lack of any particular talents, she might (and was) thought to be stupid or at least slow. As a child of fourteen, she could neither read nor write and had a hard time memorizing the simple catechism questions and answers. One would charitably classify her today as a "slow learner." Being the eldest and always willing to help with the three younger children, her parents couldn't spare her for any formal education even if they could afford it (which they couldn't). Devout Catholics as they were, they taught their children by their example of familial virtues and a solid rock-like Faith.

The reason Bernadette had a hard time concentrating, so necessary in developing study habits, was largely due to her continual ill health. Suffering from frequent, severe, suffocating bouts of asthma,made concentration on studies difficult. Nevertheless when taking classes in her late teens with other young ladies her age at the Lourdes Hospice, she did quite well, but never excelled at spelling or syntax. Her handwriting after a couple years showed signs of elegance. After four years at the Hospice, she possessed more or less the usual elementary skills of girls her age at Lourdes.

She was strong-willed and did not hesitate to correct severely her younger brothers and sister if they were remiss in their duties, even boxing their ears. She could come up with some sharp responses when pressed, indicating a wide-awake young girl, who didn't hesitate to express her mind. A Lourdes priest was told by some visitors that she returned rather sharp answers to people who sought to make her contradict herself. This was the typical way that the Pyrenean people of

Bernadette, the visionary of Lourdes, in her native Pyrenean dress. (Photo Paul Viron)

that region expressed themselves. Yet her liveliness of voice and expression never turned to harshness or bitterness. At times she could be stubborn, insisting on having her way, but not so often that her companions noticed it. She had a lively personality and was not above playing pranks on her fellow students. Among the many photographs of her at this age one can detect in some a slightly mischievous look in her dark, lively eyes.

One was immediately struck by the brilliance of her eyes. As one of her fellow religious mentioned years later, "Once you had seen them, you could never forget them. Above all you were attracted by their depth, which was truly extraordinary." The eyes that looked upon her Heavenly Mother in this life were ever focused on other realities than those of this life. Another Sister who knew her well wrote, "You had the impression that their gaze hardly rested on this earth but was

The devout parents of Bernadette: François Soubirous, gentle, simple and earnest in fulfilling his religious duties. Louise Castorot who was 17 at the time of their marriage (he 35) bore nine children. She died at a comparatively young age, but not before passing on to them her solid Faith.

mysteriously fixed on something afar off, on something enthralling that kept escaping her, and this gave her eyes and her pretty smile a touch of melancholy that still more enhanced her charm. Her smile was restrained, but you were not conscious of any effort at repression." A priest theologian sums up well the young visionary in her late teens:

"What impressed you on seeing her was an air of candor, innocence, modesty and reserve that completely enveloped her and radiated from her through her eyes, her attitude and her bearing. It was the common opinion that she had kept her baptismal innocence and had retained in all its loveliness, freshness and fragrance the lily of virginity."

When Bernadette entered the Congregation of the Sisters of Charity and Christian Instruction of Nevers on July 7, 1866, at the age of 22 the only significant change in the seer of Lourdes, if you can call it that, was in her name from Bernadette to Sister Marie-Bernard. Under the veil was the same humble and simple girl who had made giant strides in the science of the Saints, identifying with the Crucified Christ through much suffering. She who had a foretaste of heaven, in gazing upon the Queen of heaven and earth realized full well that this world offered absolutely nothing in comparison with that revelation. Indeed, it would seem that the words of Our Lady to her little child were perfectly realized in this regard: "I do not promise you happiness in this life but only in the next." She was ever homesick for her true home — heaven.

This promise of Our Lady to St. Bernadette was to be realized largely through her notoriety as the privileged seer of Lourdes which brought down upon her much misunderstanding and perhaps the envy of a few fellow religious. She never sought the limelight and hated having people fawn over her as the privileged person who saw Our Lady eighteen times. So her desire to be let alone, seek silence and obscurity was to be realized from the start of her Religious life. In her deep humility, she was happy to be considered of no account. When a Superior once inquired, "Do you not feel tempted to vainglory, having been thus fa-

Bernadette, continually in ill health in the convent, was called a lazybones by a Sister, to whom she replied, "Why, I'm doing my job! My job is to be ill." The motherhouse of the Sisters of Charity and of Christian Instruction where St. Bernadette spent the last thirteen years of her short life.

vored by Our Lady?" She answered in all sincerity that had Mary found anyone still more ignorant than she, to such a one she would have appeared. "I was like the oxen of Bétharram, who found the sacred statue. I was just *used.* What do you do with a broom?" she asked almost grimly of a nun who was staring at her. "Why, sweep with it." "And then?" "Put it back in its place." "Yes. And so for me. Our Lady used me. They have put me in my corner. I am happy there, and stop there."

She meant every word of it, and used certain ingenious stratagems to avoid attention that at times boarded on veneration. When she was sacristan visitors asked her "Oh Sister, might we see Bernadette?" Bernadette smiled, bowed and went to fetch herself, but failed to find her. "What!" one sister remarked, "You are hiding from the Bishop? And you could get forty days' indulgence if you kissed his ring." "Oh well — 'My Jesus, mercy!' There! I have got a hundred!'" The only ones whom she was really glad to see were children.

Bernadette was by nature very sensitive, and grateful for any tenderness she received, but for the most part in the convent she received "tough love" from superiors. From a strictly natural point of view, it is hard to appreciate the official policy of her novice mistresses and the mother general who felt that they had to humiliate and demean one so deeply grounded in humility, in order to keep her from being proud. Added to her intense physical sufferings, gasping for breath, constantly sick with tuberculosis of the bone and on the verge of death several times, no doubt the official snubs and lack of the usual expressions of love from her superiors caused great mental pain to one so deeply touched by the least expression of love and gratitude. But it was all allowed by God for her sanctification and the salvation of souls.

In reading the authoritative and perhaps the best biography of St. Bernadette, by *Saint Bernadette Soubirous,* by Abbé François Trochu, one is reminded that the Saint had to make strenuous efforts to practice virtue and was not exempt from the sad results of original sin. She was not without her faults and failings in patience but made no attempt to disguise these imperfections inherent in our wounded human nature. She was always sorry after a sudden flare up. During the period of formation in the novitiate her temperament was fundamentally the same, though abrupt manifestations of impatience and too ready sharp rejoinders, often quite witty, were less frequent.

After profession, the slight flashes of temper were less apparent. Yet she was reproached for being "very tenacious of her opinion." She admitted, "I have been headstrong all my life," and added good-humoredly, "Even at the grotto I had to be told twice by the Blessed Virgin to drink the muddy water. But she punished me well by making me ask her three times for her name." But judging from her own statements and testimonies of others her obstinacy had nothing to do with dissenting from that which was true and morally right.

As a religious she livened up the frequently monotonous lives of fellow novices with harmless jokes and merry witticisms. Coming as they did from the innocent mischievousness of the Saint they could hardly be considered imperfections, but rather genuine acts of sisterly charity. As one commentator remarked, "Sister Marie-Bernard's little fits of roguishness, and certain remarks that were seasoned with the garlic of the south raised the spirits and gladdened the hearts of those around her." During one of their recreations a Sister who was deeply attached to Bernadette, saw her take out a snuffbox (she took snuff at doctor's orders for her asthma). "Sister Marie-Bernard," Sister Chantal teasingly said, "you won't be canonized." "Why?" "Because you take snuff. St. Vincent de Paul very nearly missed it on account of his snuffbox." "But you, Sister Chantal, you don't take snuff, so you will no doubt be canonized?"

An admiring sister said, "Never to my knowledge did I see her fail in charity." On seeing Sister Marie-Bernard at recreation exploiting her talent for mimicking, it was clear she loved her community. Mother Elizabeth Meyrignac recalled how: "She used to join us (the novices) at recreation and make herself at home with her charming simplicity and tell us amusing stories that made us laugh uproariously — as one does laugh at that age. What happy times I owe to her! What a fund of good humor she brought us. But I must say that there was never anything unkind. It was all in good fun and left us under the charm of her saintliness."

"The stories usually concerned little incidents in the infirmary in which Dr. Robert Saint-Cyr sometimes figured. That excellent man had some little whims and mannerisms which we all knew, and Bernadette used to entertain us with imitations of him which made us laugh so much that tears rolled down our cheeks. Her mimicry was brilliant, full of delicate touches of wit and sometimes of sly roguishness." However, Mother Elizabeth did not wish to leave the reader with a picture of Bernadette as a mere entertainer, so she hastened to add:

"When recreation was ended, the dear Sister got up, bowed to us graciously and immediately resumed her grave demeanor, to bring home to us that we young novices had also to return to the silence that was our rule." Such an instantaneous return to silence at the first sound of the bell, after much merriment, demonstrates that in spite of her youthful appearance and girlish frolics Sister Marie-Bernard had a strong will and prompt control of her feelings.

In this regard, one day the pious story was being told of how St. Teresa of Avila had a vision of the Child Jesus whom she left immediately when she heard the sound of the bell calling her to some duty. To the astonishment of all the Sisters, Marie-Bernard said, "I would not have acted so." Then in her simple straight forward practical way explained, "I would have picked Him up and taken Him with me. He couldn't have been so very heavy."

There was another touching incident which illustrates her wise handling of a delicate situation. A trunk arrived at the Motherhouse along with a sweet little thing of sixteen and had been deposited in the linen room. When the girl came to the linen room the next day to claim her trunk, the sight of it reminded her of home and she began to cry. With her elbows on the table and her head in her hands she cried and cried. Sister Marie-Bernard came quietly up to her and said in a soft playful voice; "Oh, mademoiselle! What a solid vocation! It's going to grow well, this one, for I see you are watering it thoroughly. That's right, dear, water it!" As the postulant was later to say when she had become a superior in one of their houses, “These simple words had more effect on me than a sermon. I could not help laughing. I was laughing and crying at the same time. But the tears stopped almost immediately and did not return, whilst the smile remained. I even laughed so much afterwards that our Mistress told me several times: ‘You’ll have to do some Purgatory later on, my dear; you’re not serious enough.’”

Sister Marie-Bernard went to recreation out of a sense of giving rather than receiving. This was no more apparent than the great day of her religious profession, the same afternoon the newly professed were given their first appointments. When it came her turn as she knelt before the presiding prelate, Bishop Forcade asked the Mother General what assignment they intended to give her. Mother Imbert replied, “This child is good for nothing. She would be a burden on any house we sent her to.” He queried, “In that case, my poor child, what are we going to do with you?” After a short dialogue between Bernadette and the bishop before the whole assembly of Sisters and friends, it was decided out of charity to keep her at the Motherhouse. “Good for nothing?” Her fellow newly professed Sisters knew better; it was but another calculated humiliation to keep Sister Marie-Bernard humble. Nonetheless the words, “good for nothing” cut deeply. At the next community recreation, Sister Marie-Bernard intensified her efforts to be lively and cheerful as though nothing had happened though she admitted later how deeply she felt the humiliation.

Continual humiliations were her diet for at least nine of the twelve years she was in the convent. A good friend of Mother Imbert and collab-

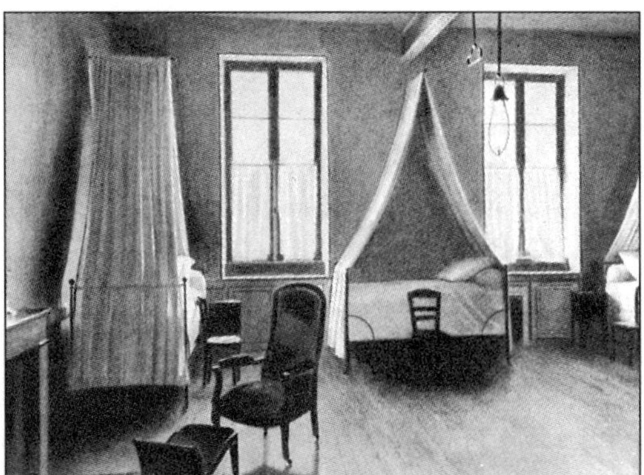

Sr. Bernard’s Mistress of Novices, Mother Marie-Thérèse Vauzou, whose treatment of Bernadette contributed so much to the establishment of her practice of heroic virtue. The room in the infirmary where the Saint died.

orator in "keeping the seer of Lourdes humble," was Mother Marie-Thérèse Vauzou, the Mistress of Novices. She came from a totally different background than the little shepherdess of Lourdes. Her grandfather and father were lawyers and she received a good education. Highly cultured, she was acquainted with the arts and social graces that meant so much to her. She showed early in life a propensity for "taking over."

The novices under her care were well liked and favored according to their "openness" to the Novice Mistress. Bernadette had already received personal direction or secrets from the Mother of God, which she was not at liberty to disclose. She guarded them tenaciously. Mother Marie-Thérèse could never gain the confidence of Bernadette, who respected her but never confided in her. This more than anything upset the Mistress who demanded the absolute trust and confidence of her subjects. It was said of this strong character that one either came to love her or fear her. Even the prosecutor at Lourdes who put Bernadette to the test (see page 95) caused Bernadette no fear or pain as did her Novice Mistress. When Bernadette returned to the novitiate after a near fatal illness, rapping on the table for emphasis, Mother Marie-Thérèse said, "Now we can hammer away at you." The novice replied: "I hope you will do it gently."

Bernadette was affectionate, warm, and popular with her fellow religious. She who had a mother's tender heart, had a favorite picture of a child at Mary's knees. "That is how we should always be with Our Lady," she said. "a child with its mother." She who had a very caring earthly mother, and could in a special way claim Mary Immaculate as her mother, now had a "Mother" of another sort. The contrast couldn't be more glaring. Moreover, due to Sister Marie-Bernard's strong commitment to her religious vows and submission to God-given authority, religious life must have given her many anxious moments on how to show respect, deference and love to a superior who responded with rebuffs and humiliations at every opportunity. But it wasn't the humiliations that cut deepest as the coldness and studied antipathy towards Bernadette which seemed so unexplainable.

It wasn't easy for a quick tempered person continually suffering from asthma attacks, which would eventually led to tuberculosis, not to be openly ill-tempered. She admitted to a friend, "I am seething inside but they don't see what's going on there," and added, "There would be no merit if one did not master oneself." She held no grudges against superiors who hurt her, showing them no less filial affection and respect. She never stopped at the persons who exercised authority arbitrarily and unjustly. She told sister Ducout, "We must always see God in our superiors. . . .I submit come what may." In her private notebook

Covered by a thin film of wax, the incorrupt body of St. Bernadette lies in a reliquary in the chapel of the motherhouse in Nevers. It was Pope Pius XI who inscribed the little peasant girl of Lourdes in the roster of the Saints by canonizing her in 1933. (Leonard von Matt Photo)

she had written, "Never regard the creature, but always see God in her."

On one occasion, a companion tried to console her for the undeserved severe treatment of the Novice Mistress. Sr. Marie-Bernard replied with deep conviction: "But I owe her great gratitude for the good she has done my soul." The irony is that one could say that Mother Marie-Thérèse more than anyone contributed to her eventual canonization. One of the consultors of the Congregation of Rites declared at the close of her beatification that nothing had done so much to establish the heroic degree of Bernadette's virtues as her difficulties with her Mother Mistress.

Her physical suffering due to deteriorating health became much worse in the winter of 1877. A tumor, and an abscess on her knee, caused her excruciating pain that kept her awake throughout the night. "They say there are saints who did not go straight to heaven because they did not desire it enough. That will not be *me.*" As she approached death, she did not think of herself as holy. "After my death," she said with naive ruefulness, "they will be saying that Sister Marie-Bernard is a *saintoun,* and leave me to grill in purgatory!" Less than a year before her death, September 22, 1878, the Feast of Our Lady of Sorrows, she made her final vows which bound her forever to Christ.

On the Feast of St. Joseph, 1879, she asked from that saint, whom she called her father, the grace of a good death. After receiving the last Sacraments on March 28, she begged pardon in a "strong voice" for all the disedification she had given the community — especially through her "pride." During Holy Week "the devil tried to frighten her." But she invoked Our Lord, "and it all went away." On April 16, she became too weak to hold her crucifix, so she asked to have it tied to her breast.

Increasingly throughout her illness, it was noticed how alive her eyes were. She answered all the prayers for the dying, and then, an hour before her departure, raising her eyes, cried three times "Oh!" in a voice, of surprise rather than pain. Her body trembled as she put her hand on her heart, and said, in a clear voice, "My God, I love Thee with all my heart, with all my soul, and with all my strength." She then took the crucifix into her own hands and kissed it, and begged pardon once more for all the trouble she had given. Indicating she was thirsty, she made for the last time her "marvelous sign of the Cross," and drank a few drops. Then she said gently, "Holy Mary, Mother of God, pray for me, a poor sinner, a poor sinner," and died very quietly during this last prayer.

With consummate simplicity, common sense and heroic love and faith, and a good sense of humor, a spin-off of her deep humility, St. Bernadette never deviated from the course that was set for her at the Grotto of Massabielle by the Lady who assured her that she couldn't promise her happiness in this life but only in the next. Yes, Bernadette had her priorities in order. The shepherdess of Lourdes was (excuse the expression) "one sharp lady."

A Lasting Impression of Lourdes by Bishop Theas

"Let us take away as our last picture of Lourdes this gathering of pilgrims who, candle in hand, sing each evening the Credo in the sacred and universal language of the Church. It is the symbol of the unity of the faith in the midst of a great diversity of races and nations on this large esplanade, before the Basilica of the Rosary, in the presence of bishops who represent the magisterium of the Church, and who at the end will give their blessing.

"Have you noticed how much the Blessed Virgin has humbled herself? After the triumphant responding of the "Ave Maria" which accompanied the torchlight procession, she who has often been proclaimed Queen, is mentioned in the great formula of faith with the simple words: *Natus ex Maria Virgine* (born of the Virgin Mary). Here we sense that Mary is present in the world of realities and that she is all powerful because of her humility."

Saint Maximilian Mary Kolbe

He Wrote about Lourdes and the Immaculate Conception

Early in 1914, while in his second year of philosophy studies in Rome, Saint Maximilian encountered the mystery and power of Lourdes. An abscess had formed on a finger of his right hand and had begun to penetrate the bone. His doctor ordered the bone to be scraped. Maximilian noted that there was even great danger of losing the finger. However, his rector gave him some Lourdes water, and the doctor himself applied it to the abscess the day before the scheduled operation. Examining the finger the following day revealed such improvement that the scraping was cancelled. After a few more medications, the finger was completely healed.

This grace deeply affected the young friar in more ways than one. It opened his eyes to the mystery hidden in the name Mary gave herself at Lourdes — "I am the Immaculate Conception." In fact in the first letter to his mother in which he describes his healing, he refers to Mary for the first time as the "Immaculata." From that period on, this was his favorite name for her, the one he almost always uses in preference to all others. This name tantalized him and became the focus of his prayer and contemplation of the mystery of Mary. It led him ultimately to discoveries and insights of profound importance not only for Mariology, but for Trinitarian theology as well. Following are a few selections from his conferences and writings that evidence his extraordinary appreciation of the events at Lourdes.

Who are You, Immaculate?

Not God, because He has no beginning; not an angel created directly from nothing; not Adam, formed from the clay of the earth; not Eve, taken from Adam. Nor are you the Word-Incarnate, Who existed from all ages and is begotten rather than having a beginning. The children of Eve did not exist before conception, hence they can all the more be called a conception, and yet you are different from them all because they are conceptions stained by original sin. But you alone are an immaculate conception.

This privilege must be dear to her, since she says of herself at Lourdes, "I am the Immaculate Conception." She does not say, "I am immaculately conceived," but "the Immaculate Conception." Hence it follows that she is Immaculateness itself, truly a Conception, for her existence began in time, but the "Immaculate Conception."

The Immaculate at Lourdes does not call herself immaculately conceived, but, as St. Bernadette herself relates, "The Lady was standing above the wild rose bush in a position very similar to that shown on the miraculous medal. At my third request her face took on a serious expression, and at the same time an expression of deep humility. . . . Joining her palms as if for prayer, she raised them to the height of her breast. . . . she looked up to heaven then slowly opening her hands and bending down towards me, she said to me in a voice in which one could sense a slight trembling, 'I am the Immaculate Conception.'"

Immaculate! The summit of perfection of a creature, Mother of God, the most God-like of creatures. The purpose of the creature, the purpose of man, is the progressive growth in likeness to the Creator, a constantly more perfect Godliness. "God becomes man so that man might become God," says St. Augustine. We imitate good, virtuous, holy people, but none of these is without imperfection. Only she, Immaculate from the first moment of her existence, knows no fault, not the least. It is she whom one should imitate and come close to. We should become hers, become her. Behold the peak of perfection in man — the Immaculate. . .

Human words have not the power to relate what she is who has become the real Mother of God. In reality, she is only a creature, but in God she is such a sublime being that one would have to grasp what God is, in order to understand who the Mother of God is. She is the real Mother of God. That is a dogma of faith. She is not a mother in name only. A mother is not the parent of only a part of her child, neither is the father the parent of a part, but both the father and mother are parents of the whole child. And so the Blessed Mother is rightly the Mother of the whole Jesus, the God-Man, and therefore the Mother of God.

Our Father in heaven is the first beginning and final end of everything. The human tongue and mind of man, in borrowing his notions from his surroundings, falters when he tries to think and speak about God. Imperfect is his notion of God, nevertheless true. We know from Divine Revelation that from all ages and forever the Father brings forth the Son, and the Spirit proceeds from the Father and the Son. This life of the Most Holy Trinity is imitated in numberless and diverse images of the creatures that come from the hands of the Triune God, according as they more or less resemble Him.

The general principle that each effect is similar to the cause has here also its full application and all the more so, since God creates from nothing. Therefore whatever is in creation is His handiwork.

From the Father through the Son and Spirit descends each act of the love of God, creating, sustaining in existence; giving life and its development both in the order of nature, as well as in the order of grace. In such a manner does God bestow His love on countless finite beings. And by no other way does the return of the creature's love ascend to the Father except through the Spirit and the Son. This does not always happen consciously, but always really. No one else, but the same God is the author of the act of love in creatures. But if this creature possesses a free will, the act does not take place without his consent. The height of a creature's love returning to God is the Immaculate. A being without stain of sin, wholly beautiful, wholly belonging to God. Not even for a moment did her will bend away from the will of God.

We name her *Lady,* but this title places us at a distance from her maternal heart.

We call her *Queen,* but here we must add that she is the Queen of hearts, the Queen of love. Her law is love, and her power is motherly love. These and similar explanations, although they are brought forward without end, will tell not even a part of what the soul feels when it is consumed by love of her. It experiences in itself that the Immaculate belongs to it more and more under every respect, and yet realizes that these are but the beginnings of knowing and loving her.

You will draw more knowledge about her and will be more inflamed with her love directly from her heart than from all human words put together. — *Taken from the book,* **Aim Higher**

The Apparitions of the Most Blessed Virgin Mary at Lourdes

Ever since orginal sin was committed, the human mind has remained in darkness so that it cannot rise to the understanding of the causes for everything. Our first parents in the Garden of Eden understood everything very well; their intellects were clear and lively; but after they sinned, all that was changed. For this reason, when God wishes to make himself known to men he gives them signs and works miracles. We find many miracles in the Old Testament, and even more in the New. When Jesus was in this world he said: "Even if you do not believe in me, believe in my works." (Jn. 10 :38).

The miracle of the Resurrection is the foundation of our faith. The disciples of Jesus were weak; even though they had seen many miracles, they all abandoned him at the time of his arrest. Only when

Jesus had risen was their faith confirmed, and were they given the courage to endure suffering and persecution.

Since Christ's Resurrection, from time to time there are recorded miracles to reinforce our faith; such were the apparitions at Lourdes. There the Immaculate chose a weak instrument to manifest her power. There were many objections; people said, "It isn't true." But all the while the miraculous fountain was flowing, and many miracles and conversions took place. What did the Most Blessed Virgin do, after establishing her credibility by these miracles? In public before a crowd of people she said who she was and personally confirmed the dogma of the Immaculate Conception which had been defined in 1854. She said of herself, "I am the Immaculate Conception." If she is indeed the Immaculate Conception, then everything which serves as a foundation for this truth is also true. Hence the apparitions at Lourdes are a confirmation of the entire Catholic Faith. This is why these apparitions of the Most Blessed Virgin at Lourdes are so important.

— Conference, Feb. 11, 1938

Her Own True Name

To Bernadette's repeated request, the Immaculate replied by revealing her true name when she said, "I am the Immaculate Conception." To no one else does such a name properly belong.

When God revealed His name to Moses, He said: "I am the One who is." (Ex. 3:14). For God exists from all eternity and through all eternity. His being is unlimited, transcending all time, under whatsoever aspect. Whatever exists apart from God is not "being" itself, but receives its being from Him. Thus the Immaculata also began to exist in time.

Among the creatures which began to exist, the angels and our first parents came into being without having been conceived. Mary, on the contrary, like all ordinary humans, began to exist when she was conceived. Jesus Christ, the Man-God, also began His human life by an act of conception. But we should rather say of Him that he was conceived, not that he is a "conception," because as the Son of God He exists without a beginning, whereas Mary, since she began in a conception, is different from Him, and like all other human beings. But from the first instant of her existence she was distinguished from all the rest of humankind by the fact that their conceptions are sullied by Original Sin, since they are conceived by descendants of our first parents who sinned; Mary's conception, on the contrary, is entirely exempt from this general law; her conception was immaculate. She, therefore, has a full right to the name "Immaculate Conception." This is indeed her true name.

— Sketch, 1940

Who Is the Immaculata?

Who is Mary Immaculate? To this abrupt question it is not possible to give a satisfactory answer, because this mystery transcends our human intelligence. In the Litany of Loretto we find many beautiful titles attributed to the Mother of God; but beautiful as they are, they are not enough. Scripture says little about her; it merely relates a few facts, like the Annunciation, the Nativity, and so on. St. John would have been able to tell us a lot more no doubt, since he was, for so many years, the witness of Mary's blessed life.

One would have to set down all the various graces bestowed throughout the history of nations, to tell of the many apparitions . . . but especially one would have to recount the story of grace in each individual soul, if one wished to give even a partial answer to the question, "Who is the Immaculata?" She is the mother of God, and her name is the Immaculata. When God showed Himself to Moses He said of Himself, "I am the One who is," (Ex. 3:14); in other words, "I am BEING itself." When St. Bernadette asked the Most Blessed Virgin her name, Mary replied: "I am the Immaculate Conception." Such is Mary, defined by her own words.

But what does the expression "Immaculate Conception" mean? The word "conception" tells us that she is not eternal; that she had a beginning. "Immaculate" tells us that from the first instant of her existence there never was in her the least conflict with God's will. The Immaculata is the most perfect of all creatures; she is the most sublime; she is most Godlike. She was immaculate because she was to become the Mother of God; she became the Mother of God because she was immaculate.

Mother of God! The human mind cannot grasp what God is; neither can we comprehend the dignity of the mother of God. It is easier to understand a title like "servant of God"; "daughter of God" is more difficult to grasp; but "Mother of God" transcends our minds completely. God calls creatures into being when He creates them. Then, in their movement of return to God these creatures draw near to Him and come to resemble their Creator more and more. God comes to his most perfect creature, the Immaculata; and the fruit of their love is Jesus Christ, the Mediator between the Creator and all creatures.

When we ask, "Who is the Immaculata?" our language is not able to furnish an adequate response. We can't even form a meaningful idea of it. True knowledge of the Immaculata can only be acquired in prayer. The purer a soul is, the greater efforts it makes to avoid sin — and if it does happen to sin, it tries its best to rise from sin and to make up for its fault by love — the more humble it is, and the greater spirit of penance it shows, the more and better will it get to know the Immaculata.

—Conference, July 26, 1939

The Immaculate Conception Spouse of the Holy Spirit

And who is the Holy Spirit? He is the fruit of love of the Father and the Son. The fruit of a created love is a created conception. Hence the fruit of this love, of the prototype of all created love, can also be nothing else but a conception. Hence the Holy Spirit is an uncreated conception, an eternal one; He is the prototype of every sort of human conception in the universe.

She is joined in an ineffable manner to the Holy Spirit because she is His Spouse; but this is true of her in an incomparably more perfect sense than anything this term can express among creatures. What kind of union is this? It is above all interior; it is the union of her very being with the being of the Holy Spirit. The Holy Spirit dwells in her, loves in her, from the first instant of her existence, and He will do so always, throughout eternity.

In what does this life of the Holy Spirit in her consist? He Himself is love in her, the love of the Father and the Son, the love by which God loves Himself, the love of the entire most Holy Trinity, a fruitful love, a conception. Among created resemblances the union of love is the closest. Holy Scripture affirms that "the two of them become one body" (Gn. 2:24). and Jesus insists, "Thus they are no longer two but one flesh" (Mt. 19:6). In an incomparably more rigorous, more interior, more essential manner the Holy Spirit lives in the soul of the Immaculate, in her very being, and makes her fruitful from the first instant of her existence and throughout her life, that is, forever. This uncreated Immaculate Conception conceives divine life immaculately in the soul of Mary, His Immaculate Conception. In the Holy Spirit's union with her not only does love join these two beings, but the first of the two [the Holy Spirit] is the entire love of the Holy Trinity, while the second [Mary] is the entire love of creation; and thus in this union, heaven is joined with earth, all of heaven with all of earth, all uncreated love with all created love; it is the summit of love.

Thus at Lourdes the Immaculate did not define herself as "Conceived without sin," but as St. Bernadette related, "She said in a voice in which a slight tremor could be detected, 'Qué soy ér Immaculada Councepsou!'"

If among creatures a bride takes the name of her husband by the fact that she belongs to him, unites herself with him, makes herself like unto him and together with him becomes the source of new life, how much more should the name of the Holy Spirit, "Immaculate Conception," be the same of her in whom He lives with a love which is fruitful in the entire supernatural economy?

Final dictation of Fr. Maximilian for a book he intended to write on the Immaculate Conception, Feb. 17, 1941, the day of his arrest by the Gestapo.

"The Two Things Go Together."

On June 3, 1858, the day of her First Communion, less than four months after Our Lady had appeared to her for the first time, a friend of Bernadette asked her: "Tell me, which of the two things was the greatest joy to you, receiving your God in Holy Communion, or seeing and conversing with the Blessed Virgin at the grotto?" Bernadette hesitated momentarily, and replied, "I do not know; the two things go together and cannot be compared. All I know is that I was intensely happy at both times." The profound and yet simple response of the 14-year-old Bernadette is an incontestable answer to those who would separate love and devotion to Mary with that of her Divine Son.

Many Protestants and even some Catholics today would claim that devotion to Our Lady stands in the way of giving total love to Jesus, that in honoring Mary we dishonor or at least give less honor to Jesus. The very same people who take such a stance usually do not understand or believe in the Real Presence of Jesus in the Eucharist. It is no accident that when there is a decline in Marian devotion, belief and devotion to Jesus in His Real Presence also decline. We might add that these two are the most fundamental characteristics of Catholics as distinguished from Protestant Christians. Mary and Jesus in the Eucharist are inseparable. It is not "either one or the other," but rather "the two things go together," as Bernadette wisely points out.

Neglect Our Lady and the surest, quickest and easiest way to her divine Son is canceled out. Ignore the Woman of Faith and our faith in the Real Presence will falter and fail as it has among many Catholics who obviously do not believe that God is present in the Eucharist since they show Our Lord so little respect and reverence. It is seen in the dethroning Jesus from the center of our churches and placing him in a less "conspicuous" place to the side to make room for the presidential chair. The lack of faith in Our Eucharist God-man which is reflected in the casual and careless attitude of so many Catholics is also shown in recent secular polls.

The following statistics are sad and frightening. In January 1992, a Gallup Poll found that two out of three Catholics do not believe that

Christ is present in the Eucharist in His glorified body, blood, soul and divinity. Thus they deny the two-thousand-year-long traditional belief going back to the upper room in Jerusalem where Jesus fulfilled the promise he had made by giving men His Flesh to eat and His Blood to drink. The Eucharist to them is symbolic of His spiritual presence. In June 1994, the New York Times/CBS national poll found that among Catholics under 45, two out of three believe that the Blessed Sacrament is merely a "symbolic reminder of Christ." Only half of the Catholics over 65 years of age still subscribe to the Church's traditional teaching on the Real Presence. If any poll were to seek the reason for such a decline they would surely find a close relationship between the decline in belief of the Eucharistic Lord with a diminution of devotion to Mary.

The inseparable bond that exists between Mary and the Eucharist is brought out in several ways. Mary and the Eucharist are intricately linked in the mind of the highest authority of the Catholic Church, the papacy, and that for two thousand years. One would be hard pressed to find a single pope, especially in our century, who did not honor Mary

"Faith in the Eucharist is not weak at Lourdes. It is, on the contrary, affirmed daily there, and in the most stirring and solemn manner. Nowhere will you find emphasis as vibrant, as enthusiastic and as drawing as at Lourdes during the procession of the Blessed Sacrament.

—Bishop Theas of Tarbes-Lourdes

and at the same time show love for the Eucharistic Lord in a special way. The great Eucharistic pope, St. Pius X, said, "The unique glory of the shrine of Lourdes resides in the fact that Mary attracts to it people from everywhere for the adoration of Jesus Christ in the Blessed Sacrament, so that this sanctuary, which is at the same time the center of Marian devotion and the throne of the Eucharistic Mystery, seems to surpass in glory all others in the Catholic Church."

Pope Paul VI, who declared Mary the Mother of the Church during the Vatican Council, wrote a definitive encyclical on the Holy Eucharist, *Mysterium Fidei,* to counteract the many deviations and false ideas of the Eucharist rampant in our day. He concluded that beautiful testimony of the **Central Mystery** of our Catholic Faith with these words:

"May the most blessed Virgin Mary from whom Christ Our Lord took the flesh which under the species of bread and wine 'is contained, offered and consumed,' . . . intercede before the Father of mercies so that from this same faith in and devotion towards the Eucharist may result and flourish a perfect unity of communion among all Christians." The Eucharist is indeed *the* sign of unity and that is why it is so wrong for non-Catholics to receive Holy Communion, for they do not subscribe to all that the Church is and teaches. They make a mockery of the Eucharist.

Our present Holy Father, Pope John Paul II, has written and spoken extensively on both the Eucharist and Mary. In his encyclical *Mother of the Redeemer* we read, "The piety of the Christian people has always very rightly sensed a **profound link** between devotion to the Blessed Virgin and worship of the Eucharist: this is a fact that can be seen in the liturgy of both the West and the East, in the traditions of Religious Families, in the modern movements of spirituality, including those for youth, and in the pastoral practice of the Marian Shrines. **Mary guides the faithful to the Eucharist.**"

All the great saints of the Catholic Church had exceptional devotion to Our Eucharistic Lord and His Holy Mother. In particular St. Peter Julian Eymard comes to mind. In the last century he was the founder of a community especially devoted to the promotion of Eucharistic Adoration. But before he founded his Order, he belonged to a Congregation that was especially dedicated to Mary in her Immaculate Conception. It was towards the end of his life that he asked his spiritual sons and daughters to address Mary and venerate her under the title of Our Lady of the Blessed Sacrament.

But perhaps nowhere is the close link between Mother and Son, Immaculate Virgin and Eucharistic Christ, more apparent than in the Marian shrines that are found throughout the world. When Our Lady came to Rue du Bac in Paris in 1830, for the first of her many modern-day apparitions, she told St. Catherine Labouré to come to the foot of the altar where great graces would be bestowed on all who ask for them. At Lourdes Our Lady asked that a church be built on the site of her apparitions which, of course, indicates that she wanted the Eucharistic Sacrifice to be celebrated there as well as Christ's Presence in the Tabernacle. In every one of Mary's great sanctuaries she is not venerated in isolation. Her fundamental role is to bring pilgrims to the foot of the altar, there to adore her divine Son.

Mary is inseparably connected with Jesus in the Eucharist, because she is our Mother, a Mother whose duty it is to nourish her children. The only food which can satisfy the hunger and the needs of her family, the Church, is Jesus in the Holy Eucharist. "Amen, amen, I say to you, unless you eat the flesh of the Son of Man, and drink his blood, you shall not have life in you. He who eats my flesh and drinks my blood has life everlasting and I will raise him up on the last day" (Jn. 6:54-55). "I am the living bread that has come down from heaven. If anyone eats of this bread he shall live forever and the bread that I will give is my flesh for the life of the world" (Jn. 6:35, 51-52). But Jesus could not give us His body to eat in the Eucharist till Mary had first given Him that body.

Mary, the humble maiden of Nazareth, carried Jesus in her womb for nine months. He who calls Himself the "Bread of Life" was born of the Virgin Mary in Bethlehem, the town whose name means "House of Bread." Mary always brings her children to her divine Son, and it is He who works the miracles at Lourdes and elsewhere, just as He did at Cana at her request.

At Lourdes every single day during the pilgrimage season at least three thousand people receive Holy Communion at the grotto. Each afternoon, in the procession of the Blessed Sacrament, Jesus passes among the sick, blessing them through the bishop or priest carrying the monstrance. It is then that the miraculous cures and the miracles of grace frequently take place. Jesus in the Holy Eucharist is again "walking" among the sick with the sick exclaiming: "Lord, if you will, you can cure me!" — "Lord, that I may see!" — "Lord, he whom you love is sick. Please come and heal him." The number of miraculous cures is small, but the spiritual cures are many. All who carry the cross after the Master and the Woman who "stood at the foot of the cross" of her dying Son are at least given the grace of resignation and peace and the ability to unit their cross with that of Our Lord's.

One of the most outstanding Eucharistic cures at Lourdes during the blessing of the sick with the Eucharist was that of Elizabeth Tembrock of Mulheim, Germany. She had been sick for over five years and eventually developed tuberculosis. Her doctor clamed there wasn't a single healthy spot in her lungs. It finally settled into the bones of her right hand. After nine operations, one finger had to be removed and the whole hand became affected, so much so the doctor suggested amputating the hand before the whole arm would have to be removed.

Though she was so sick that it seemed imprudent to take the long trip to Lourdes, she insisted on taking the risk, confident that she would be cured. After arriving at the Grotto in Lourdes on August 9 she received the grace of resigning herself totally to God's holy Will. From that moment on she had great peace and happiness, which is a common reaction among the sick who come to Lourdes seeking a physical cure, but receiving something much more valuable — peace of soul.

At the end of her pilgrimage, on August 15, the feast of Our Lady's Assumption into heaven, she fainted several times due to the severe pains in her open wounds. Her right hand was dark blue, cold as ice and so stiff that one could have broken but not bent the fingers. A great deal of matter oozed from several fingers and the flesh of one finger had decayed beyond the last joint where pus was draining from the bone.

Let Elizabeth describe what happened next: "In spite of my miserable condition I was taken to the square before the Basilica for the procession of the Blessed Sacrament. As the priest, usually a bishop, blessed the sick, prayers and invocations were said: 'Good Master, grant that I may see.' 'Lord, behold he whom you love is sick.' 'Good Master, grant that I may walk.' ' Good Master, give me health!' Up to this point

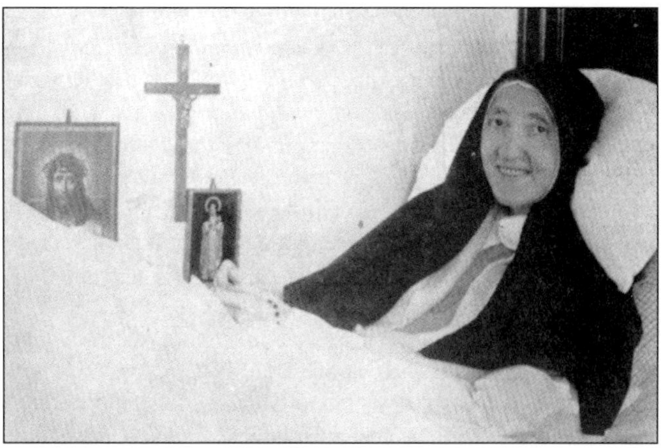

Mother Immaculata, the former Elizabeth Tembrock. After many active years in the Brazilian missions, spent the rest of her life as a expiatory victim for the sanctification of priests.

I had joined the prayers, but these last words did not pass my lips.

"The very moment the procession reached the spot where I was, what did I say? I felt as if I were in the Holy Land and Jesus, the good Master, Who went about doing good and healing the sick, saw me by the wayside and was coming towards me. I felt as if He put His hand on my head and said deep into my heart: 'My child be whole!' At that moment I lost consciousness, due to such an overwhelming happiness that my heart could not stand it.

"When I regained consciousness [after 20 minutes I am told], a thrill went through me, my fingers stretched themselves, I could move them, I could fold my hands. It was then that I cried out in a strong voice: 'I am cured!' I am cured by Our dear Lord through the intercession of Our Blessed Mother! For almost two years I had been deprived of my full voice and before I could realize it I had called out aloud. When the dressings were removed they were saturated with blood and matter, the hand however, appeared to have a pale white color, but was warm and of normal size, the fingers were nimble and the wounds closed, covered with fresh skin. For the first time in eight months I could fold my hands and make the sign of the cross. People crowded around me; everyone wished to see the hand that was cured, and wanted to press and kiss it."

The Aftermath

On the train ride home a surgeon who had accompanied the pilgrimage after asking to look at the miraculously cured hand made a public confession to Elizabeth, "During the entire journey I had been observing you and I did not expect you to reach Lourdes, as I immediately recognized your disease and its advanced stages. I knew death was at your door — and now —! Is it possible that there are people that do not want to believe in God?" At these words he pressed her hand and two big tears rolled down his cheeks. It was then he confessed, "I, too, belonged to that class of people. For a long time I had given up my faith. I said to my father, "I am going to Lourdes in order to collect material against God and His Mother. And now — next to God it is to you that I owe my conversion. I believe! I promise you to do all in my power to defend Our Blessed Mother." He kept his promise and was noted for his extraordinary devotion to Our Lady of Lourdes. Upon arriving home, a specialist who had treated Elizabeth over the years asked to see her. Elizabeth described that moving scene:

"As soon as the door opened and the next patient was to be called in, the doctor recognized me and asked me to come right in. He shook my hand and said: 'I need no longer ask you how you are for I see it with my own eyes. How wonderful and great God is! Kindly permit me to ask you this question: Could I, too, go to Lourdes, although I am a Jew?' After I assured him that there may be just as many non-Catholic doctors in Lourdes as Catholic ones he immediately made an inquiry as to the best route to the shrine. When I took leave he said to me, 'God has done great things for you. I shall send you my certificate, for I have treated you for five years without any hope for your recovery.'"

From this account we can readily see how the miracles at Lourdes and other Marian shrines are not an end in themselves but a

"This sanctuary [Lourdes] shines on the face of the Catholic world as the center of Marian devotion and as the glorious throne of the mystery of the Eucharist."
— Pope St. Pius X

tremendous witness of the power of God and an effective means of conversion. And what about Elizabeth Tembrock? She eventually founded a missionary branch of the Conceptionist Order, and spent many years in the Brazilian missions — in the last twelve years directing her congregation of sisters from a sick bed, offering her suffering as a victim for the sanctification of priests.

In conclusion; throughout the above account of Elizabeth Tembrock we see Mary and Jesus working together. In the beginning of this chapter, we showed the intimate and all embracing relationship between our Lady and our Lord in the Blessed Sacrament, especially at the Shrines of the Mother of God. We can readily see that one cannot have one without the other. To reverse the crisis of faith in the central Mystery of our Faith — the Real Presence of our Lord in the Blessed Sacrament — there has to be a return to true devotion to Mary Immaculate. When Catholics anchor their faith on these two indestructible, inseparable pillars — the Eucharist and Our Lady — then and only then will the enemy of mankind, as in the prophetic dream of Don Bosco, be defeated and a great calm and peace will descend upon both the Church and the world.

The Greatest Miracle of All

A parish priest in France had a tremendous amount of work in organizing a pilgrimage to Lourdes. Accidentally one of the train tickets fell into the hands of an unbeliever. Etienne, a giant of a man, thought this a huge joke. He decided he would make use of the ticket so that he could see the "superstition" of Lourdes at firsthand.

Etienne accompanied the pilgrimage everywhere it went in Lourdes. While the others walked with their hands folded in prayer, he sauntered along with his hands in his pockets. While others prayed reverently at the grotto or filled containers at the taps, he leaned nonchalantly against the railing in front of the grotto, gazing in amused contempt at the pilgrim's piety. What stories he would have to tell his freethinking friends when he went back home!

The only reason Etienne's peculiar behavior had escaped the notice of the priest was that the latter had been kept very busy directing the pilgrimage. Everyone else had noticed the man. While the pilgrimage was organizing to take part in the procession of the Blessed Sacrament, the priest seized Etienne by the arm. My friend, he said, you are the very man I need. We have new banner, and it is very heavy. You are strong; carry it in the procession."

He thrust the banner into the hands of the surprised Etienne. It was a great floating satin banner with the Crucifix painted on one side and the name of the parish on the other. Before the man could say a word, someone had removed his hat. Etienne shrugged his shoulders. Well why not? He had come to Lourdes as a joke; he might as well carry the joke to its conclusion. He marched off carrying the banner; on his face a cynical smile.

Once the priest moved up the line and asked Etienne if the banner were too heavy. Etienne shrugged him off, and the priest went back, singing with the rest of the pilgrims. Later the priest caught up with him again. The man appeared to be suffering from the heat.

"Let someone else carry the banner for a while," said the priest. Etienne refused roughly. The priest was puzzled. None of the parishioners had ever spoken to him in such a manner. Who was this man? A short time later, the word was passed down the line that the man carrying the banner seemed to be sick. The priest hurried to him again. The man looked white and agonized. Perspiration and tears poured down his face. Alarmed, the priest motioned for another man to come forward to take the banner.

"This banner, my friend... " he began as he reached to take it from Etienne's grasp. "Banner!" gasped Etienne, "You call this a banner! It is God on His Cross I have carried, and His sorrows have broken my heart. No, no, I will finish my Way of the Cross, and look you, then, Monsieur le Curé, I will make my submission." A cure of that kind demonstrates God's mercy more than all the cures of the body and is more typical of the spirit of Lourdes.

— Don Sharkey from the book, ***After Bernadette***

Our Lady of Lourdes

Guardian and Teacher of the Faith

Bishop Pierre-Marie Theas of Tarbes and Lourdes

In the following condensation of a pastoral letter of the late Bishop Pierre-Maria Theas we find the antidote to the crisis of faith on our day. The holy bishop shows in the message and apparitions of Our Lady at Lourdes all that is needed to strengthen and augment one's Catholic Faith.

THE BLESSED VIRGIN is our Mother. Lourdes has proven to us that Mary loves our diocese, our world, and our century with a love of predilection. She is completely disposed, therefore, to procure for her children the treasure she knows to be the most precious, the most sacred, and the most indispensable for their happiness.

The only true richness of our soul consists in the state of grace, the supernatural life, and the friendship of God. But faith is the first condition of this life: it is "the foundation and root of all justification" (Council of Trent); it is "the substance of things to be hoped for." (Heb. 11:1) Without doubt, charity is the queen of all virtues. It is inseparable from the state of grace and blends itself with holiness. Alone, it continues in the next life to be the measure of our happiness and glory. But charity presupposes faith; charity depends upon faith; charity is as it were, the expansion of faith.

WHAT IS FAITH?

It is adherence by the light of God and with the help of His grace to all that He reveals to us.

Faith is, first of all, the adherence of the intellect to an objective truth which we have learned from the revelation of God and which we hold to be true because of the authority of God who deigns to make it known to us and who can neither deceive nor be deceived. Faith bows before the dignity, the truthfulness, the holiness, the majesty of God, thus rendering to Him a priceless homage. This is the first of all the other donations that man will make of himself and it is the greatest, for it is the pride of his mind that he sacrifices. This homage is all the more meritorious inasmuch as the truths of our faith oblige us to conform our conduct to them, to mortify our passions, and to walk not in darkness but in the light.

When discord exists between one's faith and life, when through sin the soul is deprived of the state of grace, faith still remains. If the sinner has not fallen into heresy, he will continue to adhere to Catholic dogma by virtue of an intimate disposition which is a gift of God. Do not underestimate this faith, which according to the Apostle St. James (2: 7), theological language, and the Council of Trent is called a dead faith because it is not able of itself to procure eternal life. In the encyclical *Mystici Corporis* His Holiness Pius XII paternally embraces these numberless souls who "having lost charity and sanctifying grace by sin, still have the faith and Christian hope." He assures us that, "The Holy Spirit never ceases to impel them to a salutary fear and to excite them to prayer and repentance." They belong to the Mystical Body under the title of "Sick members of Jesus Christ."

This is precisely the grace of our pilgrimage (it is also a mission that is especially given to Our Lady of Lourdes) to transform this somnolent faith into charity, and to enliven the souls who up until now have not had the courage to break with sin. We could never say enough about how much this gift and virtue of faith means to us in this life. Is it not through this virtue well understood, faithfully guarded, and carried to its limits that our soul attains here its fullness, that is to say, that it realizes fully the plan of God for it? On the contrary, let it become insipid, waver, or, above all, weaken and the entire supernatural edifice crumbles, supernatural faith is compromised and our apostolate perverted.

Bishop Theas of Lourdes gives Benediction beneath the statue of the Immaculate.

Our Lady of Lourdes is the guardian of this treasure of faith; she is the inspiration and teacher of faith; she is the inspiration and teacher of the virtue of faith. She has this office by right, by desire, and by love because she is our

Mother. A mother watches over the possessions of her children even if the weakness of their age (let us understand this of the entire course of our mortal life) prevents them from appreciating what they have. In reality, at Lourdes is it not the invisible and sweet presence of Mary who, delicately and by mysterious paths, leads us to God? What a moving avowal of this fact is made by those who, at Lourdes, have passed from a dead to a living faith, from spiritual blindness to light, from unbelief to faith.

Why don't we recognize it? There is at the Grotto of Massabielle a forceful reminder of the simplicity and poverty of the Grotto of Bethlehem. Without placing the crib of the Incarnate Word and the apparitions of Massabielle on the same plane, let us remember that at Lourdes the Christian faith received something of the light of Christmas and that there is in the human framework and the story of Lourdes a little of that humble and divine poetry that St. Luke has so well expressed in his story of the Nativity.

If we consider faith from the aspect of its object, it is necessary to say that at Lourdes the perspectives of faith are at once very vast, very rich, and very simple. It is satisfying to the demands of the most able theologians, revealing to them a profundity and depth in the understanding of spiritual mysteries. Faith is also within the grasp of the most simple soul, thanks to the sensible expression that these mysteries have miraculously received there. This is why it is that the simple souls are the ones who never weary of going to Lourdes. It is they who unconsciously give the tone to the place, then direct and maintain it. Their supernatural instinct is never at fault. Others, casting off all human respect and intellectual pride, join themselves to the people and pray with them and believe with them, for it has pleased You, O Lord "to reveal these things to the little and humble and to hide them from the strong and great." (Lk.10:21)

Humble souls never have difficulty submitting themselves to the authority of the Sovereign Pontiff. More than anyone else, the Holy Father knows the dangers which menace the Christian faith in a certain epoch and in the entire world in general.* Sin is a sad reality, but the Redemption and grace is sovereignly efficacious. This is what the light

---

*** Bishop Theas recalls and quotes Pope Pius XII in his Encyclical *Humani Generis* of August 1950 "... against the false opinions which threaten to undermine the foundations of Catholic doctrine." The Holy Father puts us on guard against the "new theology which under the pretext of adapting itself to modern times mitigates the rigor and immutability of metaphysical principles. It attempts to make precise dogmatic definitions more yielding, to reverse the meaning and contents of the supernatural and its intimate structure, spiritualize and modernize the theology of the Holy Eucharist, to renovate and reconcile with modern thoughts the sentiments and doctrine of Redemption, the nature and effects of sin and several other points." One can readily see that today's deviations and dissent predate Vatican Council II. They all existed, less visibly but just as real before as now.**

of Lourdes never ceases to show us. The mystery of sin and grace are both contained in the words of the vision of March 25, 1858: "I am the Immaculate Conception." These words heard by the child, untiringly repeated by her, affirm, in a setting and circumstances that make them understandable to all, the double reality of sin and grace.

The privilege which Mary proclaimed is an exceptional grace which represents in a high degree the supernatural order and recalls all the graces that are continually offered to us. Moreover, because the Immaculate Conception is a unique privilege, it reminds us of the common law — we are all born with original sin. None of us is so strong as to be without sin. (Jn. 8: 7). That is why we reply "pray for us sinners" to the invocation, "Hail Mary, full of grace."

It is through Jesus first and principally that we receive grace which on one hand triumphs over sin, and on the other elevates us to the sublime order to which God has destined us. It is through Our Lady of Lourdes that grace of redemption is continually offered to us: grace of purification and recovery, of opposition to sin, of reparation for sin, and of compassion for sinners. The Mother of Mercy invites the pilgrims of Lourdes to this supreme form of charity which pities and relieves the most oppressive of miseries — that of sin. And when one thinks of the numberless crowds of sinners who at Lourdes pass from death to life, from mediocrity to fervor, one admires and proclaims with transports of joy the omnipotence and triumph of divine grace.

LOURDES AND THE MYSTERY OF THE EUCHARIST

Faith in the Eucharist is not weak at Lourdes. It is, on the contrary, affirmed daily there, and in the most stirring and solemn manner. Nowhere will one find emphasis as vibrant, as enthusiastic and as drawing as at Lourdes during the processions of the Blessed Sacrament. As St. Pius X wrote to Bishop Schoepfer, "this sanctuary shines on the face of the Catholic world both as the center of Marian cult and as the most glorious throne of the mystery of the Eucharist." Lourdes is truly the city of the Blessed Sacrament.

The Eucharist will always remain the mystery of mysteries. If faith consists essentially in the adherence of the intellect to a truth and a truth which goes beyond us, which is shown to us not by the logic of a reasoning, nor by the evidence of the senses, nor by a direct intellectual intuition, but by the testimony alone of God, on the word of God, then we must say that nowhere does this word weigh more than in the mystery of the Eucharist. . . .

The Christian faith of which Our Lady of Lourdes is the guardian is essentially the Catholic faith. She helps us adhere to the truths revealed by God, but presented, proposed, and defined as such by the Church. The Church, in reality, has received the complete and universal mission to teach, that is, to guard the deposit of faith, to interpret the Scriptures (which always ought to be learned at the feet of Holy Mother the Church), and to express and formulate traditions. The Church, through the liturgy, breaks the bread of doctrine while taking into account the differences of race, capacities, times, and places. We must be grateful to the Church for fulfilling with vigilance, sometimes with jealousy, the mission of distributing the bread of truth to her children. The Church has found a faithful climate for this at Lourdes. . . .

The best way to scatter darkness is to make the light shine. The characteristic of the preaching at Lourdes is the purest orthodoxy. . . . The Blessed Virgin has the interests of her Son so much at heart that she vigilantly maintains the pilgrims, priests and faithful, in the strictest and most trusting union with the Church. Who is there who has not experienced at the moment when the invocations rise from the vast esplanade towards the Blessed Sacrament (perhaps the most solemn moment of the day at Lourdes) an impression of order, of continuity, and of plenitude when the acclamation resounds: *Our Lady of Lourdes, bless the Pope, the vicar of Jesus Christ.* His absence would have left an emptiness in the intellect and even more so in the heart. . .

When our bishops come to Lourdes with their delegations (sometimes very imposing), they have the impression that they have been followed by their entire diocese, that here as nowhere else they are united to their flock in intimate trust and holy familiarity because pastors and flocks are reunited in the presence of Our Lady. Yes, truly at Lourdes the Christian people are gathered close to their hierarchy and to the Roman pontiff. Here they are more aware of that which is the object of faith: the reality of the Mystical Body, the mysterious and inexpressible bonds which unite the members of the true church, and in the first place, the bonds which attach the faithful, not only to Jesus Christ, but to the visible head of each particular church and to the Vicar of Christ, who is at the same time Bishop of Rome and Bishop of the entire Catholic Church. As you can see, at Lourdes the great Christian mysteries of grace, of the Eucharist, and of the Church are revealed in a clearer light. Let us invoke the Virgin of Massabielle as the guardian and teacher of our faith.

When our enraptured eyes look upon the white statue girded in blue which stands in the hollow of the rock, from our hearts must arise with greater spontaneity the invocation of the Litany of Loretto: *Virgo fidelis, ora pro nobis,* Virgin most Faithful, pray for us. Mary is surely the faithful Virgin, the model of perfect faith. That is why she is able to ask and obtain for us the preservation and growth of this treasure. The Gospel declares her blessed because she believed; she believed in the accomplishment of what had been told to her on the part of the Lord (Lk.1:45). She believed the word of God as transmitted by the angel, as we must believe the word of God as it comes from the Church.

For her as for us, but in a different manner, there was an area of darkness. This gave her the merit of faith. How solemn and mysterious are the words of the angel: "The Holy Spirit will come upon you and the power of the Most High will overshadow you." (Lk 1: 35) The day came when this faith caused her sorrow as she did not understand the attitude of her Son, a child, when He remained at the Temple. How natural is the reproach that she addressed to Him, "My Son, why have you done this? Your father and I have sought you sorrowing." (Lk 2:48) But above all can we imagine the interior struggle of Mary as she stood at the foot of the cross? What heroic faith she had to have to maintain in her heart, in spite of all the contrary and crushing appearances, a most confident hope in the Resurrection. Her faith, perfect and unalterable in all points, was subject to the difficulties and trials to which ours is submitted.

We know now why we should not separate the two titles: Virgin most faithful and Our Lady of Lourdes. O Mary, Model of faith during your earthly life, and now guardian and teacher of the faith at Lourdes, purify and augment our faith!

Condensation of pastoral letter of Bishop Pierre-Marie Theas, of Tarbes and Lourdes, translated by Bro. Patrick Phil, S.M.

A Marian Reprint

At the Battle of the Marne, W.W. I. . .

She Pushed Back the Germans

The National television program titled, "Alcoa Presents" opened with a court-martial of some German soldiers during World War I. The half hour program was one of a series of authentic stories of the supernatural and preternatural. The soldiers were being court-martialed for what they carelessly revealed, as "top secret." What was this "top secret" for which they were eventually shot? Each soldier told an identical story of seeing during the decisive first battle of the Marne, which checked the German advance, a Lady in white with a blue sash around her waist. Each told his version. One said that when he saw the Lady he was unable to move. The next soldier had a similar story to tell. With reason the German High Command did not wish this to be known, as the Battle of the Marne in 1914 checked the German advance which could have easily taken Paris in days.

Raymond Recouly in his careful study, "Foch, the Winner of the War," describes the brilliant leadership of Marshal Foch in the fierce four-day battle of the Marne which he held was "the greatest military victory of all time." In his analysis he attributed the victory to the Marshal's teaching of the French War School, that battles are won morally rather than by superior forces and firepower. When he ordered the attack at the Battle of the Marne, one of his generals objected that his troops were exhausted. The Marshal answered, "The Germans are still more so. You will attack."

Over and above the iron will of this indomitable soldier and his genius in making a right move at the critical time, what wasn't mentioned was the hidden and invincible power of prayer, and the place of the Sacred Heart of Jesus in the victory. Foch and many of the French soldiers wore on their uniforms an emblem of the Heart of Jesus. On the white panel of the miniature French flag was woven the Heart of Jesus as described by St. Margaret Mary and beneath it in letters of gold, "ESPOIR ET SALUT DE LA FRANCE" (Hope and Salvation of France).

Hilliard Atteridge in his book *Marshal Ferdinand Foch* (Dodd Mead & Co., NY) writes: "The religion that he was taught in his

Pyrenean home and later in the Jesuit College, was something not merely to be professed, but to be practiced. It has been a real force in the shaping of his career. (p.283). Day after day, he found time for morning Mass. . . and went again to pray before the altar (p.284). It was enough for him that he finds help in prayer and that in times of danger the Sacraments of the Church are for him as well as for the simple soldier in the ranks, the well-known way of preparing to face death as the beginning of a new life (p.285). He was more than once seen (among his soldiers on the actual battlefront) kneeling among his officers and men at the Masses celebrated under the open sky (p.284). When a telegram arrived that required his immediate attention, he was sought and found alone in a little chapel, kneeling in prayer before the Blessed Sacrament. (p.285)."

As mentioned above, Marshal Foch came from the Pyrenees. His mother had a saintly little friend whom she would accompany at times to pray a Rosary in a Grotto just outside the little town of Lourdes. The name of her little companion? St. Bernadette Soubirous. Understandably the friend of Bernadette, the Marshal's mother, brought him up to have special love of Mary and her Rosary. "Always be faithful to your Rosary," she used to tell him. "Never let a day go by without saying it devoutly." When he came to die the famous general held a Rosary in his hand.

The national French hero, who was awarded the Grand Cross of the Legion of Honor, recognized where victory came from. He used to say: "I interiorly consecrated my armies to the Blessed Virgin whose Rosary I recited every day. I think that I did not miss a single day in reciting it, including the most terrible times of battle, when I had no rest night or day. How often did I see her manifest intercession in the decisions which I made in choosing a precise tactic. Take, then, the advice of an old soldier seasoned by experience: Do not neglect the recitation of the Rosary for any reason."

Now to return to the account above of the young German soldiers being court-martialed. An independent verification of Our Lady of Lourdes appearing before the advancing German army is found in an article "Stories of the Great War" that appeared in the French magazine, *La Semaine D'Averbode* (Everybody's Weekly) of April 10, 1927. The following is a translation from the French: "A German priest wounded and taken prisoner at the Battle of the Marne died in a French ambulance where sisters were nursing. He said to them: "As a soldier, I ought to keep silence, as a priest I think it my duty to tell you what I have seen during the battle of the Marne. All of us were dumbfounded at being pushed back because, compared to the French forces, we were "legion" and quite expected to reach Paris soon. We saw the Blessed

Central focus in the Esplanade is the crowned statue of the Immaculate. On March 25, the feast of the Annunciation, Mary identified herself as the "Immaculate Conception." Two scenes separated by almost two-thousand years: "I am the handmaid of the Lord," and "I am the Immaculate Conception." Here, as at Nazareth, the same humble Virgin, recognizing how God has done great things in her. At the Lourdes grotto, as in the house of Nazareth, Mary is making the same total offering of her will to the Will of God. As one theologian points out "The mystery of the Immaculate Conception is at the heart of the mystery of our Redemption."

Virgin dressed in white with a blue sash around her waist. She was looking towards the South. She was turning away from us and her right hand seemed to be pushing us back. I saw her and a great many of our men saw her too."

In an independent account, two German officers, wounded and taken prisoners in the same battle, were in a Red Cross ambulance. A nurse who understood German accompanied them. When they entered a ward in the hospital where a statue of Our Lady of Lourdes was in a conspicuous place, they looked at each other for a few brief moments, then exclaimed, "Oh! The Virgin of the Marne." The nurse tried to get them to explain, but they refused.

A nun nursing the wounded at Issyles-Moulinaux writes: "Among the wounded soldiers was a German who it was thought would soon die. Thanks to the good care lavished upon him, he lived more than a month. He was a Catholic and gave proofs of an ardent faith. Since all the infirmarians were priests, spiritual help was not lacking. Deeply moved by the care he received, he did not know how to express his gratitude and repeated unceasingly, "'I should like to do something to thank you.' At last, on the day he received the last Sacraments, he said to one of the priests, 'I am your enemy and you treated me like one of your own. I want to do something for you by telling you of an incident which is not in our favor, but in that way I shall pay my debt to you. If I were at the front I would be shot as it has been forbidden to us under death penalty to repeat what I am going to tell you. You must have been surprised at our falling back when we had nearly reached the gates of Paris, but we simply could not go further. A Virgin was standing before us pushing us back each time we received orders to advance. We were as if nailed to the ground. We finally realized that it was the Blessed Virgin. On September 8th, the feast of her nativity, she repelled us so forcibly that we all fled.'"

In conclusion, we have a devout Catholic General, whose mother was a companion of St. Bernadette in praying the Rosary at the Grotto at Lourdes, who himself prayed the Rosary daily, consecrated his armies to the Blessed Virgin and spent an hour of prayer the first thing in the morning and another hour in prayer late at night. He and many of his men wore a Sacred Heart patch on their uniforms. He was the man who turned the tide in the battle of the Marne — but did he? There is solid evidence that besides his ardent prayers and military genius, he had a Woman behind him who had all the power of God behind her, and didn't hesitate to use it at the appropriate time in answer to prayers.

—Compiled from several sources by the editor

Bernadette Speaks from the Heart

The Blessed Mother is so beautiful that, when one has once laid eyes upon her. One would joyfully die in order to see her again.

How favored you are in being sent to care for the poor and miserable. Learn to love your little orphans. Do all to make them comfortable and. above all, teach them to love God.

Pray for all sinners. The Blessed Virgin insisted so much on the necessity of praying for sinners.

Perhaps we do not mortify ourselves sufficiently. Let us try to do more. I will always do what costs me most. Great sickness is always a special privilege from your Divine Spouse. God requires victims.

The simple Gospel stories affect me most.

O Mary, my Blessed Mother. grant that love may motivate my every action and my accepting suffering. My God, I promise you, with the assistance of your grace, to show my love for you by accepting without a murmur the trials and disappointments you may send me, whether through my superiors or my companions or even through the evil one himself.

O Jesus, help me realize more fully the jealousy of the Divine Lover, detach my affections from creatures, may my affections raise me up and bind me to You.

At least I can accept with joy privations. sufferings and humiliations like Jesus and Mary, and offer them up for the glory of God. For the love of Our Lord I will show special affection toward those who may have been the cause of mortification for me.

Our Lord gives a crown of thorns to his friends on earth, do not look for anything better.

We ought always to behave with the Blessed Virgin like children at their mother's side. You can never love her, the divine Mother, enough. If you only knew how good she is! One day I shall see her again, this dearest of Mothers.

Put yourself under her protection, you will never do so in vain. Place yourself in the heart of Mary and remain there: make it your home while here on earth. O Mother, in your heart I come to bury my anguish and to seek strength and courage!

Not my will, but your will be done. Blessed Mother, as it is always that of Jesus. Let us always submit ourselves to the will of God. I desire only God's holy will. What sacrifice! It is no sacrifice to leave this miserable earth. where it is so difficult to serve God.

Whenever I am suffering, I will ever come and seek refuge in your heart, sweet Mother, and pray you not to let me perish. but to grant me the grace to bear all with resignation and confidence, and suffer lovingly, as you did. O Mother, may I, like you, remain at the foot of the cross. if such be the will of your dear Son! O Mother, offer me to Jesus!

O Mother, come to my aid! Grant me the grace to die to myself so that I may no longer live except through and for my Jesus.

What folly to draw back when our Lord seeks our hand to nail it to the cross! Henceforth, the more I am crucified, the more I will rejoice. No, no, not consolation, but strength and patience. My God, give me, I pray you, the love of the cross! I will bear the cross, concealed within my heart, with courage and generosity.

O my God, if I may not shed my blood or give my life for you, at least let me die to all that is displeasing to you! For the love of Jesus I will do violence to my feelings even in the smallest matters. My Jesus, how I love you!

O Jesus, give me, I implore you, the bread of patience to support the grief which tortures my heart. O Jesus, your will is to crucify me....your will be done." Give me the bread of strength that I may be able to suffer. Grant that I may see you alone in all things and forever.

My Divine Spouse has given me a predilection for the humble and hidden life. He has often told me that my heart will know no rest till I have sacrificed everything for Him. . . .O folly of follies to attach myself to anything other than Him. I am happier, with my crucifix, on my bed of pain than a queen on her throne.

Heaven! Heaven! Let us determine to go to heaven, let us work for it, suffer for it! Everything else is of no value. You don't seem to know that dear St. Joseph is now my father. I have asked St. Joseph for the grace of a happy death. It all counts for heaven.

My God, I love you with all my heart, with all my soul and with all my strength. Holy Mary, Mother of God, pray for me, a poor sinner. *(These were St. Bernadette's last words.)*

PART V

Pontmain, January 17, 1871

Our Lady of Hope

- Meeting the "Conflagration" of the Nineteenth Century
- Pontmain — The Lady of Hope
- Other Providential Events

Left: The Barbedette barn. Right: The Pontmain seers, left to right: Eugene, Joseph, Jean Marie and Françoise.

Left: Parish church and Guildecoq house along side of it. Other side of Square, the Barbedette barn.

Pontmain, 1871

Meeting the "Conflagrations" of the 19th Century

It is interesting to note that the optimists of the nineteenth Century who held infallible the *dogma* of "progress" carefully omitted the Church. World leaders and political scientists, of a liberal bent, felt sure that the Church would never survive the century. With nationalism on the rise, the little Papal States under their king, the Pope, which divided the northern part of Italy from the southern part, were continually threatened by revolutionary movements intent on uniting the north and the south and swallowing up the Papal States into a "greater" Italy. The Pope's influence in the political sphere was nil and the Papal States along with the Pope were considered by many to be moribund.

It was expected that once the Church had no territory or army to act as a buffer to prevent outside governments from meddling in Church affairs, the sovereignty of the Popes, along with the Papal States, would soon come to an end. They were right about the Papal States, but absolutely wrong about the papacy, which without any territory of its own, actually became stronger and more influential than ever before.

To those without the Faith it seemed quite plausible in the early part of the 19th century that the Papacy would not survive. Pope Pius VII was taken prisoner to France by Napoleon, and lived in exile from Rome for almost a decade. When the Pope excommunicated him, the French leader remarked, "Does he expect now the guns of my soldiers to drop from their arms?" They actually did in the freezing disastrous winter retreat of his armies from Russia. The ailing, aged Pope eventually returned to Rome in triumph.

When Pope Pius IX was elected Pope in 1846 amidst great popular acclaim as a modern, "liberal" Pope, it was unthinkable that within the short space of two years revolutionaries converging on Rome would assassinate his Prime Minister, Count Rossi, and force the Pope to flee from Rome for his life. That was but the beginning of countless threats against the Church and the saintly Pope Pius IX in one of the longest pontificates in the history of the Church. Nor was Italy alone in experiencing great political unrest.

Following the French revolution the nineteenth century was a period of continual revolutions throughout Europe. They were for the most part engineered by radical liberals who cared little for law and order, much less stability. In fact they fomented the opposite in order to bring down established, stable governments. As such they were against the State and the Church — at enmity with both.

The industrial revolution at that time played into the hands of the revolutionaries. Newly rich, ruthless entrepreneurs were responsible for grave social injustices and imbalances between the *haves* and the *have nots*, between the working class and the capitalists. This exploitation of the working class was played up by Karl Marx in his *Das Capital.* From this he developed his theory of class warfare and his radical socialism or Communism. The exploitation of the working class happened so suddenly and was of such magnitude that the Church was caught off guard and slow to react.

It was only towards the end of the century that Pope Leo XIII with his social encyclicals took up the cause and plight of the working class, and exposed the evils of laissez-faire capitalism. Unfortunately by then the church, associated with the tottering crown, was unjustly held responsible for the miseries of the working class and thus lost many Catholics, especially the workers of France.

Yet, it was to France, the cradle of nineteenth century revolutions, that Our Lady came to checkmate forces that were intent in destroying the Church. During the period from 1830 to 1871, four major apparitions of Our Lady took place in France — Rue du Bac, Paris (Miraculous Medal), 1830; La Salette, 1846; Lourdes, 1858; and Pontmain, 1871. In this second, updated edition of the book which was originally titled, *You Will Make This Known to My People*, we have added the apparition of Our Lady of Hope at Pontmain to give a more complete picture of how Mary's intervention in nineteenth century France set the stage for the apparitions at Fatima and the Age of Mary we are now experiencing — the culmination of which will be the triumph of her Immaculate Heart as promised at Fatima and the Social Reign of the Sacred Heart of Jesus.

The first phase of Our Lady of Pontmain as she appeared over the house of Augustin Guidecog. About twenty feet above the center of the roof Eugene Barbedette saw a tall, beautiful Lady. Her dress was blue, much darker than the blue of the surrounding sky and was covered with golden stars. It fell in loose folds to her feet. Over her head was a soft black veil and on that she wore a golden crown. Her face was small and was incomparably beautiful. She appeared to be about twenty years old. Her arms were at her sides and the palms of her hands were turned out, similar to the image of the Miraculous Medal.

Below: An airial view of the town of Pontmain with the large Basilica of Our Lady of Hope dominating the scene. Nearby are the House of the Oblates of the Oblate Fathers to the left is the pilgrims guest house operated by Sisters.

Pontmain – Our Lady of Hope

Bro. Francis Mary Kalvelage, FI

At the time of Our Lady's apparition to the six French children, aged two to eleven, Pontmain was a typical small town in western France, about two hundred miles from Paris. However, it was exceptional in one way. All agree that the Parish priest of Pontmain, Curé Guerin, was a pious man who gave himself unstintingly to the spiritual welfare of his five hundred parishioners. His effort, in the thirty-five years he was their shepherd, was blessed with deeply religious people who never worked on Sundays and were never heard to take the name of the Lord in vain. The children respected their elders and were well instructed in the Faith by Religious Sisters.

Such was not the case throughout France as indicated in the chapter, "A Mother Weeps for Her Children" (page 47) in this book. Both at Paris and La Salette, Our Lady had warned the people of France of impending disasters if they did not repent and return to the practice of their Faith. At Lourdes, she cried out, "Penitence! Penitence!" Penitence in this broad sense of the word means, amend your lives and make sacrifice in reparation for one's personal sins and the sins of all men. Though there was a change of heart among many Frenchmen after La Salette, and thus the predicted chastisements of revolutions, crop failures, famines and infant mortality were lessened, many still continued in their sinful ways.

Some of the most brilliant minds the world has ever seen — French journalists, writers, scientists, college professors, and government leaders, in their intellectual pride — arrogantly ignored God and despised religious practices, leading many ordinary Catholics astray. As so frequently happens in world history, God allowed the scourge of war and the humiliation of enemy conquest and occupation to straighten out His people. In 1870, the Franco-Prussian War broke out. The Prussians under the Iron Chancellor Bismarck invaded France and surrounded Paris in the fall of 1870. By December, the Parisians were under daily bombardment, starving, desperate and in deadly fear of a violent death at any moment. People in eastern France were under occupation while other parts of France lived in terror of being invaded.

Millions of French people turned to Mary, their mother and protector in their hour of trial. At Our Lady of Victories church in Paris, as well as at La Salette and Lourdes large crowds gathered to seek her intercession for their beloved country. In parish churches, in homes throughout France, the ordinary people — peasants, workingmen, small shopkeepers —turned to Mary by the thousands. They fervently prayed the Rosary. She heard their prayers and was touched.

In the northwest corner of the department of Mayenne, bordering Brittany, in the little village of Pontmain the Barbedette family prayed fervently for the end of hostilities. Their eldest son, Auguste, was in the army in September 1870. The two remaining sons of the Barbedettes, twelve year old Eugene and ten year old Joseph, were pious and prayerful lads who were gifted by a vision of Our Lady on January 17, 1871.

Tuesday, January 17, 1871, began in much the same way as other days in the Barbedette household. The father woke the boys at six o'clock in the morning. They did their household chores and then recited a Rosary for their brother in the army. After breakfast they went to the village chapel to make the Way of the Cross for their brother's intention. Then they served Mass. After Mass, they joined in the public prayers for France and her army. The Curé often reminded his people, "Let us add penance to our prayers, and then we may take courage. God will have pity on us. His mercy will surely come through Mary."

That evening around 6:00 PM a neighbor, Jeannette Detais, stopped by to pass on some news about Auguste, their soldier son. She found the father and the two boys in their barn with mallets preparing fodder for their horses. The noisy work was discontinued while she and Mr. Barbedette conversed, affording Eugene a break. He walked over and looked out the barn door.

As he later related, "I just went to see what the weather was like." He was suddenly transfixed, his whole attention focused above a neighbor's house. About twenty feet above the center of the roof he saw a tall, beautiful Lady. Her dress was blue, much darker than the blue of the surrounding sky and was covered with golden stars. It fell in loose folds to her feet. She wore dark blue slippers fastened with golden ribbons. Over her head was a soft black veil and on that she wore a golden crown. Her face was small and was incomparably beautiful. She appeared to be about twenty years old. Her arms were at her sides and the palms of her hands were turned out, similar to the image of the Miraculous Medal.

The Lady was smiling at the boy. As he was gazing in awe, Jeannette Detais, who had delivered her message, came to the door of the barn beside Eugene. Excitedly he said to her, "Look, Jeannette, and tell me what you see over Augustin Guidecog's house!"

"My goodness, Eugene, I can't see anything," she replied to the boy who gazing intently at the starry sky. Eugene called his father and brother over. The father could not see anything either, but Joseph exclaimed excitedly,

"Oh, I see a beautiful tall Lady!" He then described her dress in detail.

"My poor boys," the father said, "you don't see anything; if you did we could see it too." He told the boys to come back and finish their chores. To Jeannette he said, "Be sure and not mention in the village what the children say they saw."

"You need not fear," Jeannette answered.

The boys obediently returned to their work, but had hardly done so when the father told Eugene to look again. The Lady was still there. Then the father told him to get their mother, maybe she would see something. Upon arriving at the door where her son Joseph was clapping his hands rapidly and at the same time crying out,

"Oh, how beautiful she is! Oh! How beautiful she is!" His mother gave him a nudge saying, "Be silent! Everyone is looking at us." By that time a small crowd had gathered.

Eugene turned to his mother. "Mother," he said "look over at the house of Augustine Guideco; do you see something?"

"No. I absolutely see nothing." Struck by the strong conviction of what they were seeing by the tone of their voices and knowing her sons were incapable of lying she suggested that the family kneel and say five Our Fathers and five Hail Mary's in honor of Our Lady. After they had prayed the mother asked them if they still saw the Lady.

"Yes," replied the children, "It is the same."

"Then," she said "I am going to get my glasses, Perhaps I will then see something." She carefully arranged her glasses but in vain. Defensive and cross, she reprimanded the children, "Definitely, you see nothing! You must finish preparing the horse food. You are little liars." They finished their chores in five minutes and the father called them in to supper. They came slowly, with reluctance walking backwards as they faced the Lady. For the first time it cost them much to obey and leave the beautiful Lady. The boys rushed through the meal in order to return to the Lady who was smiling and patiently waiting for them. They fell to their knees and again recited the five Our Fathers and five Hail Mary's. They then returned to the house exclaiming, "It is the same. . . The Lady is the same size as Sister Vitaline."

"Then," Mrs. Barbedette said, "I'll ask Sister to come over. She is better than you. If you see something, she will surely see it too." The nun arrived, but she saw nothing unusual.

"How is it possible you don't see!" exclaimed Eugene. "The apparition is so brilliant. Don't you see those three bright stars forming a triangle?"

"Yes, I see them."

"Well, the highest star is right over the Lady's head; the other two are on a level with her elbows." These three stars were seen by everyone that night. They were never seen again.

Mrs. Barbedette accompanied the nun back to the school. There they found three little girl boarders sitting around the fire. "Children," Sister said, "go with Mrs. Barbedette. She will show you something."

"What is it?" they inquired. "Come and see" she replied. "For my part, I see nothing." The three children set off. Even before reaching the barn, eleven-year-old Françoise Richer exclaimed, "I see something bright above Augustin Guidecog's house!" When they reached the barn door, Françoise and nine-year-old Jeanne-Marie Lebosse cried out together, "Oh, the beautiful Lady, with her blue dress and golden stars!" They described the vision exactly as the Barbedette boys had. The third child saw nothing.

The news spread rapidly, and soon about eighty people — virtually half the population of the village — and the teaching Sisters gathered at the barn door. Sister Mary Edward, much to her sadness, like the rest of the adults saw nothing. She suggested, "Since only the children see, we must get other, younger children." She ran to the house of Mr. Friteau who had a delicate little six-year-old grandson, Eugene. Carried and wrapped in his grandmother's mantel he too beheld the vision, but the sickly child was not allowed to stay long in the cold air. He died a few months later. A two-year-old girl, daughter of Boitin the shoemaker, when brought into the presence of the apparition began clapping her little hands exclaiming "Le Jesus! Le Jesus." These were the only words she knew to describe such a sight. Her mother tried in vain to distract her by showing her other objects, but she always turned her eyes back to the apparition.

The good Curé, when informed of the apparition by the excited Sister Mary Edward, was deeply moved. He repeated her words, "A wonder! An apparition! The Blessed Mother! My Sister, you make me afraid." At first a little reluctant to go, his servant, elderly Jeanette, already had prepared a lantern, saying, "We must go see. . ." As the pastor arrived at the barn door, the children cried out all together, "Oh! something is happening!"

A small red cross formed over our Lady's heart. The apparition became surrounded by a frame or oval of a darker blue than the robe. Four sockets were attached to the inside of the frame. Each socket held an unlighted candle, two at the height of her knees and two at the height of her shoulders. The four children all related these wonders. One simple gentleman said that if he had a telescope he was sure that he too could see what the children were seeing. He was brought one, but for all his efforts he still saw nothing. This incident provoked laughter among the crowd, and they began to talk loudly and joke.

Eugene Barbedette, who stood in the middle of the road cried out, "She is looking sad." The other children confirmed that she had stopped smiling and was sad. The Curé commanded silence and reverence and said, "if the children only are privileged to behold the celestial vision, it is because they are more worthy than we." He then suggested that they pray. Everyone knelt, some in the barn, others outside. No one seemed to mind the bitter cold or the deep snow. Sister Mary Edward led in the recitation of the Rosary.

Left: Our Lady of Pontmain appears surrounded by a frame or oval of a darker blue than the robe. Four sockets were attached to the inside of the frame. Each socket held an unlighted candle. In the next phase of the apparition she raised her hands (right).

Suddenly the vision began to grow larger. "She is twice as tall as Sister Vitaline now!" the children exclaimed. The blue oval was now proportionally extended. The stars in the sky appeared to move aside, as if to allow the Lady to rise. Then they ranged themselves beneath her feet, two by two outside the frame. There were about forty of these stars, and they were visible only to the children. Soon other stars appeared at a distance from the apparition and they fastened themselves on her dress.

"Oh, there are so many stars the Blessed Virgin will soon be gilt all over," one of the children exclaimed. Our Lady smiled during the recitation of the Rosary. As she smiled her open mouth revealed brilliantly white teeth. When the Rosary was completed, Sister Mary Edward began the *Magnificat*. Before the first verse was sung the children cried out, "Something new is happening!"

A plain white band had unrolled itself at the feet of the Lady. It was about a yard wide and it extended the length of the roof of the house. The first stroke of a letter appeared, then the entire letter. The letter was in gold.

"It's an M!" the children cried. "And now there is another letter—it's an A!"

The word "mais", meaning "but" was formed and remained alone for almost ten minutes. During this time Joseph Babin, a fellow townsman, arrived. He shouted to the crowd the frightening news that the Prussians were at nearby Laval. The news made no impression at all on the crowd. As one lady said, "They could be at the entrance of the village and we would not be afraid." When the man was told of the apparition, he too joined the group in their prayers. Before the *Magnificat* was concluded other letters appeared. The children read aloud the golden letters, "**But pray, my children.**"

By now the children were besieged with questions by the Curé, the Sisters and the crowd. They answered without the least hesitation or contradiction. Everyone was deeply moved. No one openly questioned nor laughed now. Many were in tears. The Lady was smiling again. The good Curé requested they sing the litany of Our Lady. At the first invocation, the children cried out, "Look again something is happening; there is a letter "D." More letters appeared on the white band. The new message was, **"God will hear you in a short time."** One can well imagine the joy and emotion of the crowd in receiving this good news. The children related that the lady looked at them and was smiling. They joyfully cried out, "Look she smiles," and then laughing themselves they cried out, "Look she is laughing now."

Next the *Inviolata* was sung. A second line of golden letters began to appear on the white writing space. As they finished singing, "O sweet and beloved Mother of Christ" the children read "**My Son. . .**"

"It is really the Blessed Virgin," they cried. "Yes, yes, it is Mary! It is Mary!" The emotion that filled the hearts of all present cannot be described. Many were in tears. When the sentence was completed it read, **"My Son permits Himself to be moved**." And as to give special emphasis, a large golden underlining, slowly formed beneath this line. The completed message now read, **"But pray my children, God will hear you in a short time. My Son permits Himself to be moved."** This was Mary's message of hope from her Divine Son and the source of great consolation to her afflicted children of France. No words could have been more welcome or prophetic.

The following excerpt from the most accurate account of Pontmain written by Father Richard just a few days after the apparition of January 17, 1871 summarizes well that stirring reaction of the privileged seers and devout crowd.

"'Look she's laughing!' they cried out. And they jumped joyously, clapping their hands, repeating a hundred times with an expression which would be impossible to communicate in words, 'Oh, how beautiful she is! Oh! How beautiful she is!' The crowd laughed and cried at the same time. They saw on the faces of the children, so full of expression and so sincere, a reflection of the smile which caused them such transports of Joy."

At the Curé's suggestion, the people sang the canticle *Mother of Hope*. Sister Edward sang the verse so appropriate to the occasion, "Mother of Hope, of name so sweet, protect our country, pray for us, pray for us!" During the singing of this hymn the Blessed Mother lifted her hands to the height of her shoulders, and moving her hands she seemed to be keeping time with the song. Towards the end of the eight verses, the words at the feet of Our Lady gradually faded away.

After singing another song the children's faces became extremely sad reflecting the sad expression of Our Lady. "Look," they said "she becomes sad again." Then, "look again something is happening."

A red crucifix approximately 2 feet high appeared about a foot in front of our Lady. She took it in her hands and held it out toward the children. At the top of the cross appeared the words **Jesus Christ** in red letters on a white band. After each verse of the hymn, the *Parce Domine* was sung. Our Lady, sad and recollected, was seen praying with the people.

At that point a star shot up from beneath the Virgin's feet and lit the candle at the lower left, then the top one, and then passed over her head and lit the two candles at the right side. It rose again, passed outside the blue circle and came to a stop to remain suspended over Mary's head.

When Sister Edward led the recollected and prayerful crowd in the singing of the *Ave Maris Stella* the crucifix disappeared and the vision assumed the attitude of the Immaculate Conception or of Our Lady on the Miraculous Medal with her hands extended. On each of the shoulders were seen small white crosses about eight inches high.

When the hymn was finished the Curé said: "Now let us all recite our evening prayers."

During the examination of conscience the children's eyes, which never left the smiling face of the Madonna, noticed a white veil rising from beneath Mary's feet and little by little hiding the vision from view. Finally her face, still smiling down upon her children, disappeared. Only the crown with the stars remained. The four candles around the great blue circle remained burning to the end.

"Do you still see anything?" the Curé asked.

"No, Monsieur le Curé. All is over." It was a quarter past nine. The apparition had lasted more than three hours.

And what about the Prussians, who were just a mile outside of the city of Laval on that fateful day of the 17th? With but a small band of exhausted soldiers defending the strategic unfortified city of Laval, the German commander-in-chief assured the bishop of Le Mans on January 17th, "This evening my troops are in Laval." For some inexplicable reason the Prussians never took Laval. The official records of the German high command state that exactly from the evening of January 17th the Prussian troops didn't move a single step further to the west of France. That very night a formal and unexpected order prevented General Schmidt from taking Laval. The night of the 17th the Prussian troops were only a mile from Laval. The very next day they were at Vaiges, twelve miles back from Laval! This retreat is inexplicable and may be considered the great miracle of Pontmain. Besides the prayers of the good people of Pontmain for peace there were other significant events that happened on January 17 (see the following short chapter).

Our Lady was indeed good to the promise that, ". . . God will hear you in a short time."

An armistice was signed on January 27, just ten days after the apparition. France lost the war and had to pay a heavy indemnity, but the bloodshed was over.

The devout visionaries seemed to respond in one way or another to the grace of the apparition. Eugene Barbedette became a diocesan priest and was made rector of Chatillon-sur-Colinont until his death in 1927. Joseph became an Oblate of Mary Immaculate, the order that was put in charge of the shrine at Pontmain. He died at the house of his Congregation in 1930. Françoise Richer, though not a nun, worked as a domestic servant and an assistant teacher in various obscure country schools. Her last years were spent in the service of Abbé Barbedette. She died in 1915. Jeanne-Marie became a religious of the Holy Family Sisters and died at Bordeaux in 1933.

On February 2, 1875, the first Bishop of Laval, Bishop Wicart, approved the devotion to Notre Dame d'Espérance de Pontmain. The barn was converted into an oratory. A great twin-spired gothic church was begun in 1872 on the spot of the apparitions and was completed in 1900. Raised to the rank of a minor basilica by Pope Pius X, it was built as a thanksgiving offering by the provinces of the western part of France preserved from Prussian invasion. The village of Pontmain is just a short 27 miles south of the famous Mont St. Michel, the medieval shrine of Saint Michael which juts out dramatically into the ocean off the coast of Normandy. Pilgrims come in large numbers and the usual number of cures take place there as at other Marian shrines.

What is the unique significance of the apparition of Our Lady of

Left: Next, a star shot out at her feet to light the candles; Our Lady became sad as a red Crucifix appeared about a foot in front of her. She took it in her hands and held it out to the children. Right: In the last phase two white crosses appeared on her shoulders.

The sanctuary of the Basilica of Our Lady of Pontmain which was consecrated on October 15, 1900. It was build in thanksgiving by the provinces of the western part of France who were spared from invasion.

Below: The interior of the Barbedette barn which has been turned into a chapel.

Hope of Pontmain? First, unlike the first two apparitions of Our Lady in the 19th century France — the Miraculous Medal apparitions at Rue du Bac in Paris and at La Salette — which contained prophecies of coming chastisements if men didn't amend their lives, at Pontmain Our Lady focused her motherly attention on her faithful French people with a message of hope in their time of great trial.

At Pontmain she was *the* Woman of the Gospels who spoke little and prayed much. It was her silence, smiles and laughter that spoke a language of love and joy, which were simply inexpressible in human words. The golden words written by the invisible hand of Our Lady were few in number and pointed directly to her Son. She, the Handmaid of the Lord, acknowledges that the one and only cause of her intercessory power is, "**My Son [who] permits Himself to be moved.**" As such she makes it clear in ourage of ecumenism that non-Catholics need not fear Catholics being too devoted to the Blessed Mother. By her example of prayerful silence, humility and ultimate dependence on Jesus, Our Lady sets an example for us all to imitate.

Throughout the apparition the hands of Our Lady were for the most part extended as on the Miraculous Medal, thus symbolizing the Immaculate Conception and Mary Mediatrix, Co-redemptrix and Advocate, from whom all graces flow. The rich symbolism in the various phases of the apparition, especially in the movement and positioning of the stars, have an iconographic meaning which would appeal to the Eastern Church. The two white crosses on the shoulders of Our Lady, one to the east the other to the west, also seem to point to the possible reconciliation of the Orthodox Church with the Church of Rome, effected through their common devotion to the Blessed Mother.

The bright star at the feet of Our Lady which lit the four candles in the oval background remind us of the star on the lower part of the tunic of Our Lady of Fatima. It is said to represent the name of one of the great heroines of the Old Testament, Queen Esther, whose name means star. She saved her people from the evil Amman who wanted to wipe out the Jews during the time they were in Babylonian captivity. In a much deeper, fundamental, spiritual way Mary saves her children, the people of God, from the snares of the great adversary of mankind, the devil, and his minions, intent on their destruction. All of this points out the purpose and continuity of Mary's apparitions, the salvation of immortal souls. As Bishop Paul Richard points out in the preface of the book, *What Happened at Pontmain*, "An entire spirituality unfolds from the apparition of Pontmain which is inexhaustible."

In conclusion, the first word of the message at Pontmain, **"But"**, is of utmost importance. Mary's ability in catching her Son's attention is conditioned by trustful prayer to her for the favors we seek. **"But pray my children."** In today's world, torn by wars, revolutions, and persecutions of the Church, Our Lady of Hope is ready and more than willing to help us toward world peace, **but** we, her children, must pray.

Other Providential Events

As if to focus greater attention to Pontmain several providential incidences occurred in other parts of France on January 17. The first had its beginning in the year 1848 when the pastor of Saint-Brieuc established the "Archconfraternity of Our Lady of Hope" for the salvation of the Church and of France." It was here that the hymn, *Mother of Hope,* was composed, the very same hymn sung a number of times during the apparitions of Pontmain. This was but the beginning of a unique connection between Pontmain and Saint Brieuc.

Thirty-two years later, as the Prussians advanced towards Brittany, disasters and defeats mounted in France. The people of Mother of Hope sanctuary at Saint-Brieuc wasted no time in turning to Our Lady Hope in what seemed to be a hopeless situation by making a solemn vow on the evening January 17th at 5:30 PM. They prayed fervently that evening until 9:00, approximately the same hours (unknown to them) that Our Lady was appearing in Pontmain. These providential connections filled the heart of the holy elderly founder of the Archconfraternity of Our Lady of Hope in Saint-Brieuc with joyful thanksgiving.

The majestic Basilica of Pontmain.

The second instance is tied in with the shrine Our Lady of Victories church in Paris, a church already well known because of its devotions to the Immaculate Heart of Mary. On the night of January 17th, during the time of the apparition, Father Amodru announced to the people present in the church of Our Lady of Victories that at this very hour as he spoke to them, the Blessed Virgin was saving France. A solemn prayer service had begun that evening and was concluded on

January 28th, the date the Armistice was signed.

The following is an excerpt from a letter to Father Amodru, which was inspired by the sermon given by him, "I have just come back from Our Lady of Victories church, profoundly moved by the words which, in an evidently inspired improvisation, you spoke this evening to the numerous faithful united at the foot of the altar of Mary. You said that at that moment a thought presented itself to your spirit. 'We are all going to publicly and solemnly beg the most Blessed Virgin to come to our aid and we will not cross the threshold of this holy temple consecrated to her glory without solemnly promising to offer to her a silver heart, which will recall to future generations that today, between 8:00 and 9:00 in the evening, an entire nation is prostrated at the feet of Our Lady of Victories and has been saved by her...'"

One must understand the background of this church of Our Lady of Victories to fully appreciate this prediction coming at such a critical time from this church in the center of Paris and France. During and after the French revolution this church fell into bad times. Eventually it was returned to the Church and a pastor assigned it. But the pastor, Fr. Des Gennettes, try as he might, could not get the people to return to the practice of their Faith. At a Sunday Mass, December 3, 1836, he was so discouraged at the small congregation that he was tempted to resign. During the Canon of the Mass he heard a strong, distinct voice tell him, "Consecrate your parish to the Most Holy and Immaculate Heart of Mary." Afraid he imagined it, he heard the command again during his thanksgiving.

He not only consecrated his parish to the Immaculate Heart but went one step further by drawing up statutes for a Confraternity of the Holy and Immaculate Heart of Mary, and on the following Sunday inaugurated it. He was overwhelmed by the response. It was the first time the church was filled in many years with a crowd of over 400. The parish continued to flourish from that time on. Approved by Rome, the Archconfraternity of the Immaculate Heart of Mary spread rapidly throughout France and the world, followed by a great wave of devotion to the Sacred Heart of Jesus. This led in turn to a National Vow of the French People to build the Sacred Heart Basilica on the Hill of the Martyrs (Montmartre) overlooking Paris. At the end of December 1870 the formula of the vow was printed, and it was released to the public on January 11th, just a few days before the apparition in Pontmain.

The basilica was a direct result of the request and promises made by the Sacred Heart in His apparitions to St. Margaret Mary Alacoque many years before, but the conditions of which were not fulfilled by the French nation until then. It is also noteworthy that it was at this very time that St. Joseph had been proclaimed the Patron of the Catholic Church (December 8, 1870).

For Further Reading

The Woman Shall Conquer *by Don Sharkey* In the author's own words, "This book is an attempt to tell the story of the Blessed Virgin in the modern world." Don Sharkey, a former reporter, tells the story of the great Marian shrines and approved apparitions of Our Lady from Guadalupe (1531) to Vatican Council II in a very interesting and factual way. At the same time the author's deep love of Our Lady and his knowledge of Mariology shines through it all. Franciscan Marytown Press, 1600 West Park Ave., Libertyville, IL 60048 (5.95).

A Grace Called La Salette *by Fr. Jean Jaouen, M.S.* (Translated into English by Fr. Normand Théroux, M.S.) This 370 page book authored by a La Salette Missionary priest, is the most authoritative and inspirational book on La Salette. It is available from the La Salette Fathers, La Salette Publications, Attleboro, MA 02703 (11.50) Also available from their book store (same address): **La Salette** *by Roger Castel* Beautifully illustrated book of the awesome setting of Our Lady's shrine in the French alps (3.00). **The Beautiful Lady of La Salette,** a large color comic book style story book on La Salette, with a number of color illustrations of the shrine as well. (3.00).

Bernadette Soubirous *By Abbé François Trochu.* This 390 page book is the most complete biography on Saint Bernadette. She comes alive in the writings of Abbé Trochu who is also the author of the definitive biography on the Curé of Ars. It is well illustrated, with 69 photos taken from the time of the apparitions to the present. Tan Books and Publishers, Inc., P.O. Box 424, Rochford, IL 61105.

A Light Shining On the Earth A commemorative booklet recently published by the Daughters of Charity on the occasion of the 50th anniversary of the canonization of St. Catherine Labouré. A biography of the Saint which covers the apparitions as well as the symbolism and other related stories on the Miraculous Medal. The large 8.5" by 12" page formate allows for large illustration. Further information write to: Central Shrine of Our Lady of the Miraculous Medal, 475 Chelten Ave., Philadelphia, PA 19144-5785.

St. Catherine Labouré of the Miraculous Medal *by Fr. Joseph Dirvin*, The Vincentian priest has given us a concise and accurate book on the Saint and the story of the Miraculous Medal. Tan books and publishers, Inc. P.O. Box 424, Rochford, IL 61105.

The Academy of the Immaculate Books

All Generations Shall Call Me Blessed *by Stefano Manelli, F.I.* A scholarly easy to read book tracing Mary's role in the Old Testament through prophecies, figures, and symbols to Mary's presence in the New Testament. A concise exposition which shows clearly Mary's place in the economy of Salvation.

Totus Tuus *by Msgr. Arthur Burton Calkins* Provides a thorough examination of the Holy Father's thoughts on total consecration or entrustment to Our Lady based on the historic, theological and scriptural evidence. Vital in clearing away some misunderstandings about entrustment and consecration.

Jesus Our Eucharistic Love *by Fr. Stefano Manelli, F.I.* A treasure of Eucharistic devotional writings and examples from the Saints showing their stirring Eucharistic love and devotion. A valuable aid for reading meditatively before the Blessed Sacrament.

Virgo Facta Ecclesia *by Franciscan Friars of the Immaculate* is made up of two parts: the first a biography on St. Francis of Assisi and the second part on the Marian character of the Franciscan Order based on its long Marian tradition, from St. Francis to St. Maximilian Kolbe.

Not Made by Hands *by Thomas Sennott* An excellent resource book covering the two most controversial images in existence: the Holy Image of Our Lady of Guadalupe on the tilma of Juan Diego and the Sacred Image of the Crucified on the Shroud of Turin, giving scientific evidence for their authenticity and exposing the fraudulent carbon 14 test.

For the Life of the World *by Jerzy Domanski, O.F.M. Conv.* The former international director of the Knights of the Immaculata and Guardian of the City of the Immaculate in Poland examines Fr. Kolbe's Eucharistic, spiritual life as a priest and adorer of the Eucharist all in the context of his love of the Immaculate.

Padre Pio of Pietrelcina *by Fr, Stefano Manelli, F.I.* This 144 page popular life of Padre Pio is packed with details about his life, spirituality, and charisms, by one who knew the Padre intimately. The author turned to Padre Pio for guidance in establishing a new Community, the Franciscans of the Immaculate.

Come Follow Me *by Fr. Stefano Manelli, F.I.* A book directed to any young person contemplating a Religious vocation. Informative, with many inspiring illustrations and words from the lives and writings of the Saints on the challenging vocation of total dedication in the following of Christ and His Immaculate Mother through the three vows of religion.

Saints and Marian Shrine Series

Edited by Bro. Francis Mary, F.I

A Handbook on Guadalupe This well researched book on Guadalupe contains 40 topical chapters by leading experts on Guadalupe with new insights and the latest scientific findings. A number of chapters deal with Our Lady's role as the patroness of the pro-life movement. Well illustrated.

St. Thérèse: Doctor of the Little Way A compendium of 32 chapters covering many unique facets about the latest Doctor of the Church by 23 authors including Fr. John Hardon, SJ, Msgr. Vernon Johnson, Sister Marie of the Trinity, OCD, and Stephanè Piat. The 174 page book is well illustrated.

Padre Pio — The Wonder Worker The latest on this popular saint of our times including the two inspirational homilies given by Pope John Paul II during the beatification celebration in Rome. The first part of the book is a short biography. The second is on his spirituality, charisms, apostolate of the confessional, and his great works of charity.

Marian Shrines of France On the four major Marian shrines and apparitions of France during the 19th century: Our Lady at Rue du Bac (Paris), La Salette, Lourdes and Pointmain. Shows how already in the 19th century Our Lady checkmated our secular, Godless 20th century introducing the present Age of Mary. Well illustrated.

Marian Shrines of Italy The latest in the series of "Marian Saints and Shrines," with 36 pages of colorful illustrations on over thirty of the 1500 Marian shrines in Italy. The book covers that topic with an underlying theme of the intimate and vital relationship between Mary and the Church. This is especially apparent in Catholic Italy, where the center of the Catholic Faith is found in Rome.

Special rates are available with 10% to 50% discount depending on the number of books, plus postage. For ordering books and further information on rates to book stores, schools and parishes:

Academy of the Immaculate
P.O. Box 667
Valatie NY 12184
Tel. /Fax (518) 758-1594
E-mail: mimike@pipeline.com.

Quotations on bulk rates shipped directly by the box from the printery, contact: Friars of the Immaculate, P.O. Box 3003, New Bedford, MA 02740, (508) 984-1856, FAX (508) 996-8296, E-mail: ffi@marymediatrix.com.